CW00799173

# THE **COVERS**

Featuring the art and notes of J.G. Jones

With color artist Alex Sinclair

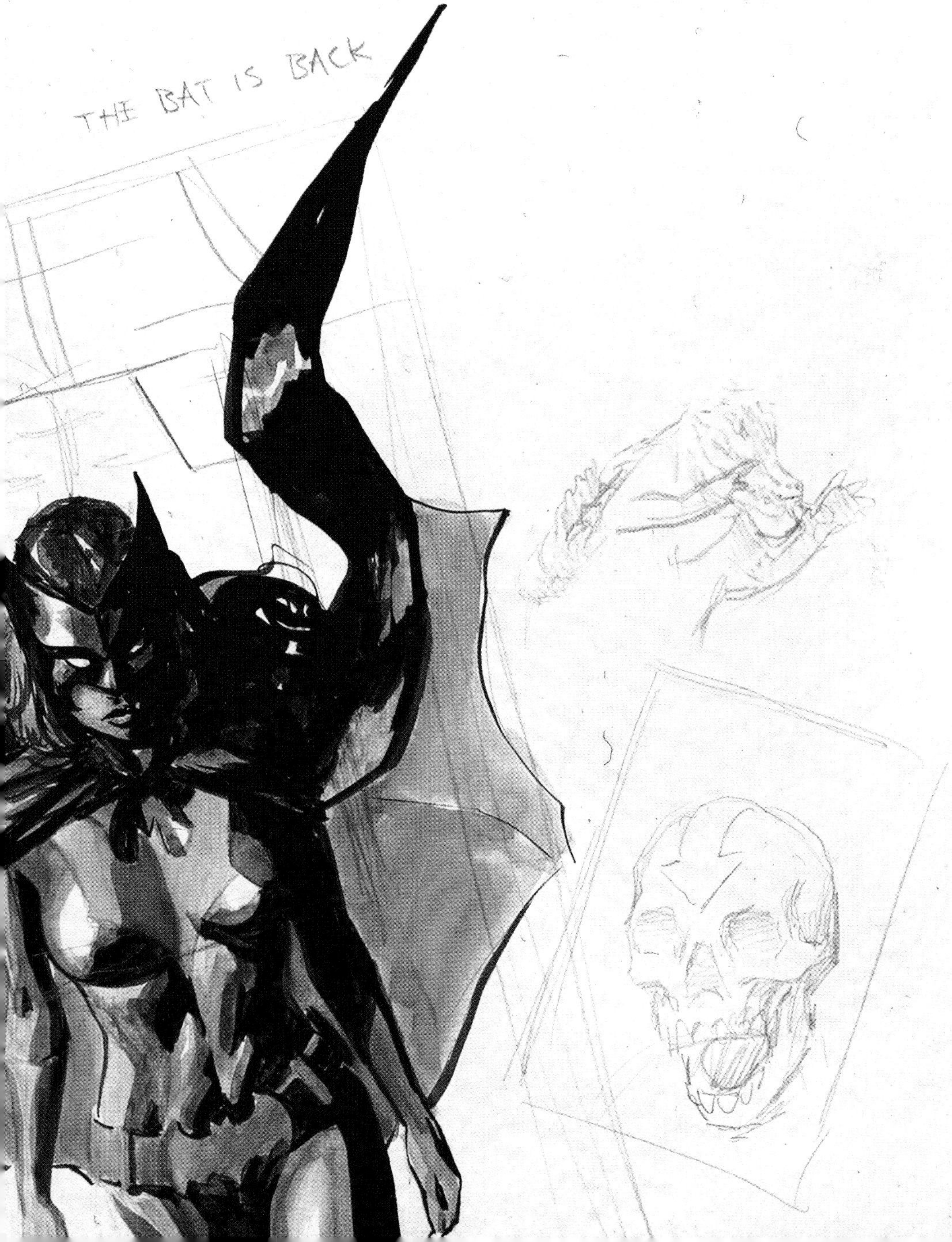
THE BAT IS BACK

Dan DiDio Senior VP-Executive Editor    Stephen Wacker  Michael Siglain Editors-original series
Anton Kawasaki Editor-collected edition    Robbin Brosterman Senior Art Director
Louis Prandi Art Director    Paul Levitz President & Publisher    Georg Brewer VP-Design & DC Direct Creative
Richard Bruning Senior VP-Creative Director    Patrick Caldon Executive VP-Finance & Operations
Chris Caramalis VP-Finance    John Cunningham VP-Marketing    Terri Cunningham VP-Managing Editor
Alison Gill VP-Manufacturing    Hank Kanalz VP-General Manager, WildStorm    Jim Lee Editorial Director-WildStorm
Paula Lowitt Senior VP-Business & Legal Affairs    MaryEllen McLaughlin VP-Advertising & Custom Publishing
John Nee VP-Business Development    Gregory Noveck Senior VP-Creative Affairs    Sue Pohja VP-Book Trade Sales
Cheryl Rubin Senior VP-Brand Management    Jeff Trojan VP-Business Development, DC Direct    Bob Wayne VP-Sales

*Cover art by J.G. Jones with Alex Sinclair*

13

Stained Glass with inverted "S"

← Green Lantern

meta- → morpho

Hawk- → woman

Green ← Arrow

## CONTENTS

## INTRODUCTION

Get ready to be amazed. You're going to see something that just can't possibly be.

Take an artist — one of the most talented, most in-demand artists working in comics today — and chain him to his drawing table. Coerce him into painting one cover every week for a full year. Fifty-two covers in fifty-two weeks. Because these covers will be the face of a new, high-profile WEEKLY comic book from DC (called **52**, get it?), and they have to be enticing, dramatic, and absolutely memorable. Because the storyline of this weekly comic is so important, and the frequency with which it ships so unprecedented in this industry, the book can't ship a single day late or the whole "stunt" will be blown. Everyone is expecting DC to fail, so it's important that no deadline is missed, or else it will lead to a domino effect, causing the tightly knit storyline to unravel. A lot of effort and money ride on this all happening like clockwork. If one creator trips, we all fall.

So we start looking for that cover artist. The list of illustrators who are talented enough to create the kind of images we want is short. The list of artists who can actually deliver work on such an extremely tight, demanding deadline is even shorter. Enter J.G. Jones.

I knew J.G.'s brilliant work on the Wonder Woman hardcover THE HIKETEIA and before that from the *Black Widow* miniseries that he painted for that *other* company. **52** editor Steve Wacker suggested J.G. to me and our boss, Dan DiDio, and we all agreed that he was the only guy for the job. Since J.G. (his friends call him Jeff) lived in the next town over from me, we decided to meet for coffee and chat about the **52** cover gig. That Saturday cup of coffee would turn into about twenty get-togethers over the course of the coming year. Now, understand, Jeff is one of those artists who ALWAYS carries his sketchbook around with him. Everywhere. So, when we'd meet for coffee, I just couldn't help but thumb through his incredible sketches. Whereas most artists' sketches and cover designs tend towards nothing more than stick figures, Jeff has the rare ability to be able to bang out the most beautiful little cover comps you've ever seen. He's got such facility drawing the human (and inhuman) form that it's no big deal to whip up five or six full-color cover concepts for each cover. And all smaller than the size of a baseball card. It was a much harder job for me and Steve to pick which sketch to go with, since they were all so consistently inspired.

It's absolutely impossible that Jeff got every single cover in on time without the slightest hiccup, but he did. It's doubly impossible that he created such an astounding, high-quality body of work, but he did. With each cover, Jeff broke new ground, reinventing the wheel each time he sat down at the drawing table. Many of these images have become classics. The one with Black Adam sitting on a throne is a fan favorite, as are the close-up of Lex Luthor's face on issue #3, the one that featured the very first image of Batwoman (and which every major newspaper in America reprinted), the 1950s horror poster pastiche "The Beast Who Came to Dinner," the toe-tag cover on issue #34, and of course, the first and last covers of the series. Classics all. With this series of covers, Jeff entered that rarefied stratosphere with Steranko, Bolland, Hughes, Ross, Adams, Kubert, and a handful of others as one of the great cover artists in comics history.

Time for a tip of the hat (like the cover for issue #48) to Alex Sinclair, the guy who colored all of these covers. Alex maintains that it was his absolute joy to work over Jeff's grayscale paintings, but I'm sure his brain is still stinging and eyes are still bleary from Jeff's rather complex wraparound cover for the final issue. Honestly, I can't imagine any colorist doing nearly as good a job on this series as Alex did.

Now comes the inevitable part: "Hey Jeff," I say, "you know, we should collect all of these covers and the accompanying sketches in a nice book when you're all done."

"Yeah, that would be great," says Jeff in that Southern drawl of his.

The next Monday, DiDio comes to me and says, "Hey, we should collect all of Jeff's **52** covers in a book when he's all done."

"Great idea," says I.

The very next day, Wacker and I are chatting over lunch and he comes up with a brainstorm: "Gee, we really should see if we can collect all of those **52** covers once Jeff is done."

"Brilliant!" says I.

I often feel that the best book you can publish is the one you'd want for your own collection. I've cleared a spot on my bookshelf for this one.

So, sit back with a cup of coffee and get ready to marvel at Jeff's gift. For a Southern boy, this guy can freaking draw.

Mark Chiarello
Editorial Art Director
DC Comics

P.S. Hey Jeff, let's do it again!

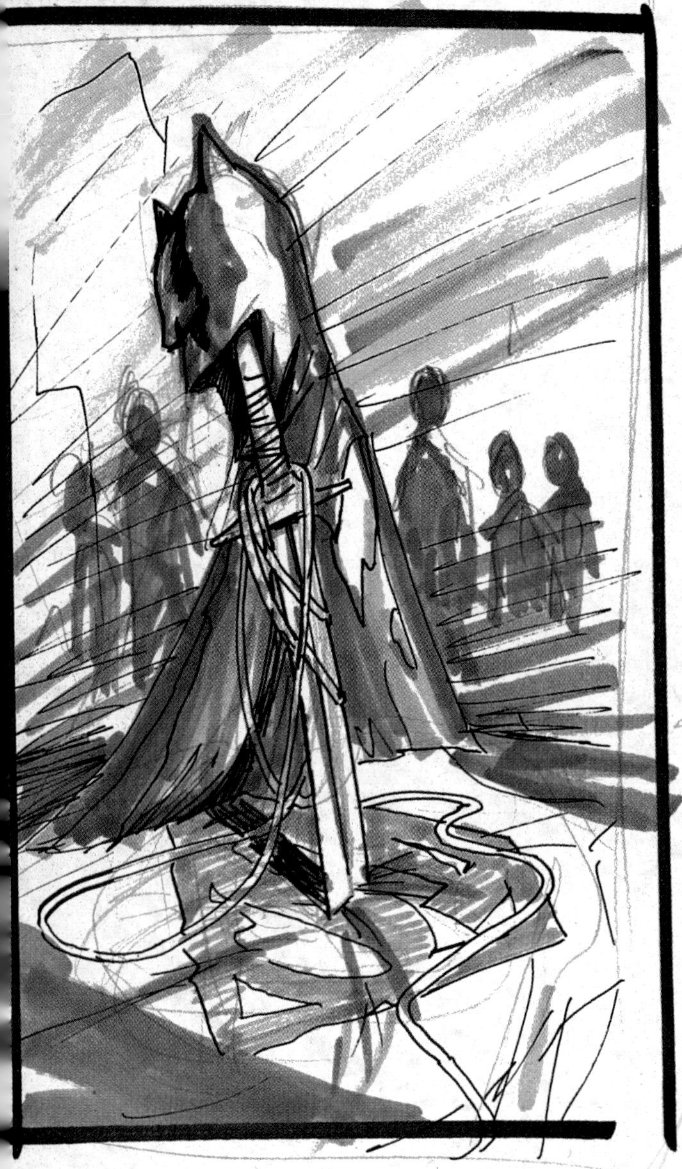

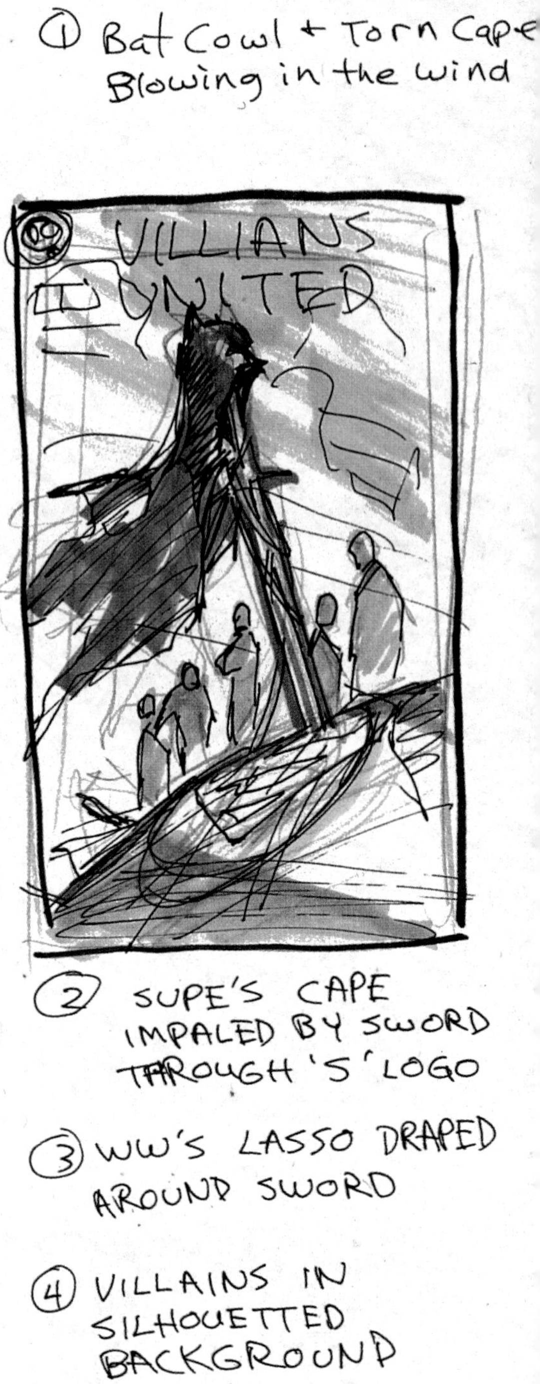
① Bat Cowl + Torn Cape Blowing in the wind
VILLIANS UNITED
② SUPE'S CAPE IMPALED BY SWORD THROUGH 'S' LOGO
③ WW'S LASSO DRAPED AROUND SWORD
④ VILLAINS IN SILHOUETTED BACKGROUND

## WEEK ONE

The cover for the first issue was tough for a number of reasons. I had to set the proper tone for the entire series while illustrating the absence of Superman, Batman, and Wonder Woman from the world. Also, I wanted to introduce some of the main cast members that we would be following throughout the yearlong series. And I had to accomplish all of this in one succinct, iconic image.

After a number of abortive efforts, I stumbled across an old, unused sketch for a VILLAINS UNITED cover (a series I did before this) that fit the bill perfectly with just a few modifications.

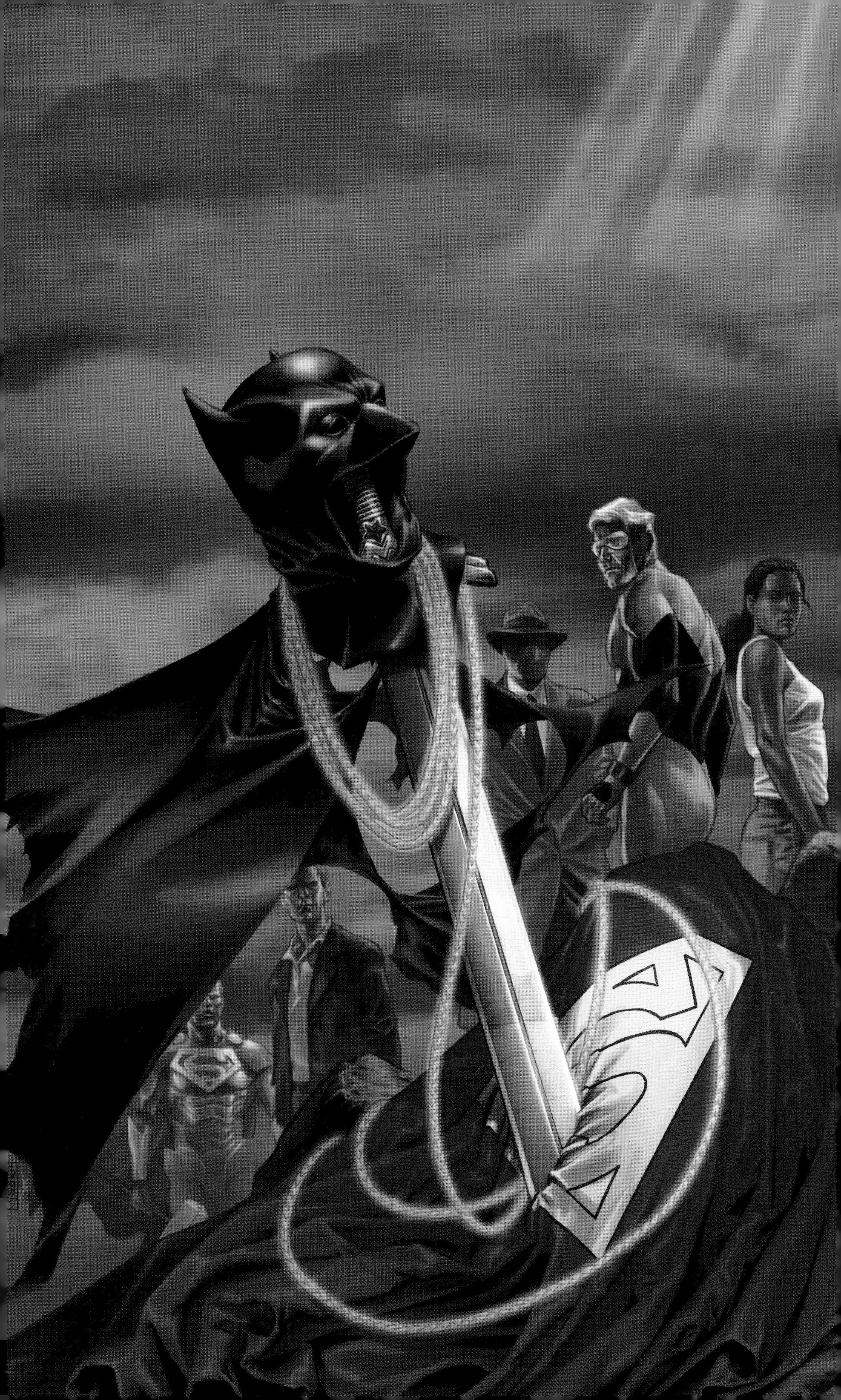

Product Placement Bottled Water or sports drink

Booster Gold flashes a million $ smile for the cameras and crowd of reporters pressing in. WEARING A NASCAR-style jacket covered in corp. logos from sponsors. Flashbulbs from cameras. Maybe he's holding a kid he saved in his left arm

## WEEK TWO

This cover was taken directly from a sketch that I did in one of the first 52 plotting sessions. I love the idea of Booster Gold in a NASCAR style jacket, covered in corporate logos. I wanted to show him as incredibly crass, soaking up the media adulation — the ultimate sellout.

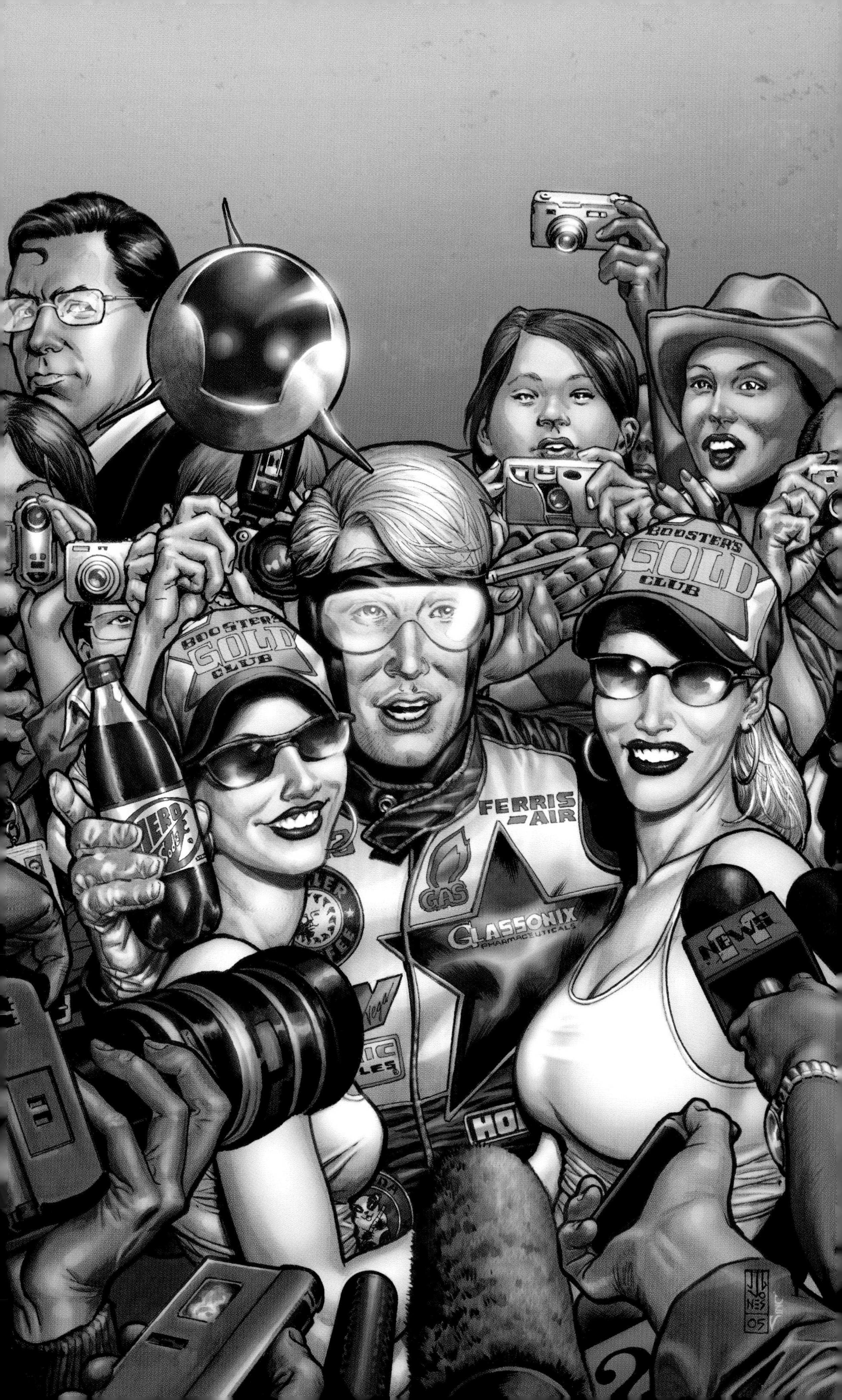

BOOSTER'S GOLD CLUB
BOOSTER'S GOLD CLUB
FERRIS AIR
GAS
GLASSONIX PHARMACEUTICALS
NEWS

52
Luthor: Good vs Evil
Parallel Worlds-
Fact or Fiction?

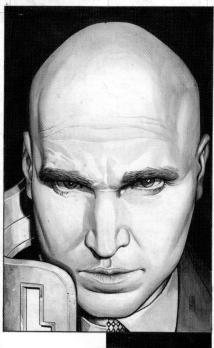

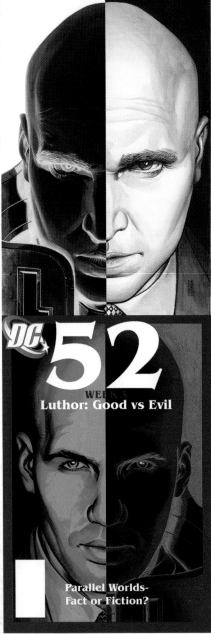

## WEEK THREE

I wanted this to look like the cover of a newsweekly magazine, like *Time*. I had originally designed it with a red border and white lettering right across the middle of the page, which would pose the question, "Lex Luthor: Good or Evil?" I split the halves into red and blue to emphasize the dichotomy.

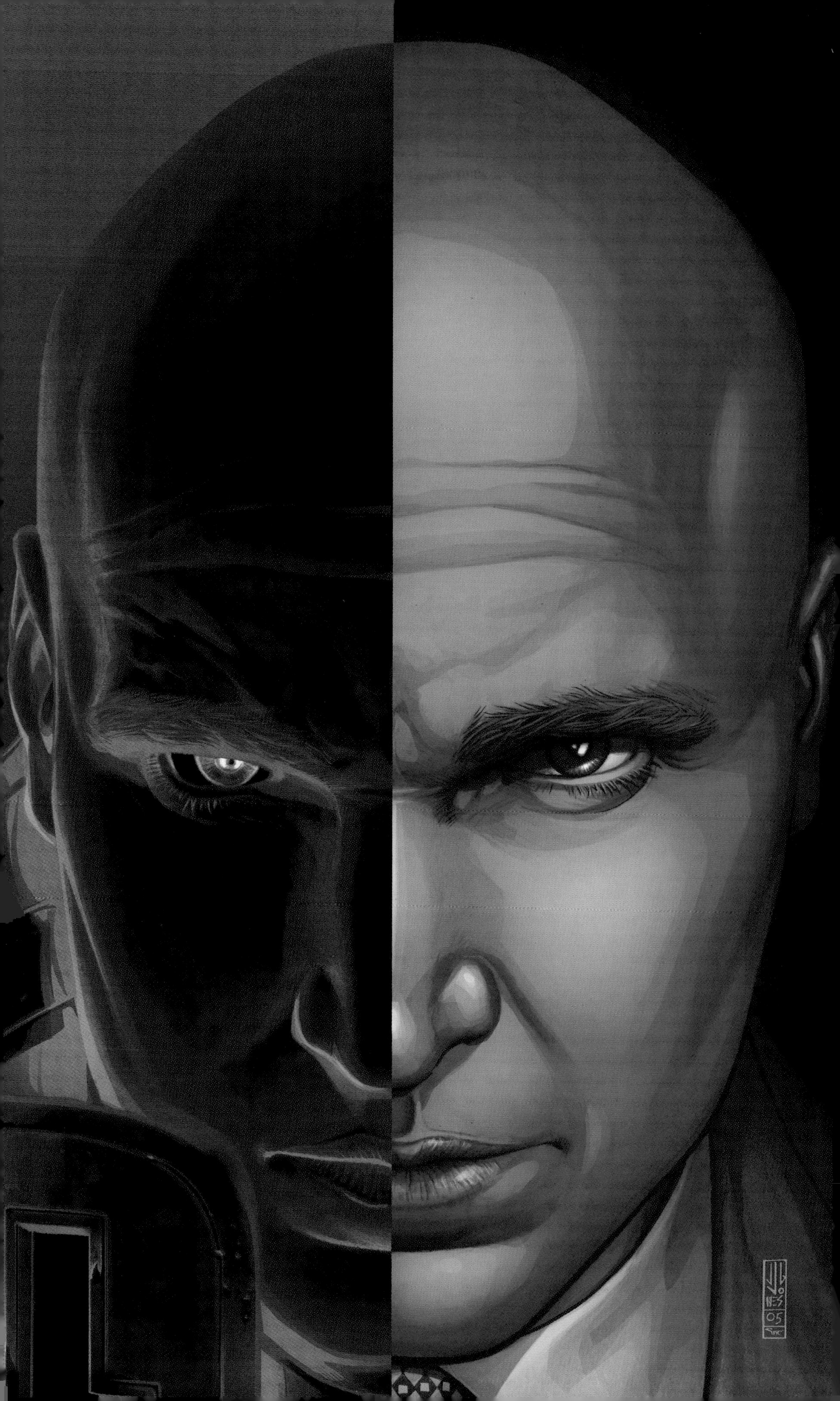

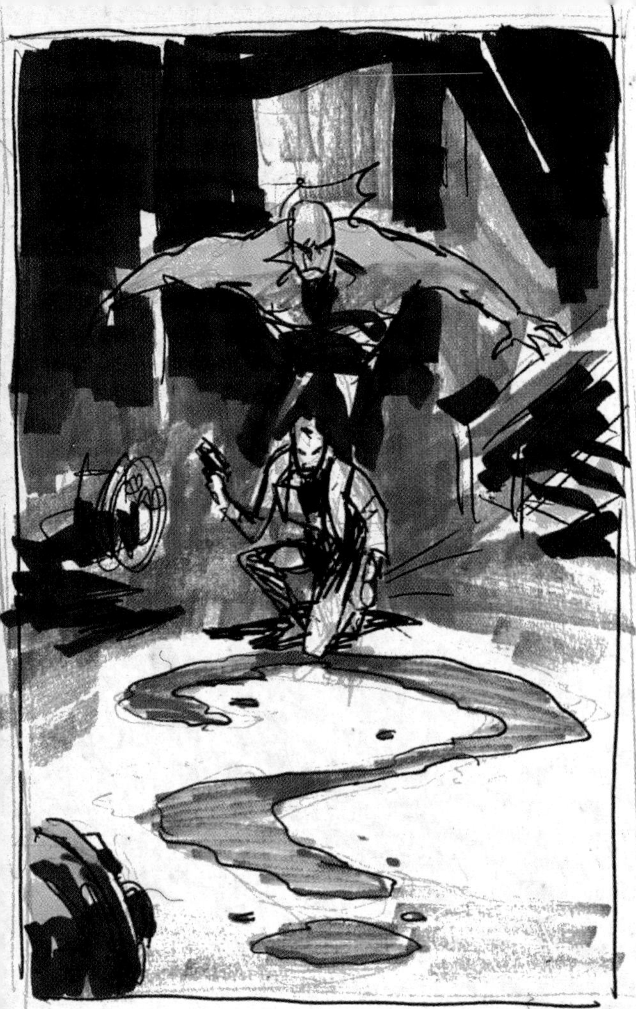

**WEEK FOUR**

Here I was establishing the incipient relationship between Renee Montoya and the mysterious figure known as The Question. I wanted to use the question mark not only as a symbol, but as a graphic element dominating the composition, so the obvious answer was to make the shape as a blood stain on the floor.

Montoya kneeling,
Gun Drawn, investigates
a darkened warehouse.
Big Genetic Monster
emerging from
Shadows behind her.
Blood on floor forms
a question mark

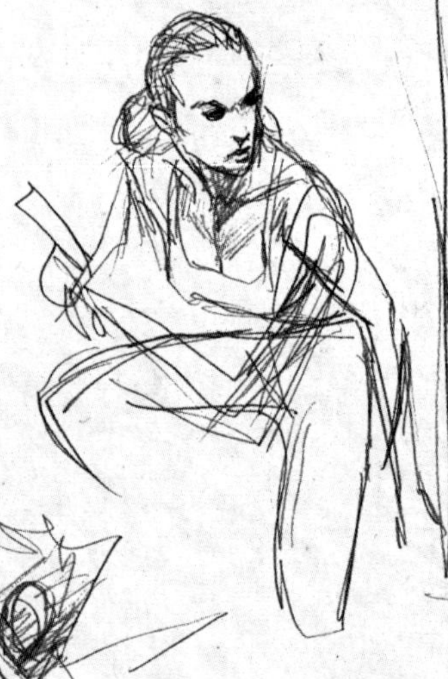

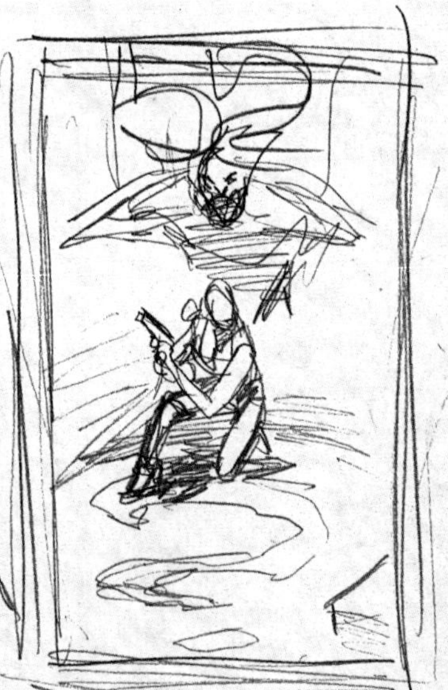

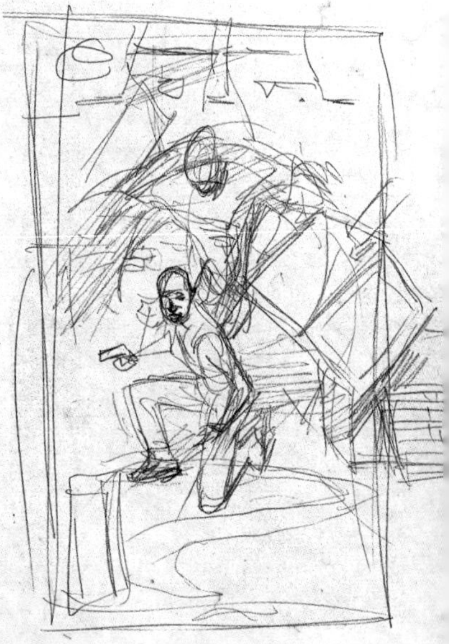

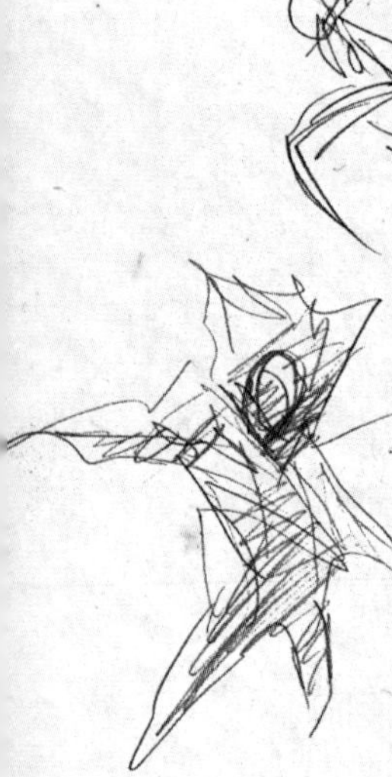

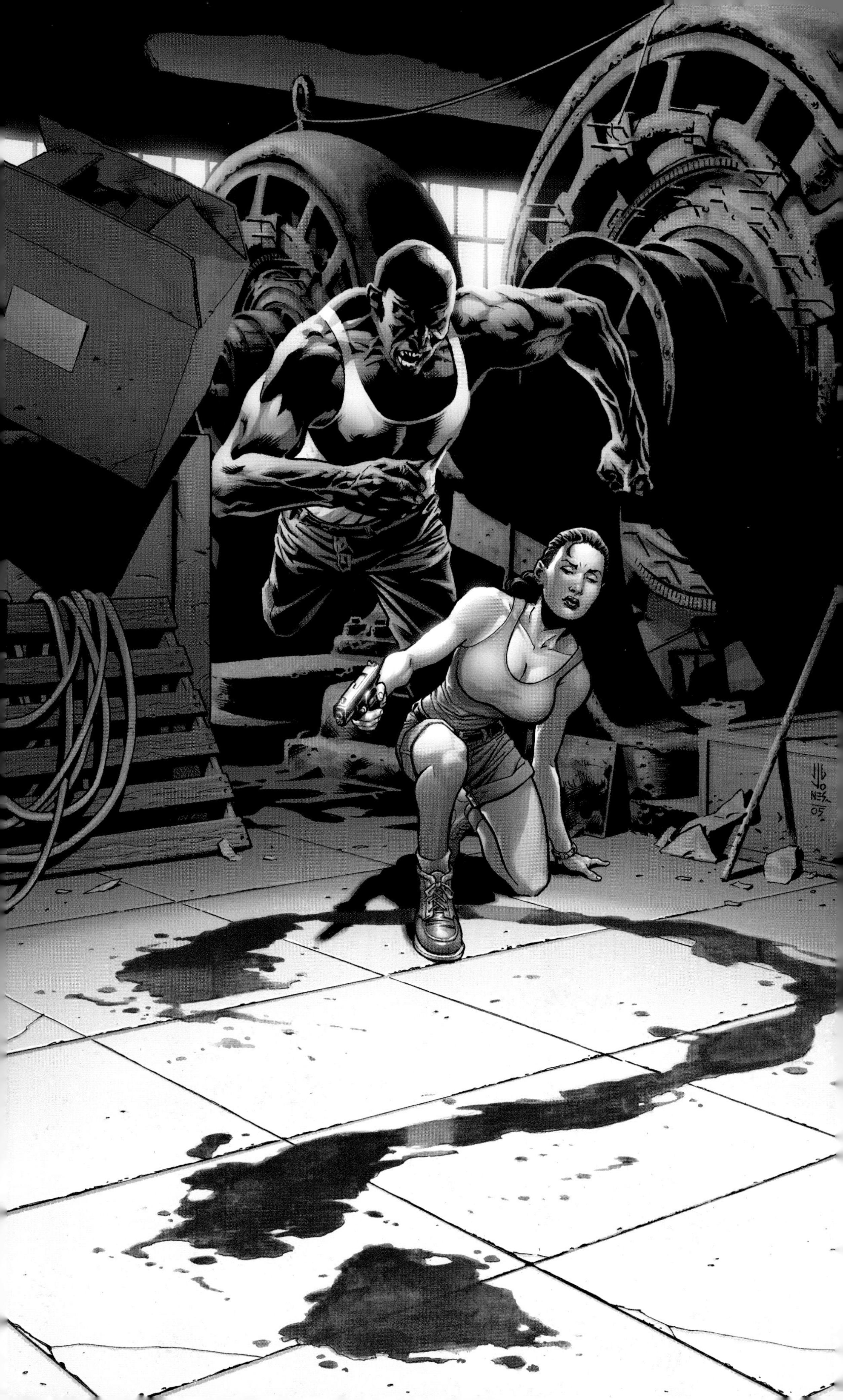

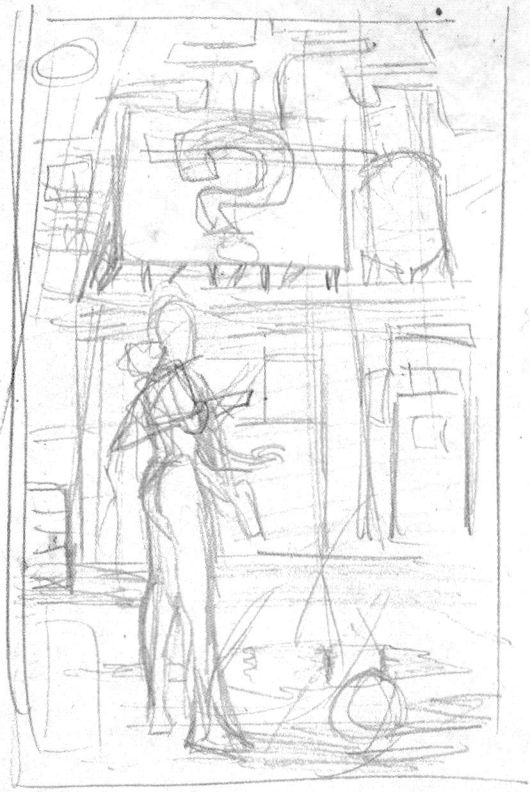

## WEEK FIVE

Initially, I was not sure what to do for this issue's cover. 52 layout artist Keith Giffen had an idea to depict an EMT worker pinned beneath a giant feather. It's a terrific image, but a bit abstruse, since we had not yet introduced Hawkgirl into the story.

In the end, I thought that it would be fun to draw a giant, thrashing, fifty-foot-tall woman. If that doesn't get your attention, I don't know what would.

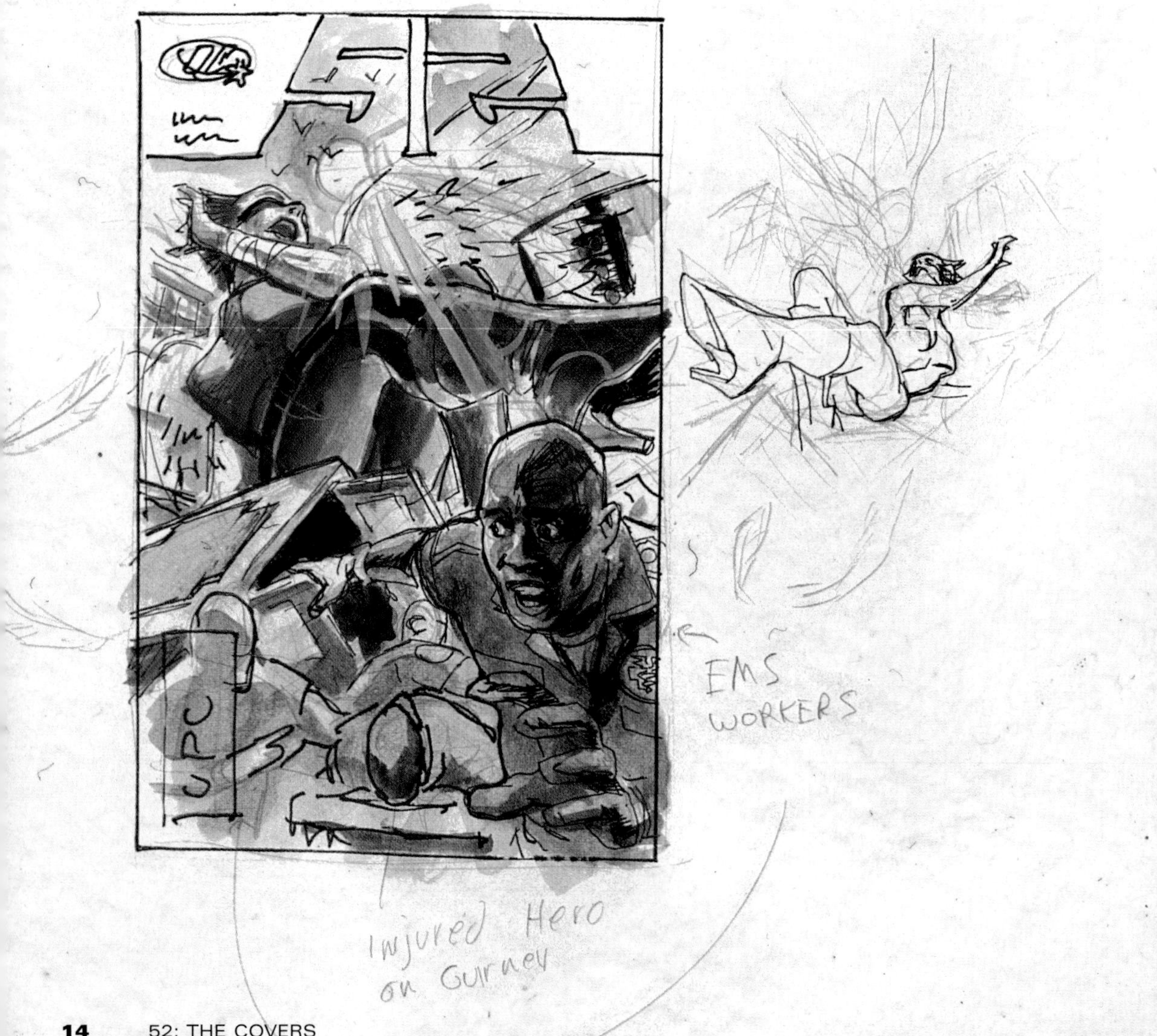
UPC
EMS WORKERS
Injured Hero on Gurney

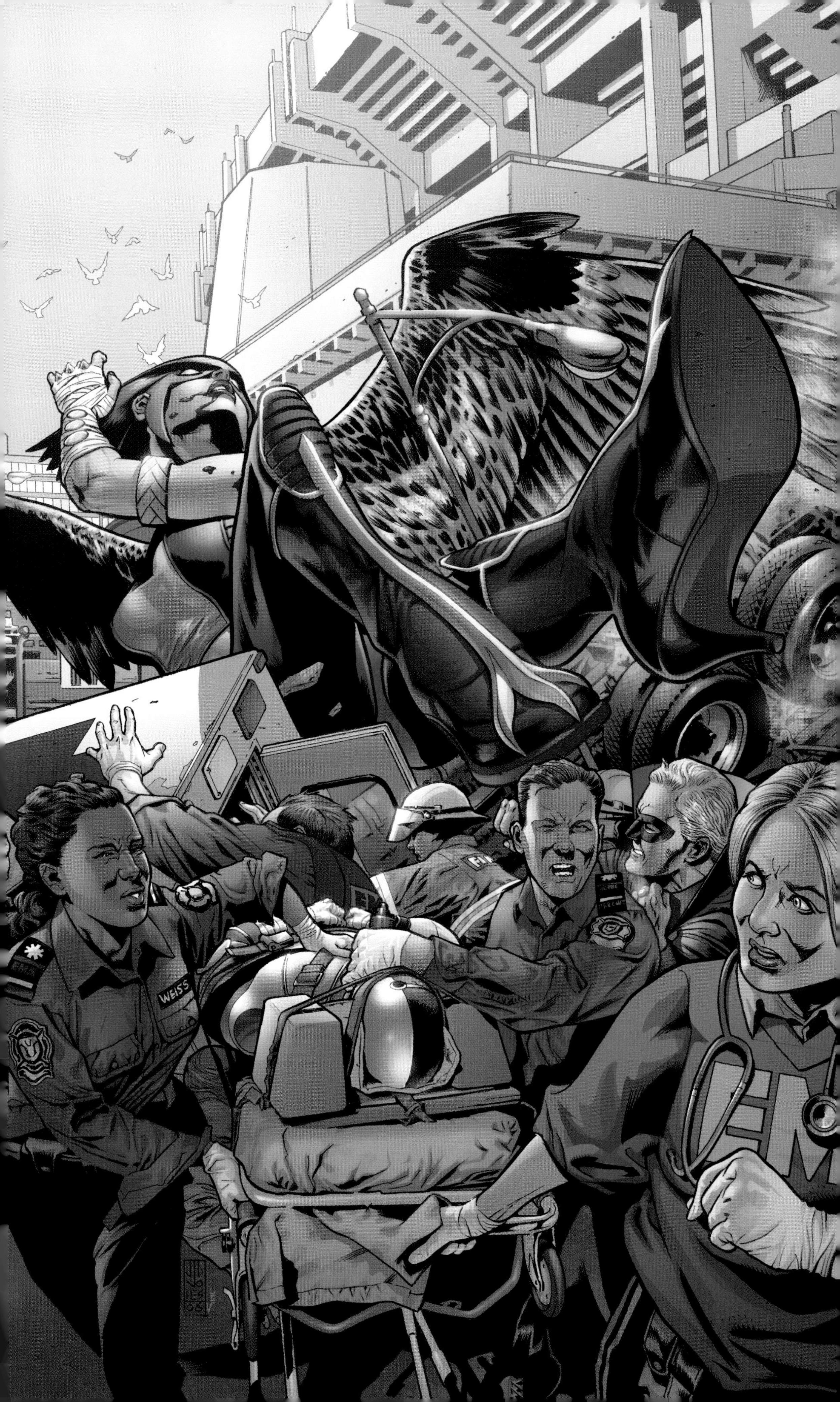
WEISS

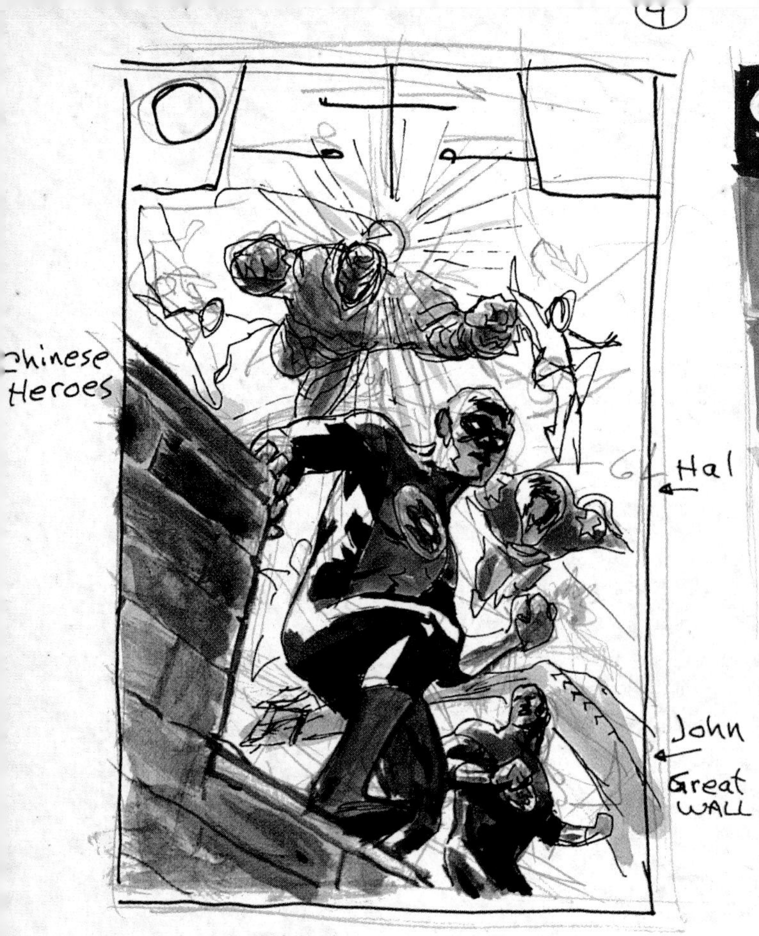
4
Chinese Heroes
Hal
John
Great WALL

Battle Above China ⑤

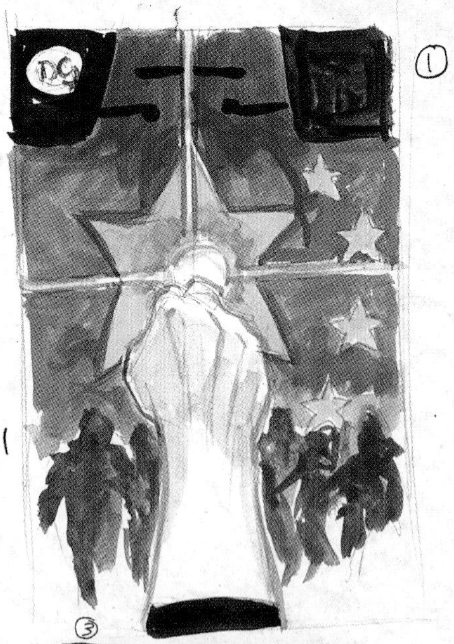
1

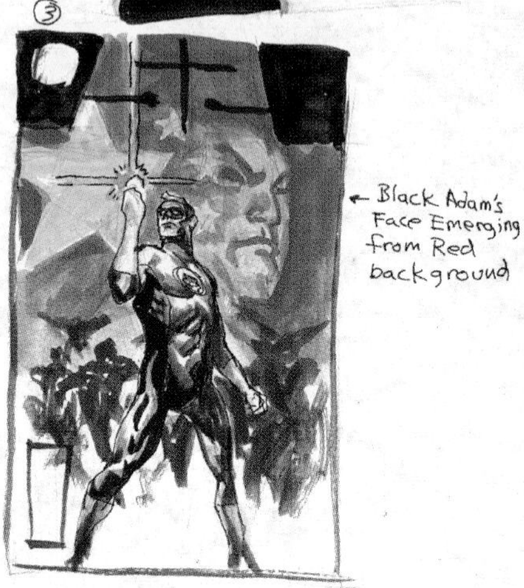
3
Black Adam's Face Emerging from Red background

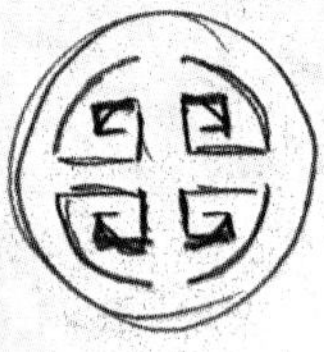

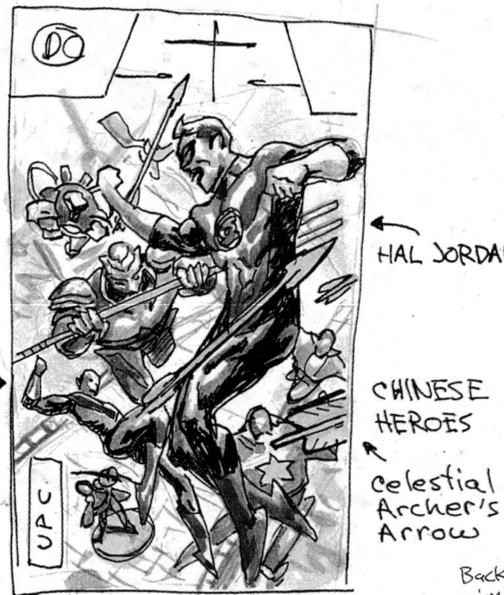
HAL JORDAN
JOHN STEWART
CHINESE HEROES
Celestial Archer's Arrow
UPC

Above Great Wall

## WEEK SIX

I must have done about twenty color sketches for this cover before Mark Chiarello chose to go with the movie poster image. This was the introduction of The Great Ten, the Chinese superhero team.

I like the way the red of the Chinese flag in the background contrasts with the green of Hal Jordan's costume in the final colored version.

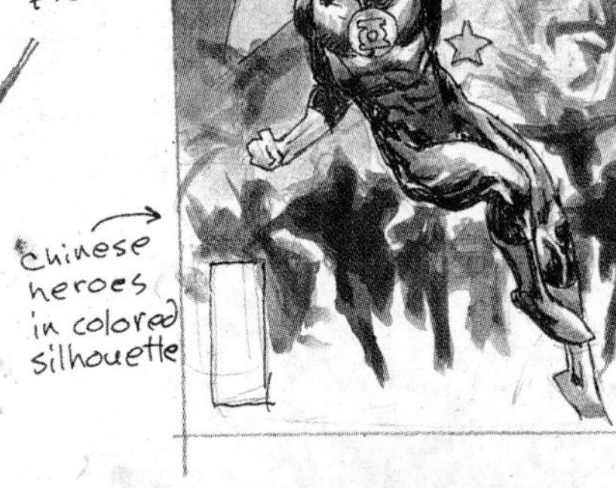
2
Background mimics Chinese Flag–
Yellow Stars on Red Field
Chinese heroes in colored silhouette

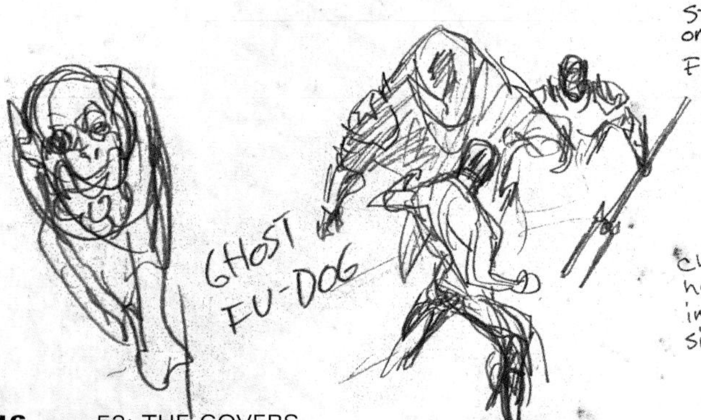
GHOST FU-DOG

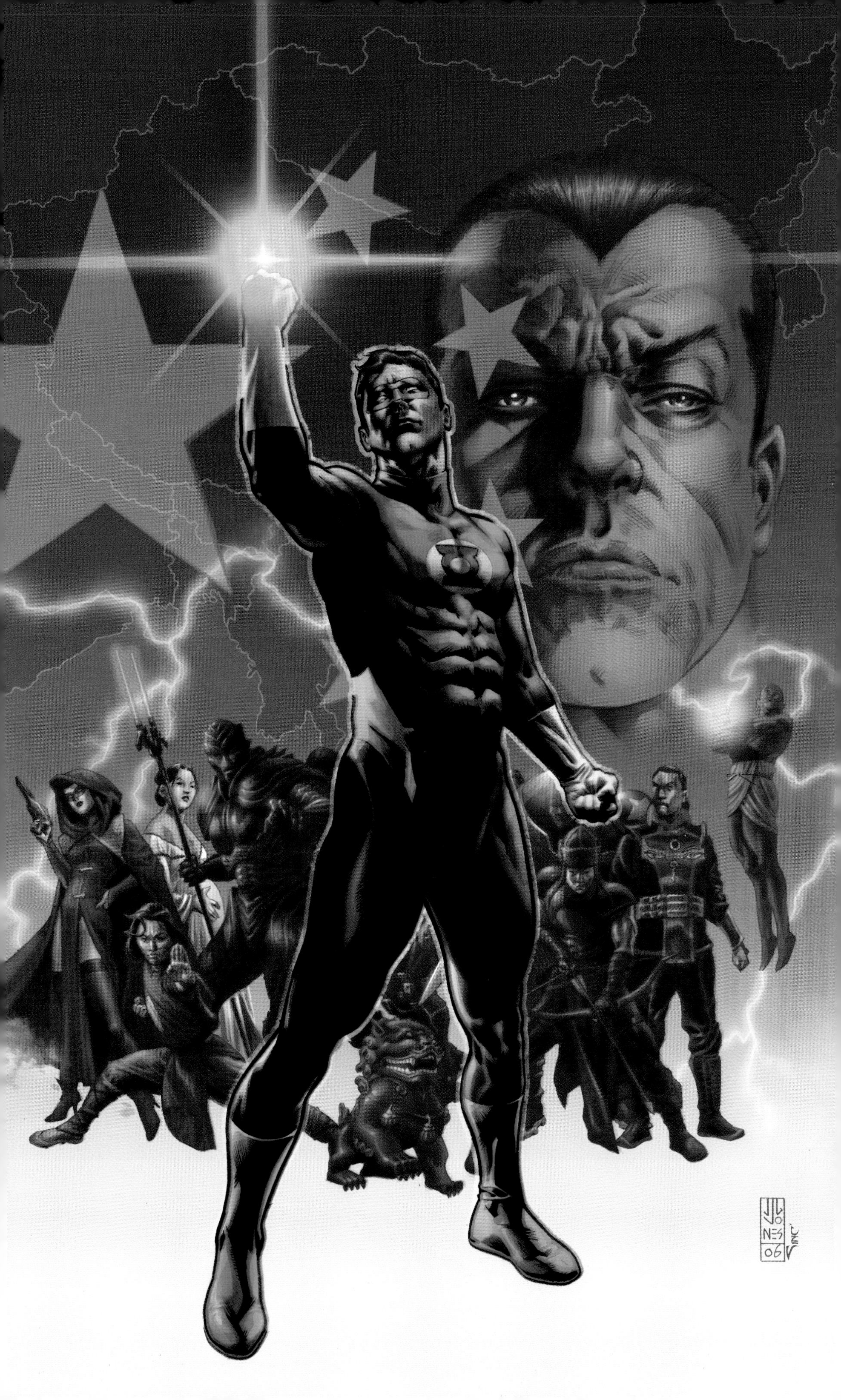

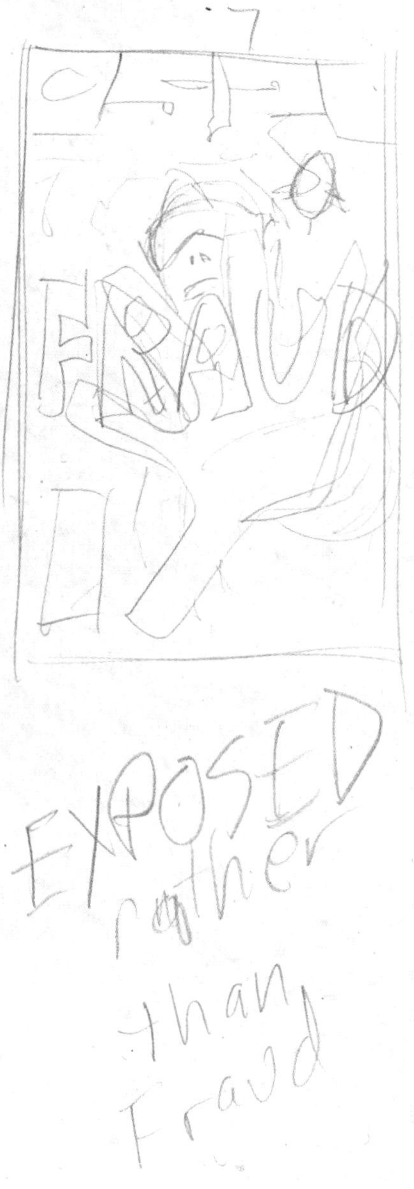
FRAUD
EXPOSED rather than Fraud

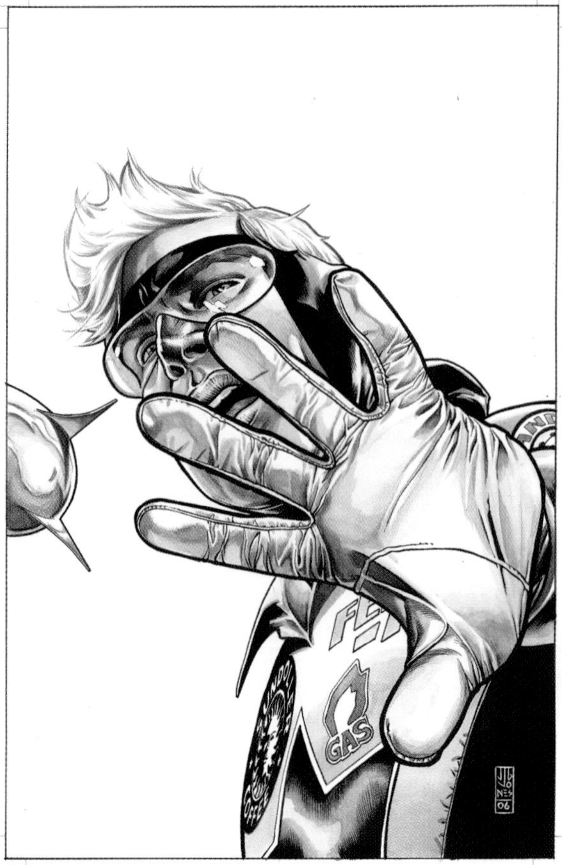
GAS

**WEEK SEVEN**

Unlike issue 6, the idea for this week came to me immediately. To illustrate his imminent implosion, I went with a "gotcha" paparazza shot of Booster on the cover of a celebrity tabloid. His hand is up, fending off the cameras, and he's clearly annoyed.

After having Alex Sinclair color the piece, we decided that it worked better in newsprint halftones. Slapping the giant, red "EXPOSED" across the cover added the final insult to injury.

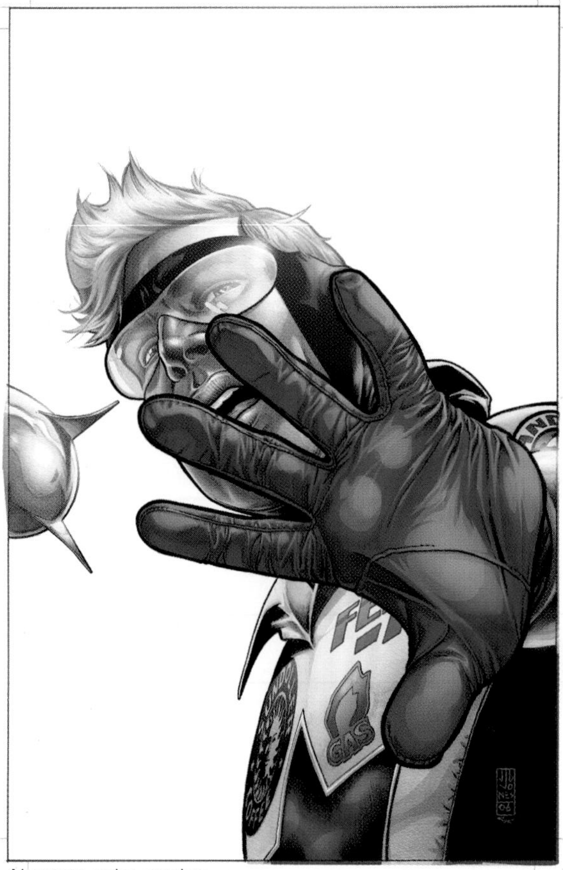
GAS

Alternate color version

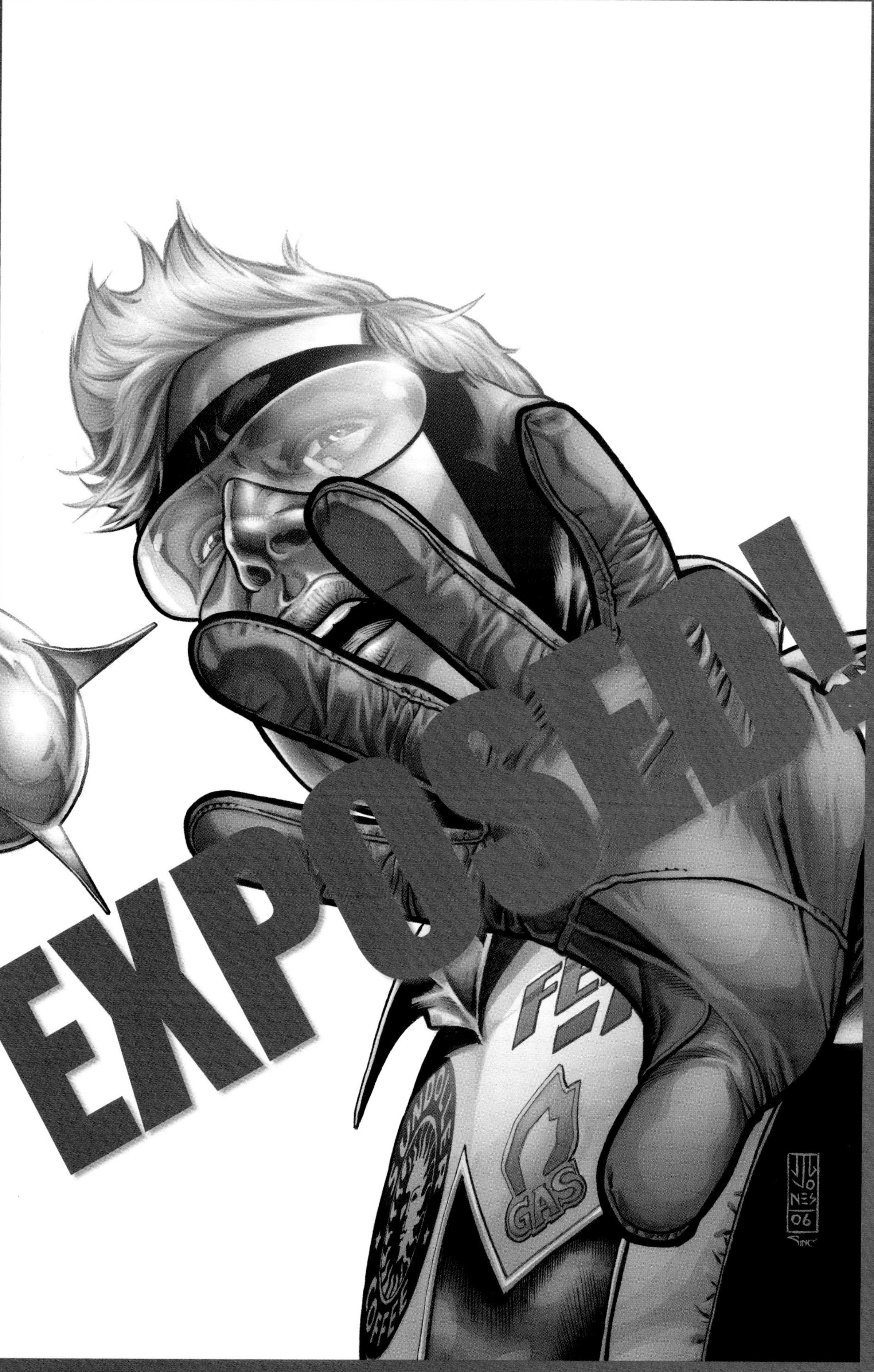
EXPOSED!
FL
GAS
COFFEE
JG JONES 06

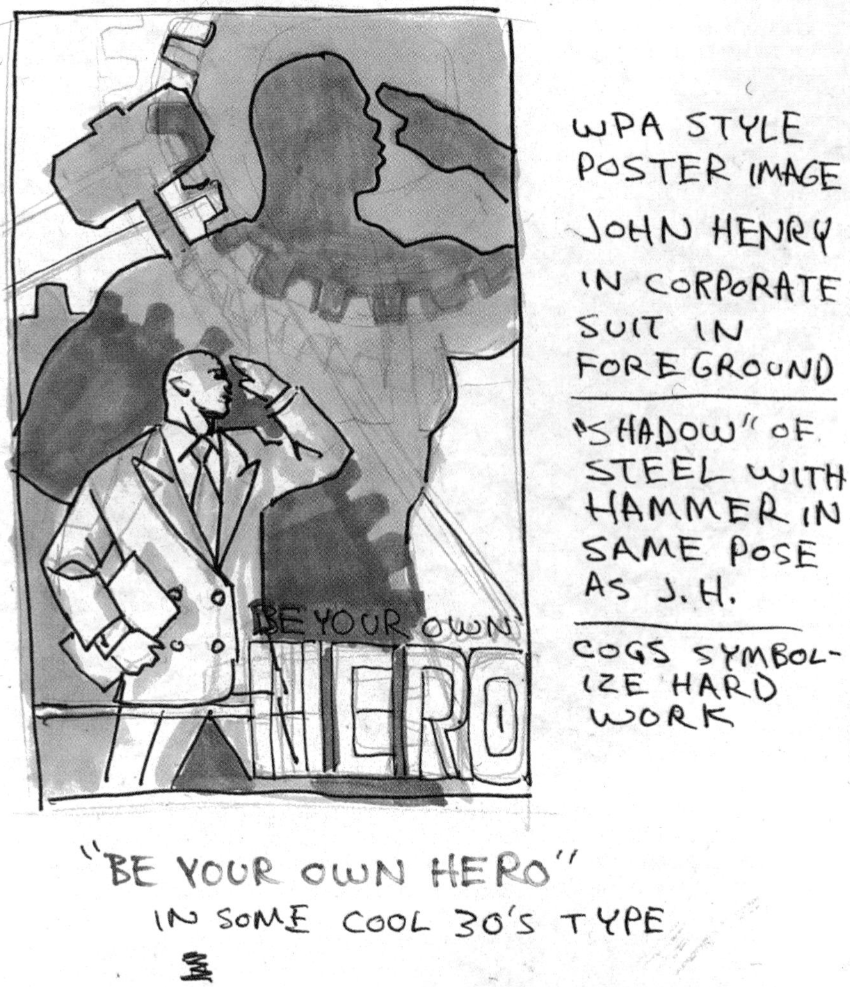
BE YOUR OWN
HERO
WPA STYLE POSTER IMAGE
JOHN HENRY IN CORPORATE SUIT IN FOREGROUND
"SHADOW" OF STEEL WITH HAMMER IN SAME POSE AS J.H.
COGS SYMBOLIZE HARD WORK
"BE YOUR OWN HERO"
IN SOME COOL 30'S TYPE

**WEEK EIGHT**

To illustrate John Henry Irons's nobility and work ethic, it seemed natural to adopt the style of a Depression era WPA poster for this cover. I put him in his blacksmith's apron, holding his hammer to depict him as a working class hero. He is willing to hold fast to his ethical code of hard work, eschewing the shortcuts to easy success offered up by the nefarious Lex Luthor.

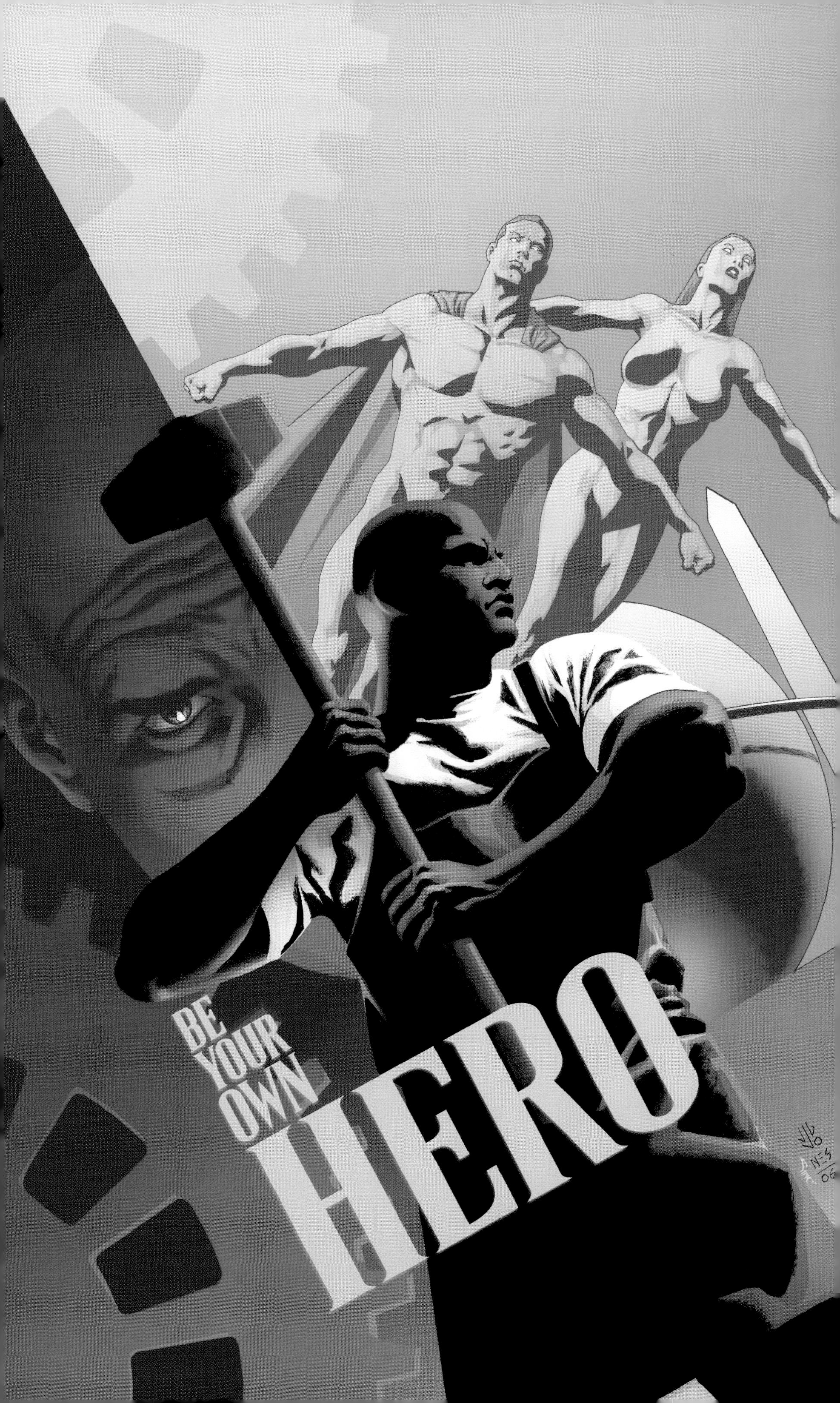

BE YOUR OWN
HERO

#9
Devilance

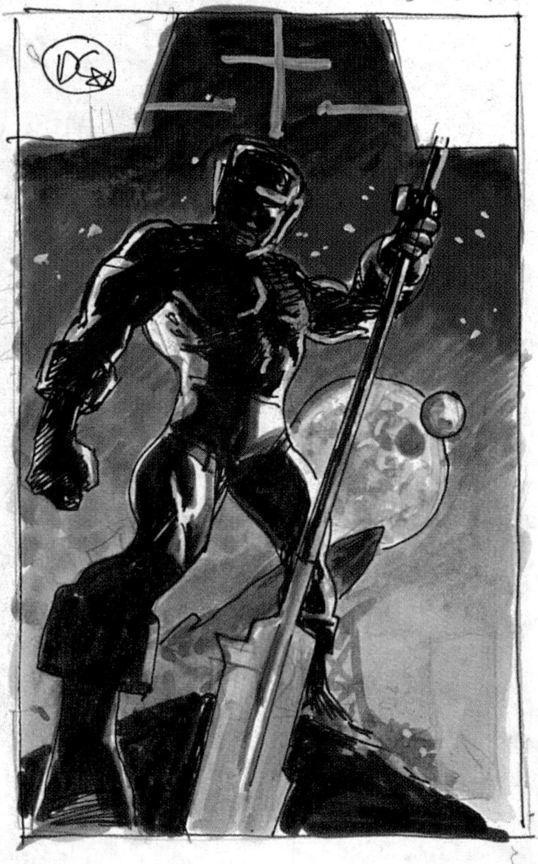

## WEEK NINE

Our space heroes encounter the giant celestial god Devilance on a remote planet halfway across the galaxy. This was just pure fun, and I was trying hard to channel my best Frank Frazetta. I love Alex's color and light effects on this image. It looks like candy.

Devilance

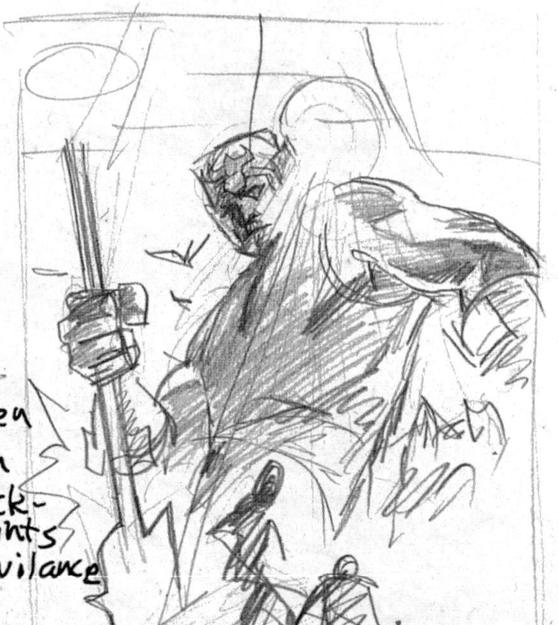

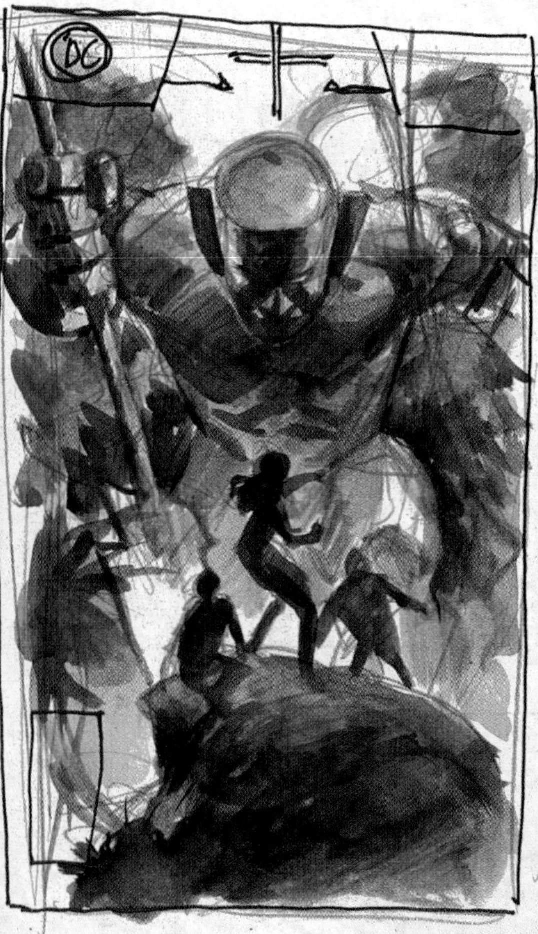

Alien
Sun
back-
lights
Devilance

Alien
Jungle

Mist Between
Giant + Foreground
figures

Foreground Figures
in silhouette to hid
identities

move blade to right
abit →

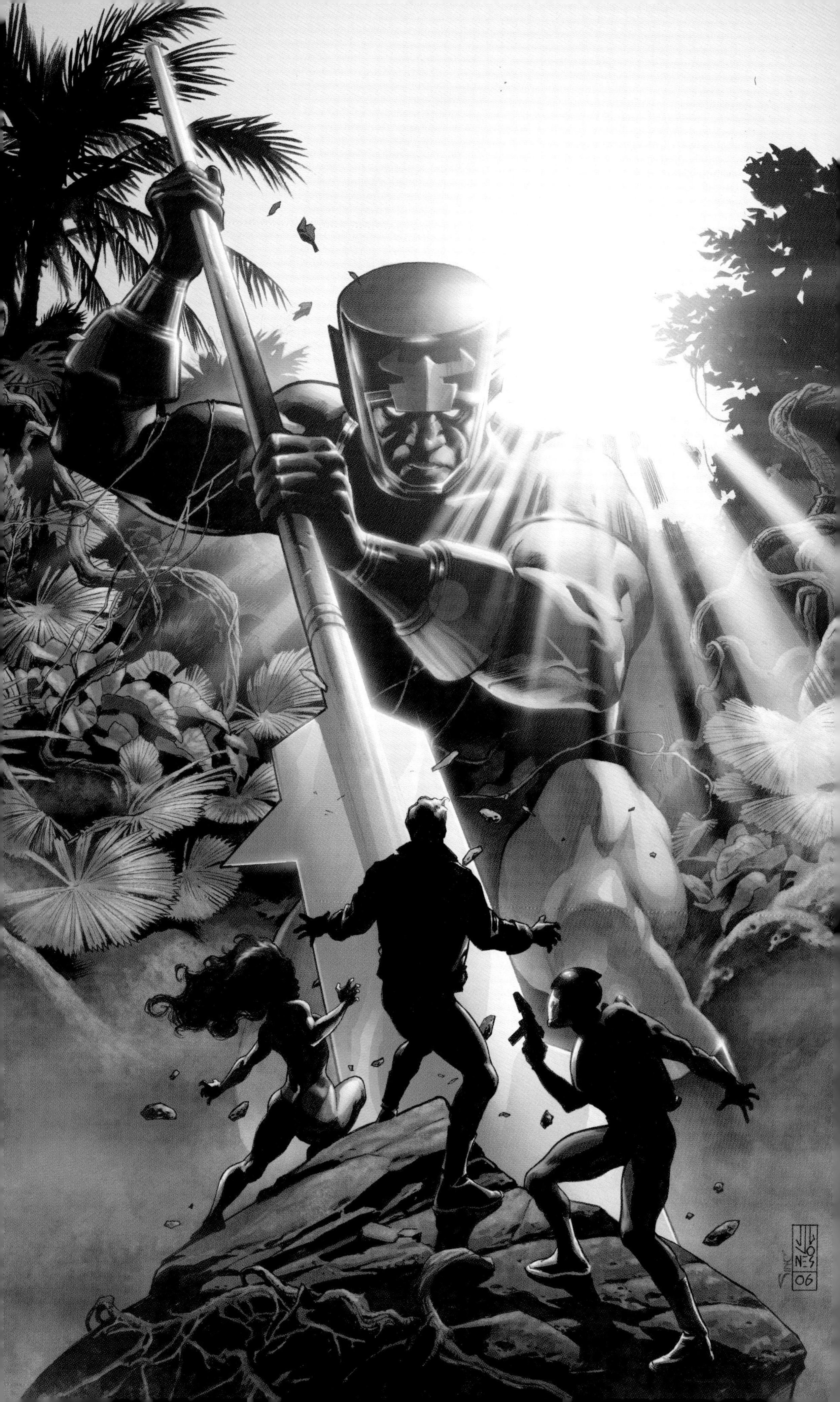

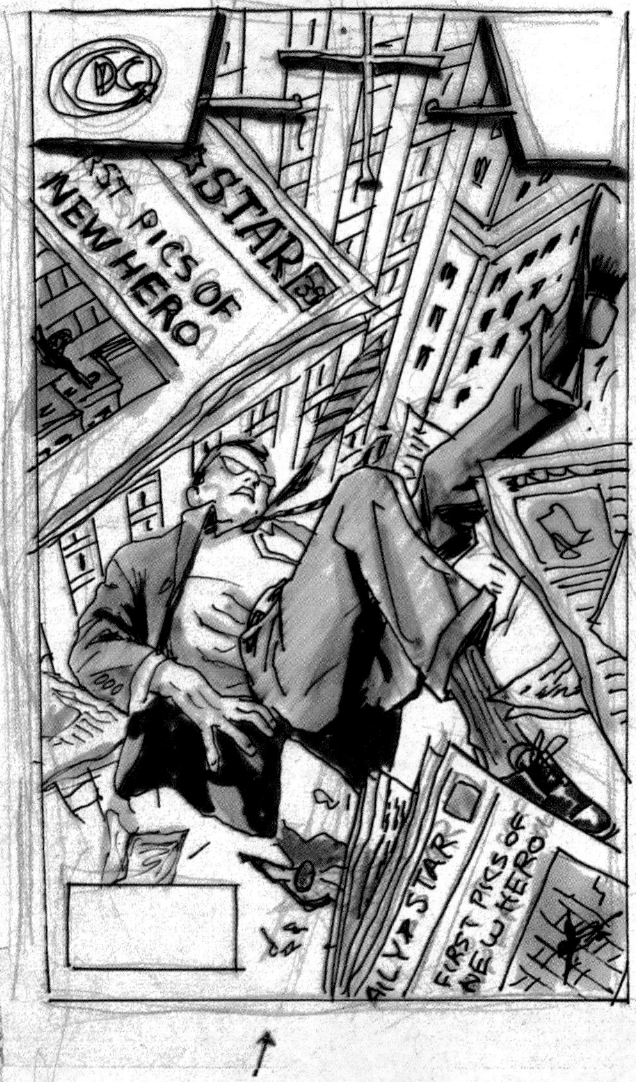
DC
STAR
FIRST PICS OF NEW HERO
DAILY STAR
FIRST PICS OF NEW HERO

CLARK KENT FALLING FROM BUILDING, Daily Star Newspapers flying about. On the newspages are Headlines and photo of the New Superhero, SUPERNOVA

**WEEK TEN**

This concept came to me in the first planning session. I wanted to depict Clark in mortal danger and in need of rescue — a clear reversal of his normal role as rescuer. The falling newspapers introducing the new hero Supernova were a clever way to do a bit of storytelling. Now we know the identity of that figure flying to Clark's rescue.

SUPERNOVA APPROACHING FROM BELOW

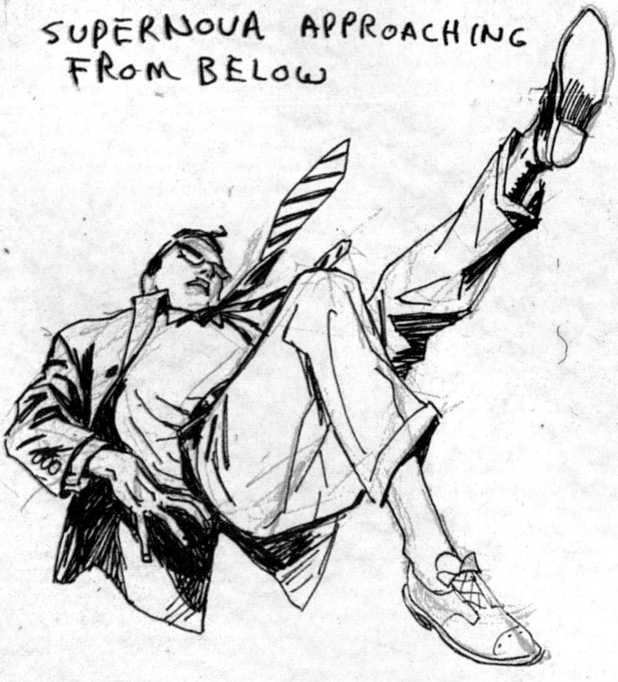

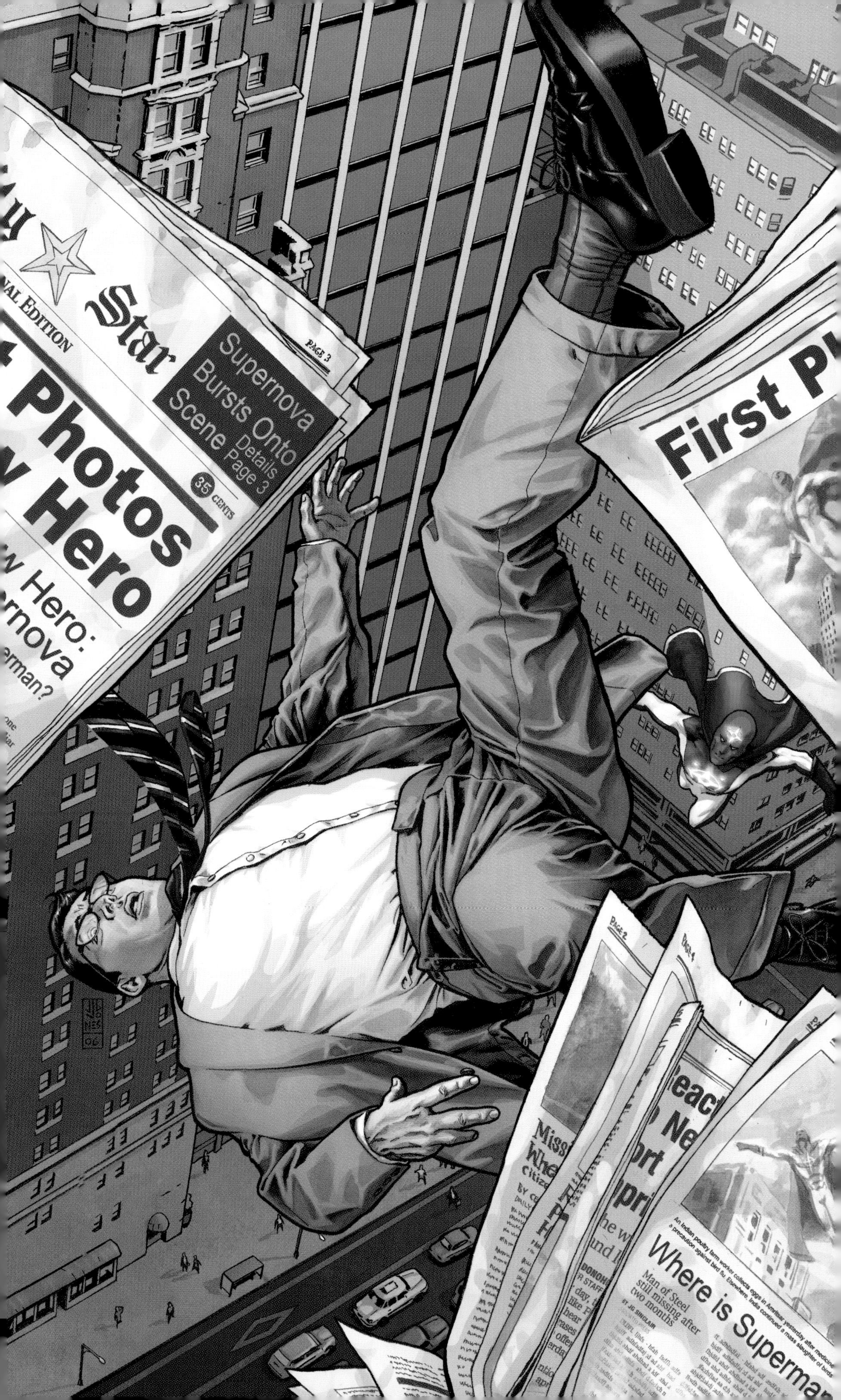

Star
NAL EDITION
PAGE 3
Supernova Bursts Onto Scene
Details Page 3
35 CENTS
Photos
Hero
Hero:
rnova
erman?
First P
PAGE 2
PAGE 4
Where is Superman
Man of Steel still missing after two months

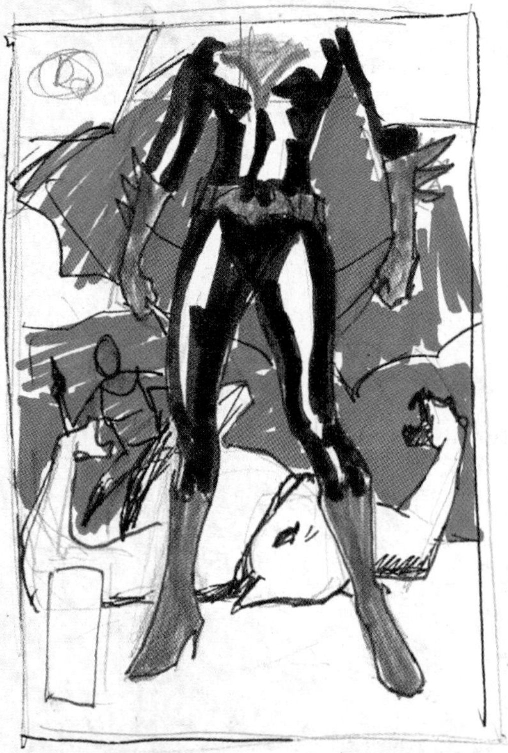

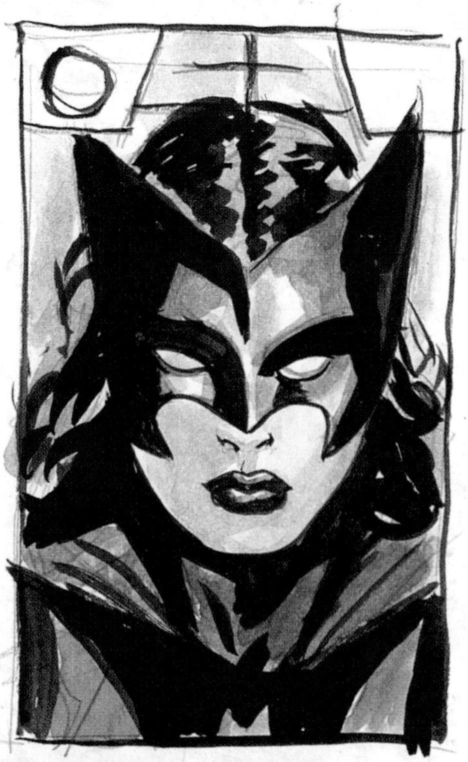

## WEEK ELEVEN

I struggled to find the best way to introduce the new Batwoman. After any number of sketches, we decided to just throw her into the middle of the action, battling some genetically mutated beasts. The cover is from Montoya's point of view, looking past her hands holding her service pistol. That was sort of inspired by first-person shooter video games.

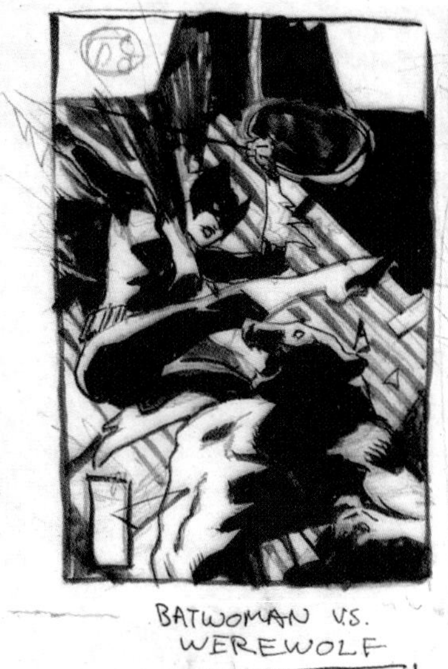
BATWOMAN VS.
WEREWOLF

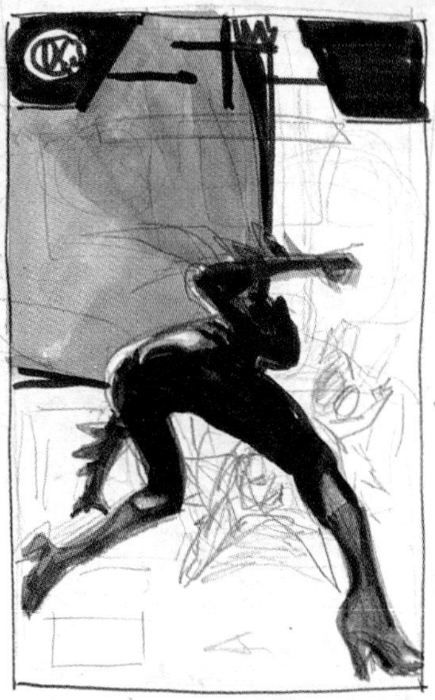

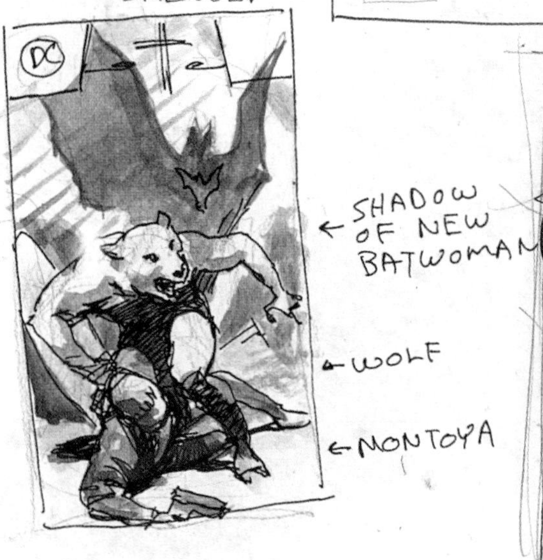
SHADOW OF NEW BATWOMAN
WOLF
MONTOYA
THE BAT IS BACK

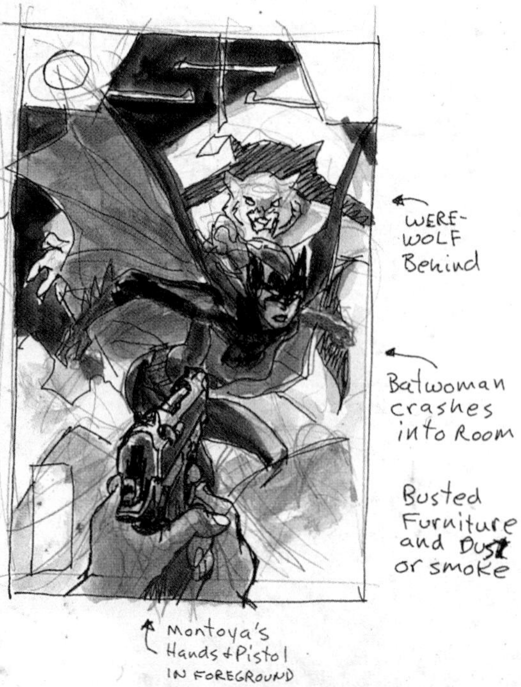
WERE-WOLF Behind
Batwoman crashes into Room
Busted Furniture and Dust or smoke
Montoya's Hands + Pistol IN FOREGROUND

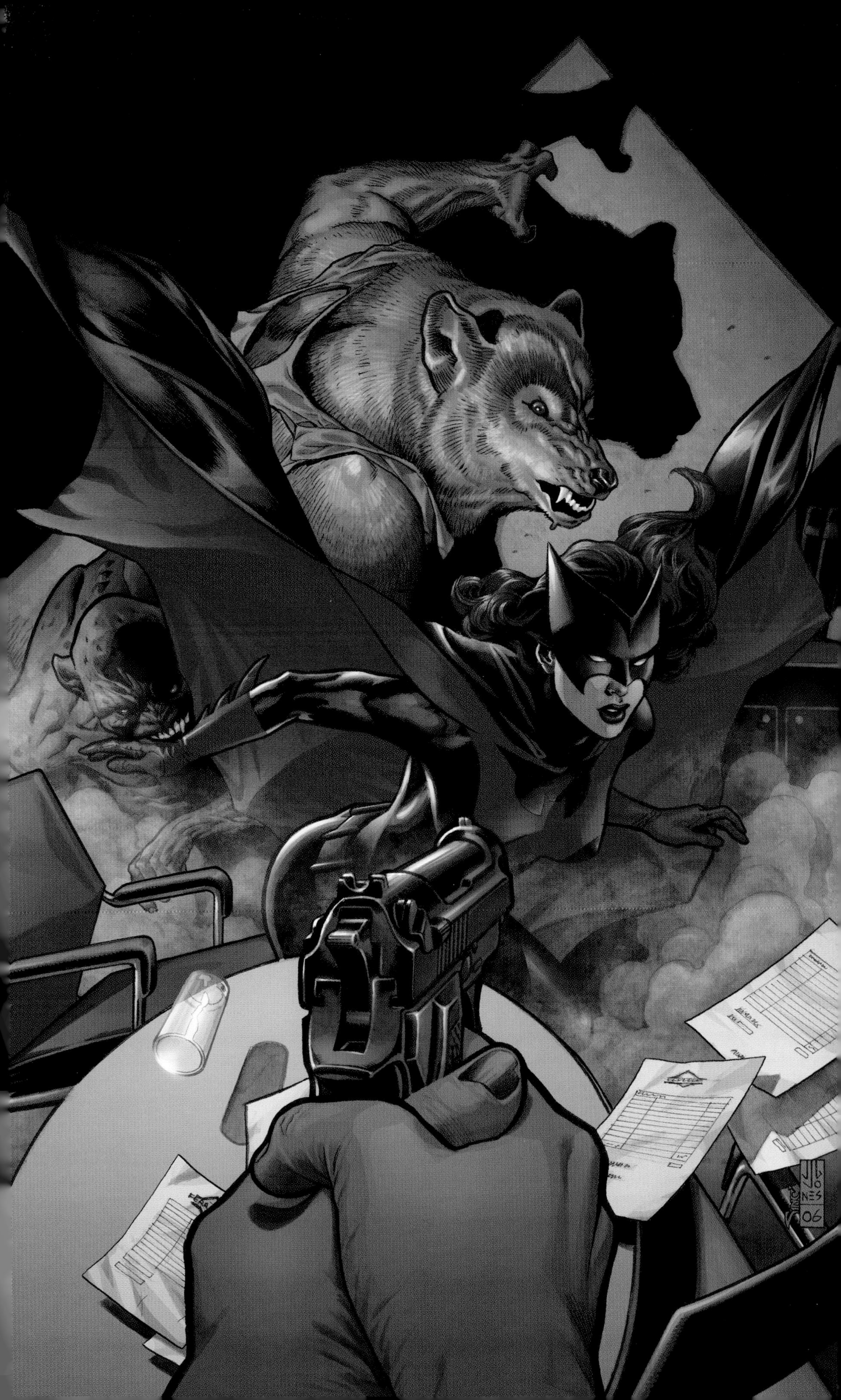
JG JONES 06

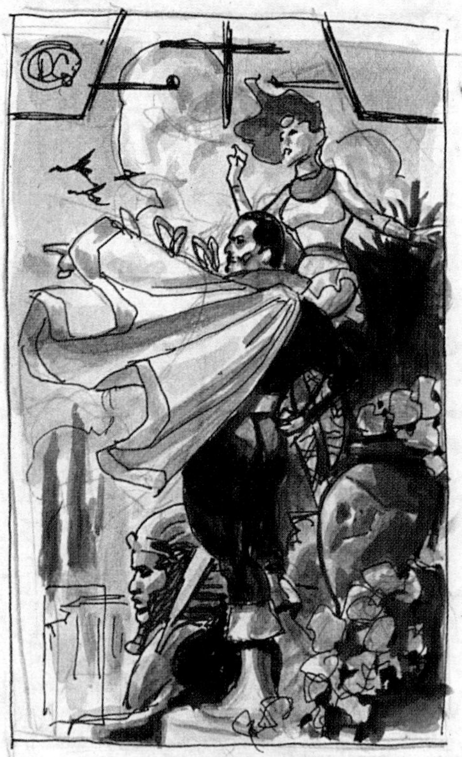

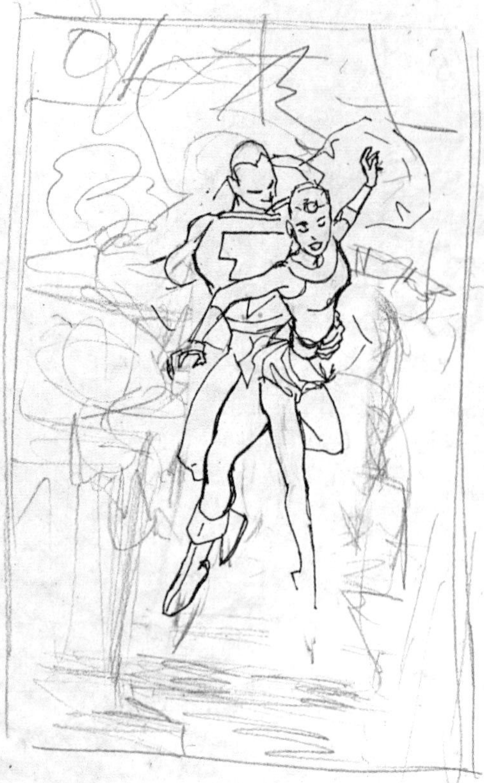

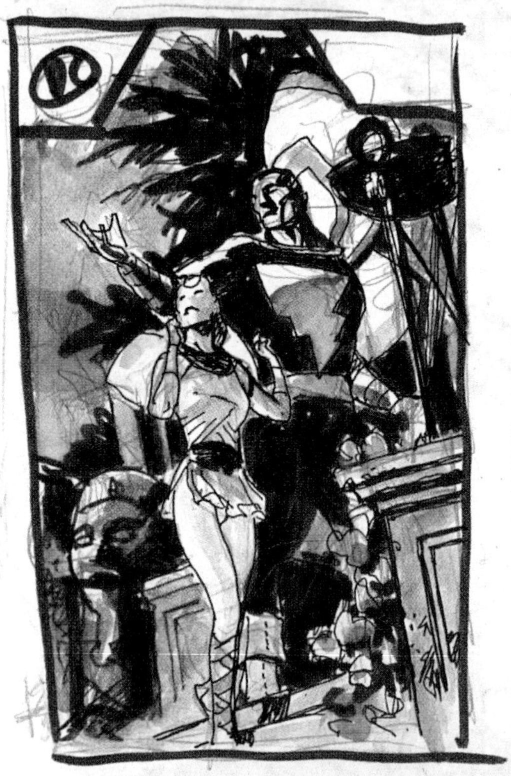

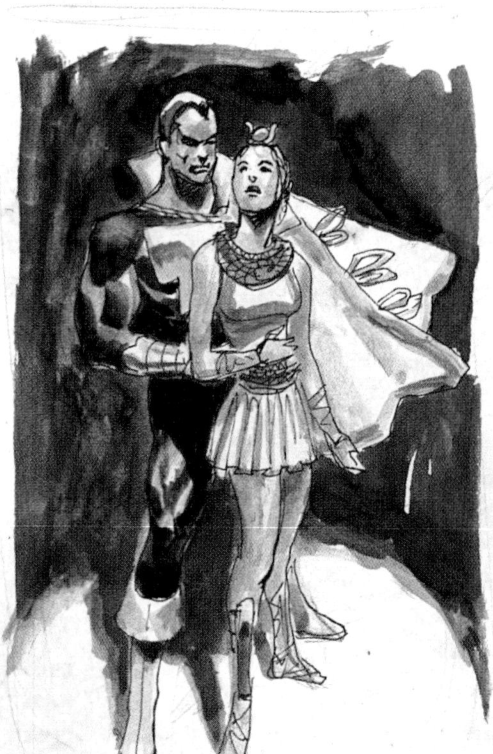

## WEEK TWELVE

This generated more concept sketches than any other cover in the entire 52 series. I wanted to choose exactly the proper image to depict the budding love between Black Adam and Isis. In the end, I went with a simple, black and white, yin-yang design, which I think works well.

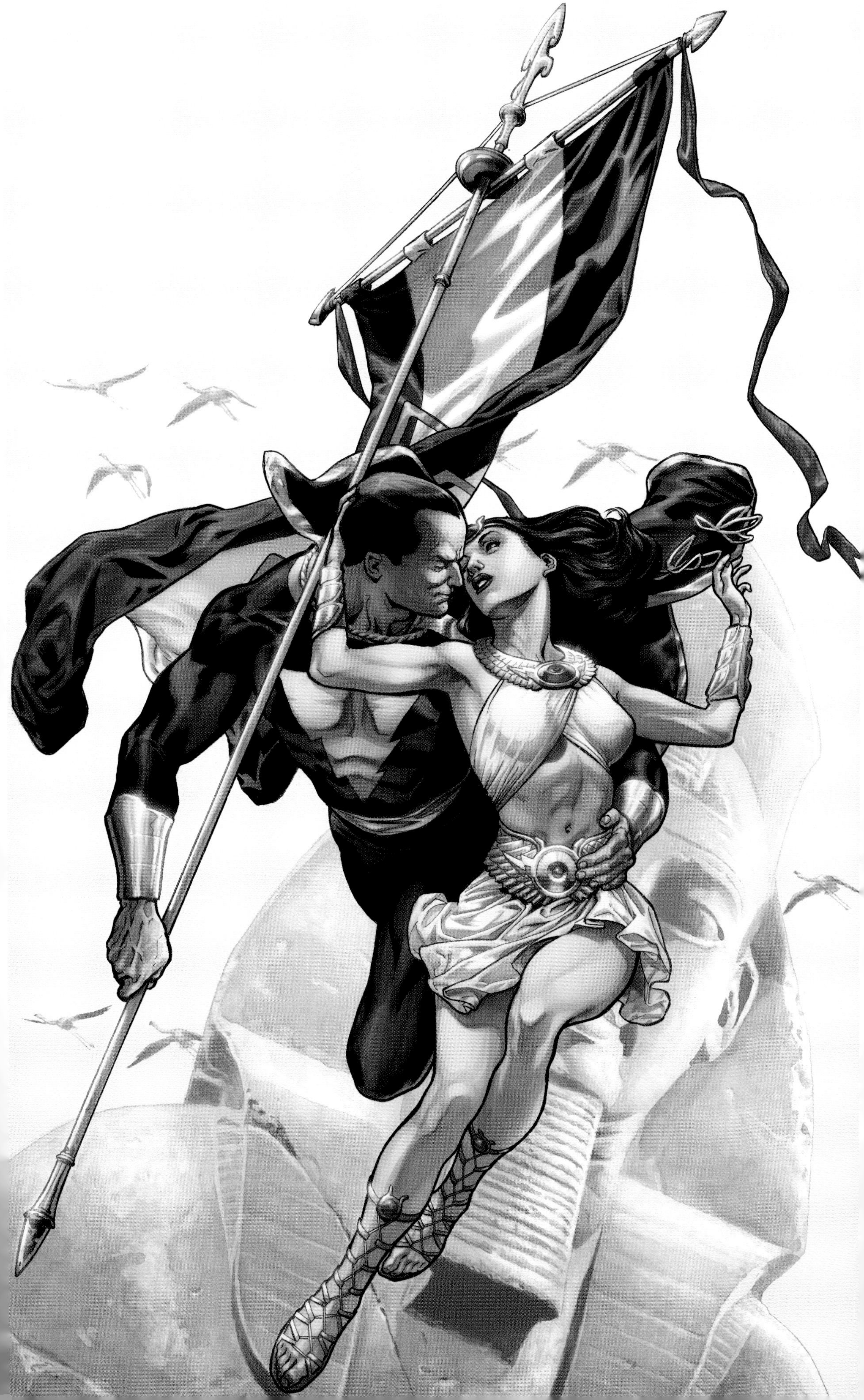

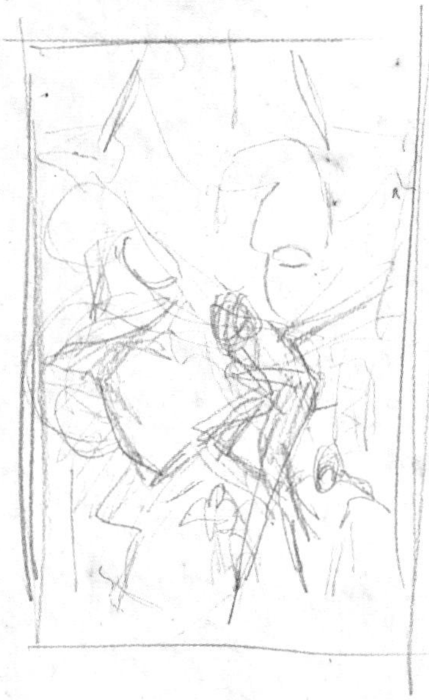

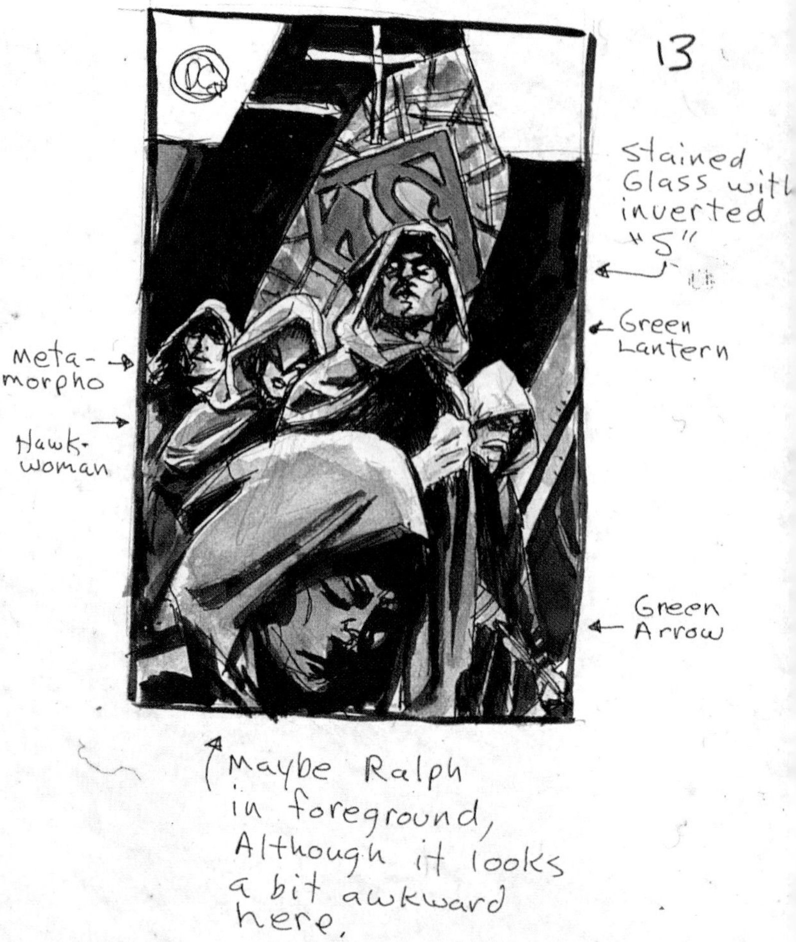
13
Stained Glass with inverted "S"
Green Lantern
Meta-morpho
Hawk-woman
Green Arrow
Maybe Ralph in foreground, Although it looks a bit awkward here.

## WEEK THIRTEEN

Although we made a few changes from the original sketch, the final cover maintains its most prominent feature, the large stained glass window with the inverted red "S," the symbol of the Cult of Conner.

I took Ralph's head out of the foreground and replaced it with a candelabra to provide moody lighting. Hawkgirl was switched to Azrael, since she was unavailable for duty in this issue.

Tilting the whole composition made the whole thing more visually dynamic.

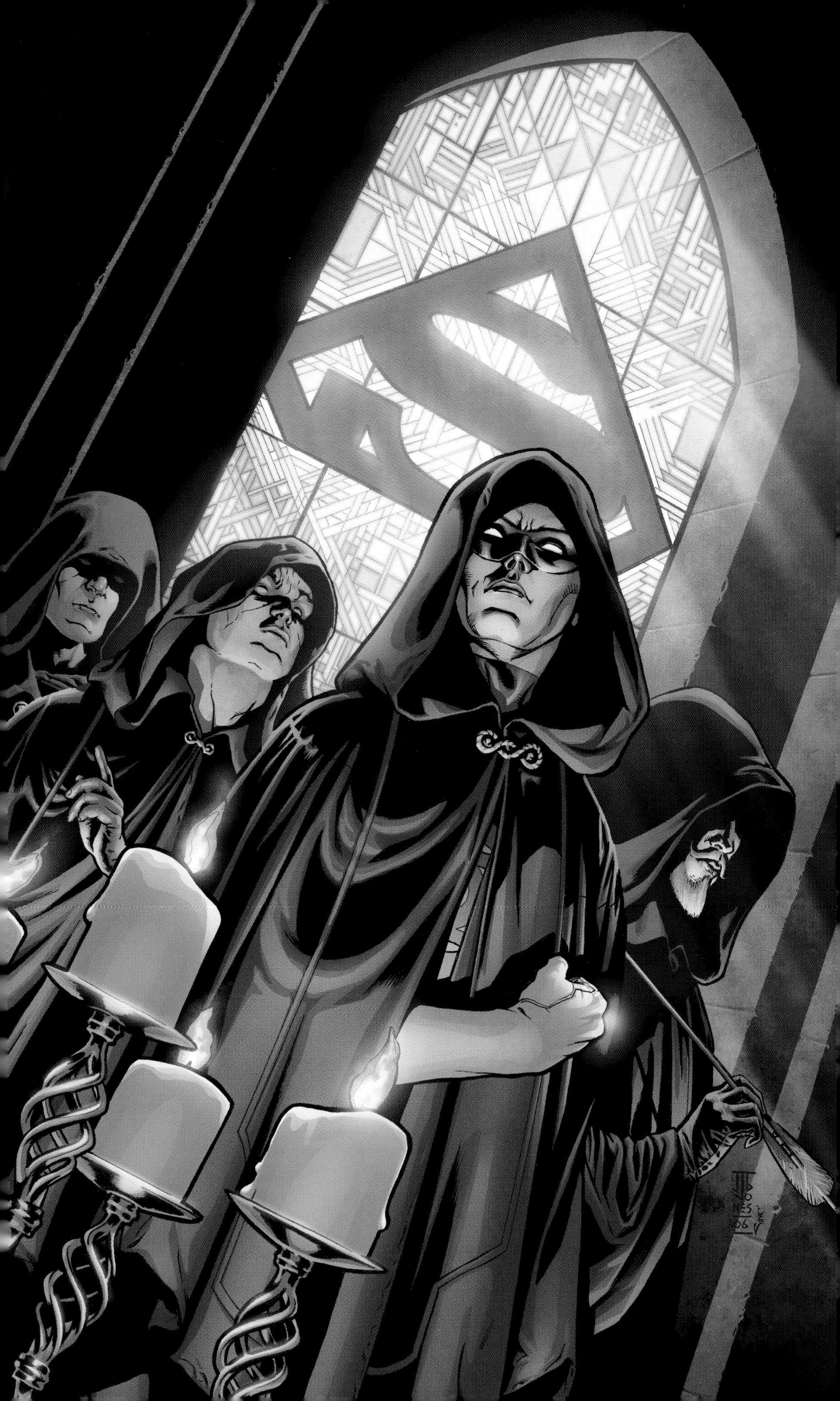

# 52 LOGO AND TRADE DRESS DESIGN

## by John J. Hill

Graphic designer John J. Hill reveals the steps to creating one of the most eye-catching logos and trade dress to hit comics stands.

52
week one

**Logo concepts:**
"As is the norm with most logo projects, I'll start off with anywhere from three to six "sketches" to get a general direction down. Compared to most logos, this was a bit more challenging because there are only two characters in "52"... in order to make this work it would have to be bigger and bolder than usual."

**Trade Dress concepts:**
"I was developing the logo as well as the trade dress (the overall design of the cover), so the next step was to take some of the logos I thought were most successful and apply them to full cover ideas. The general concept was to do something similar to a weekly magazine cover, also including a blurb and possible thumbnail image of the backup story. I definitely wanted to lean more to the non-traditional side and include some larger shapes to anchor the logo and elements instead of the usual floating look."

DC
52
week one
no. 1
$2.99 US
$3.99 CAN
PLUS:
A HISTORY OF THE DC UNIVERSE PT. 1 BY
FRANK MILLER
JOHNS • MORRISON • RUCKA • WAID • CLARK • MILLER

**Trade Dress 1:**
"This was a simple, classy version. I was thinking about the *New Yorker* and *New York Magazine*, if they were revamped to be less conservative visually."

JOHNS • MORRISON • RUCKA • WAID • CLARK • MILLER
DC
WEEK ONE
no. 1
$2.99 US
$3.99 CAN
BONUS:
FRANK MILLER


**Trade Dress 2:**
"I liked this version a lot. The dimensionality of the logo and overlapping artwork popped nicely. I think the multiple curvy shapes ended up being a bit too complex. Not knowing what JG was going to be doing with the art, this idea could have caused a lot of problems week after week. Ideally, when creating a logo, you should be able to drop any artwork into a template and it should work with very little tweaking."

52
WEEK ONE
no. 1
JOHNS • MORRISON • RUCKA • WAID • CLARK • MILLER
MARCH 1, 2006
$2.99 US
$3.99 CAN
BONUS:
A HISTORY OF THE DC UNIVERSE PART 1 BY
FRANK MILLER

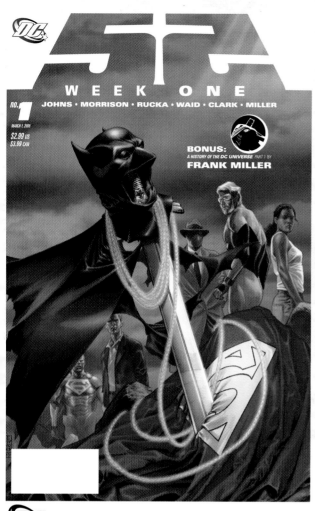

**Trade Dress 3:**
"Obviously this is the direction we ended up going with. Using the negative space for the logo would definitely ensure each issue looking unique."

$2.50 US
$3.50 CAN
May 10, 2006
52
WEEK ONE
IT STARTS
HERE!
DIRECT SALES
52thecomic.com
WHERE ARE SUPERMAN, BATMAN, AND WONDER WOMAN?...

**Final Logo and Trade Dress template:**
"This was the final version that I handed off... note the addition of the "ticker" at the bottom and bevel to help pop the logo more. At the end of the day the date and price moved to the top right, no thumbnail would be used for the backup feature blurb, and the week would reflect the issue number instead of an actual "no. 1" and the like."

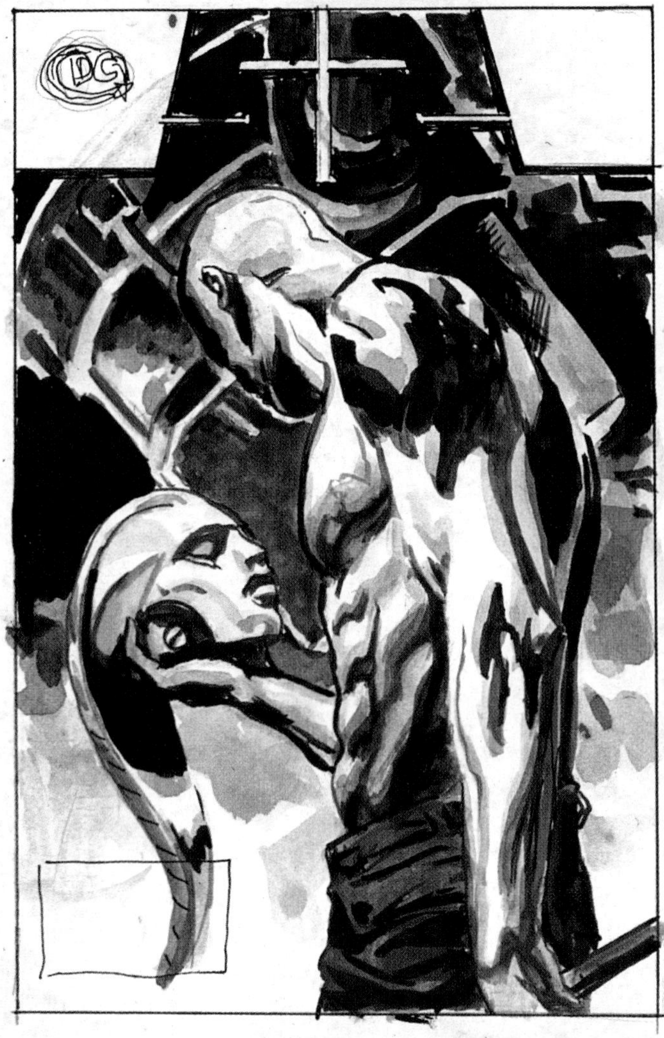

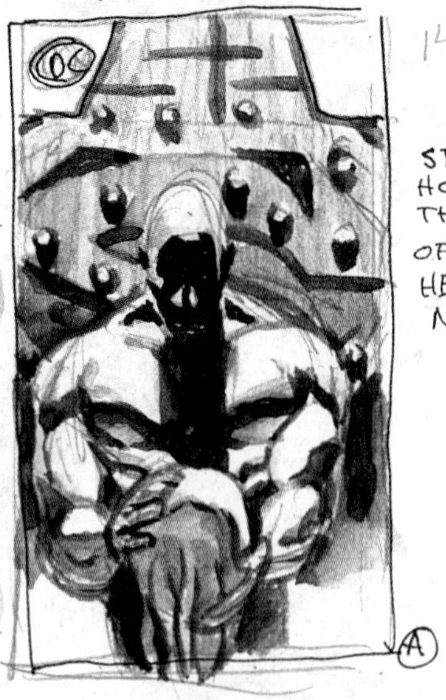
14
STEEL HOLDING THE HELMET OF THE ARMOR HE'S MADE FOR NATASHA
A

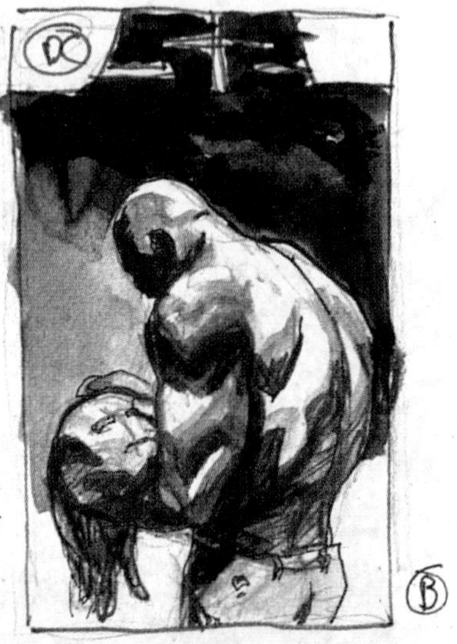
B

ISSUE 14 SKETCHES

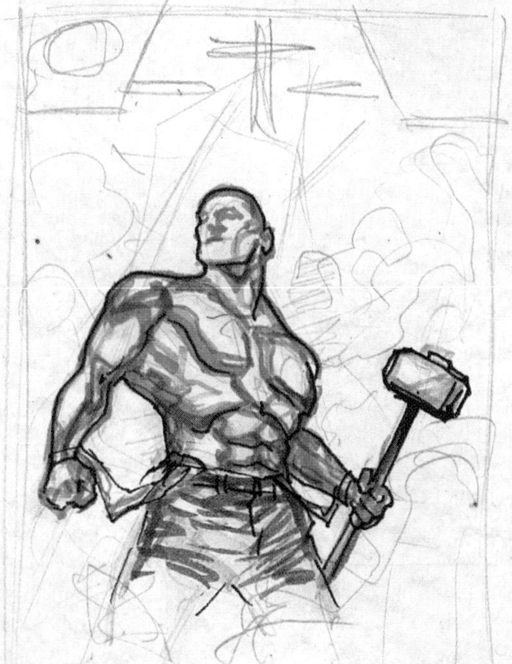
Steel Skin Steaming Shirt Burned away clearing Smoke

STEEL 'DOC Savage' cover

## WEEK FOURTEEN

I think that this was editor Steve Wacker's favorite cover. It's a poignant moment with a chrome-skinned Steel gazing sadly at the face of the armor he has created for his niece Natasha, who has abandoned him to join Lex Luthor's new superhero team. Here he is left alone with only his misgivings and regrets.

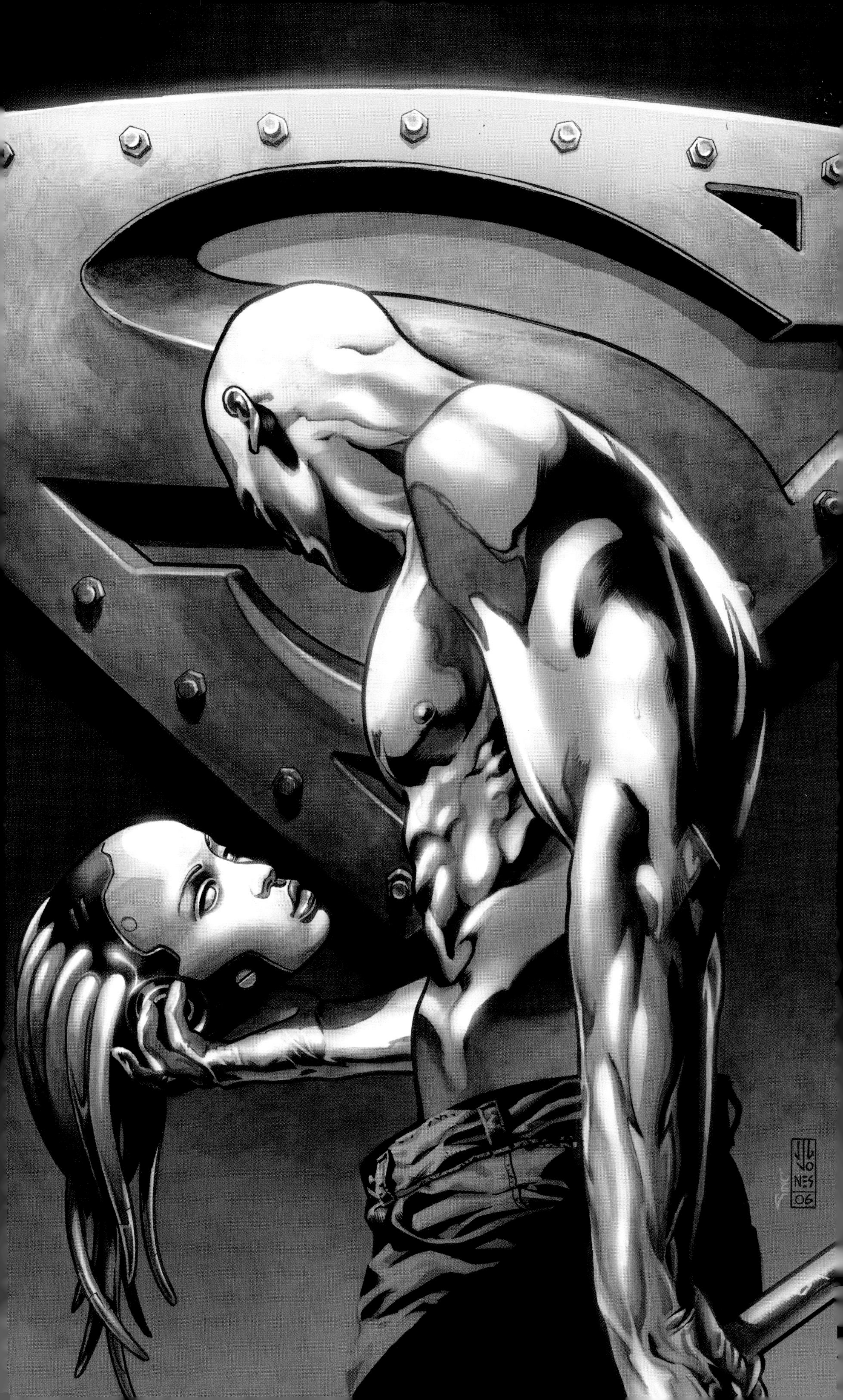

# #15

## WEEK FIFTEEN

I first did a number of sketches of Booster in an epic smack-down battle before realizing that an oblique approach worked much better for this cover. I pared it down to the most essential story elements: Booster's broken goggles, the drops of blood that imply an awful fate, and the cryptic, hovering figure of Supernova reflected in the lenses.

I love doing this kind of storytelling with just a single image. As soon as I sent this sketch in, Keith Giffen called in with almost exactly this idea for the cover. Weird.

15

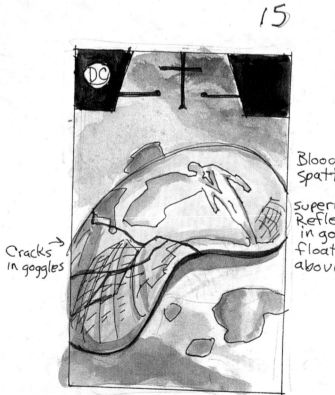

Blood
spatter

Supernova
Reflected
in goggles-
floating
above

Cracks →
In goggles

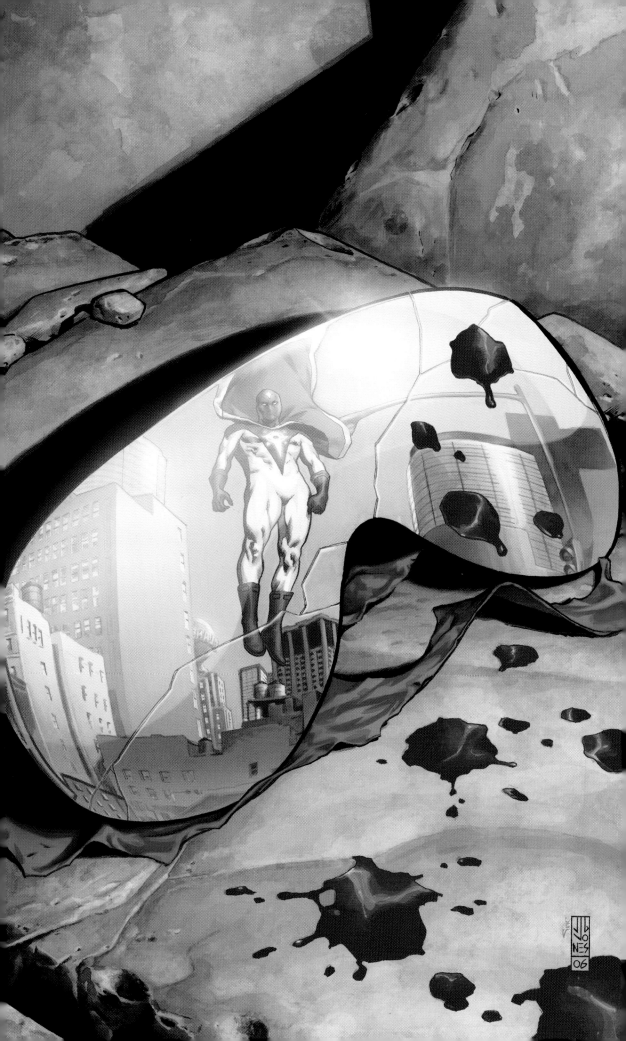

Bunting

Poster of
B.A.&Isis
celebrating
the wedding

Flower petals
raining down

Montoya
with
Intergang
Pistol

## WEEK SIXTEEN

I had to find a way to depict Montoya and The Question on the same cover with Black Adam and Isis, even though the two pairs do not directly interact in the issue. My solution was to put Montoya and Question in front of a banner featuring the images of Black Adam and Isis. The banner is a propaganda poster announcing the wedding of the couple.

The flower petals raining down are an indication that Isis is nearby, possibly flying overhead near where Montoya is pointing her blaster.

16

This one

x wall should have
glazed tiles
(see orientalist
painter book
for ref.)

Variation
with Gun
aimed &
Vic in fore-
ground

More energetic
pose

Poster in
Back on wall

flower petals,
etc

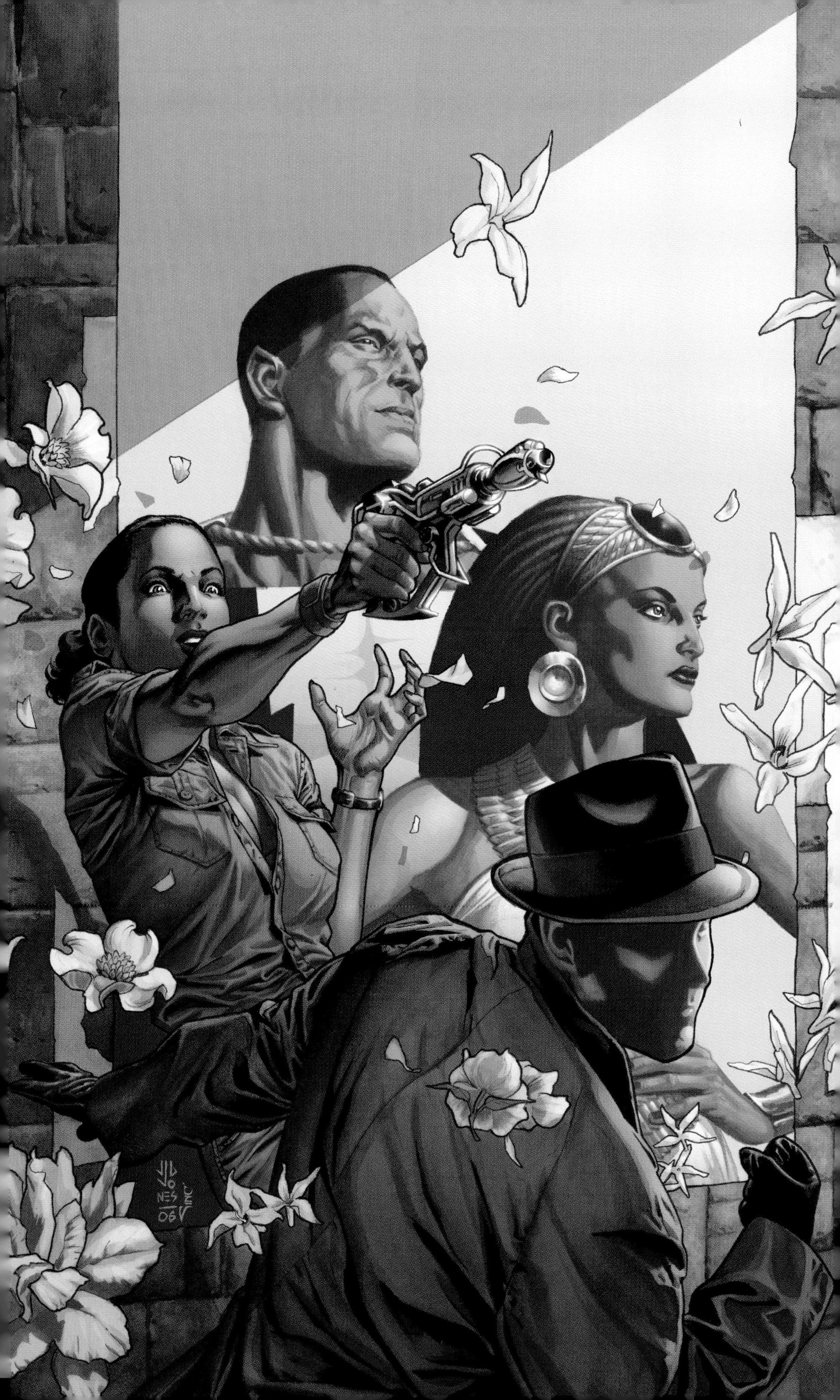

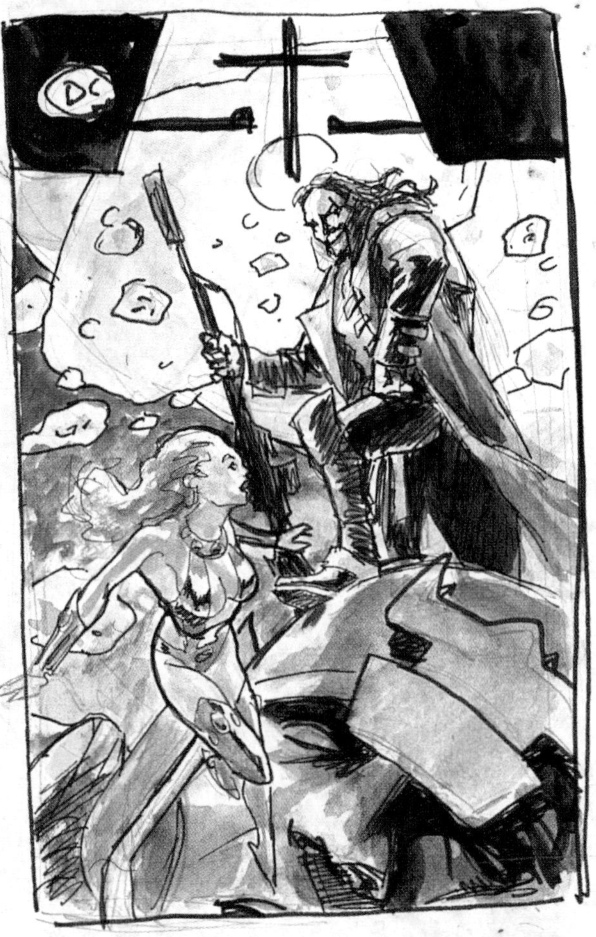

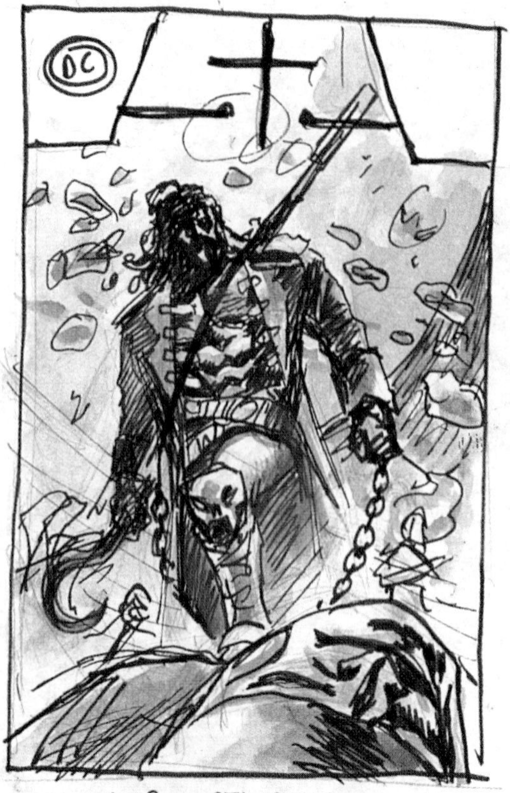

LOBO STANDING ON THE BODY OF Devilance- Starfire in background

## WEEK SEVENTEEN

It's our old pal Lobo. In keeping with those hilarious old Lobo covers of yesteryear, we did a goofy little riff on the first 52 cover. This was a fun one for me. I have a buddy who loves Lobo, and, luckily, he looks enough like the last Czarnian to pose for me...complete with cigar.

Starfire

ADAM STRANGE

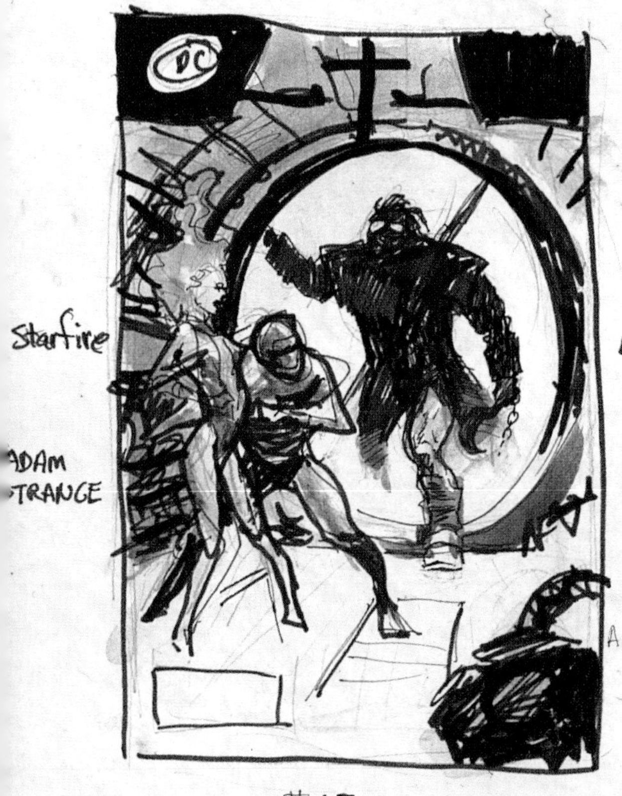

LOBO

Asteroids

#17 "FRAZETTA" COVER

Giant Planeto

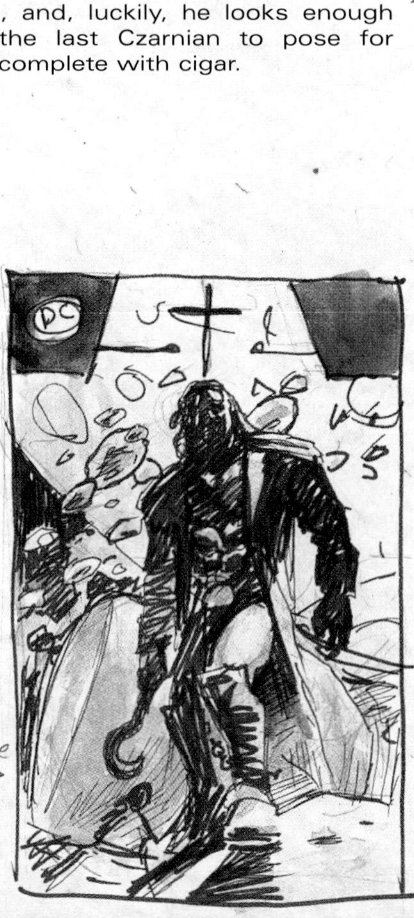

LOBO IN Backligh

Head of Devilance →

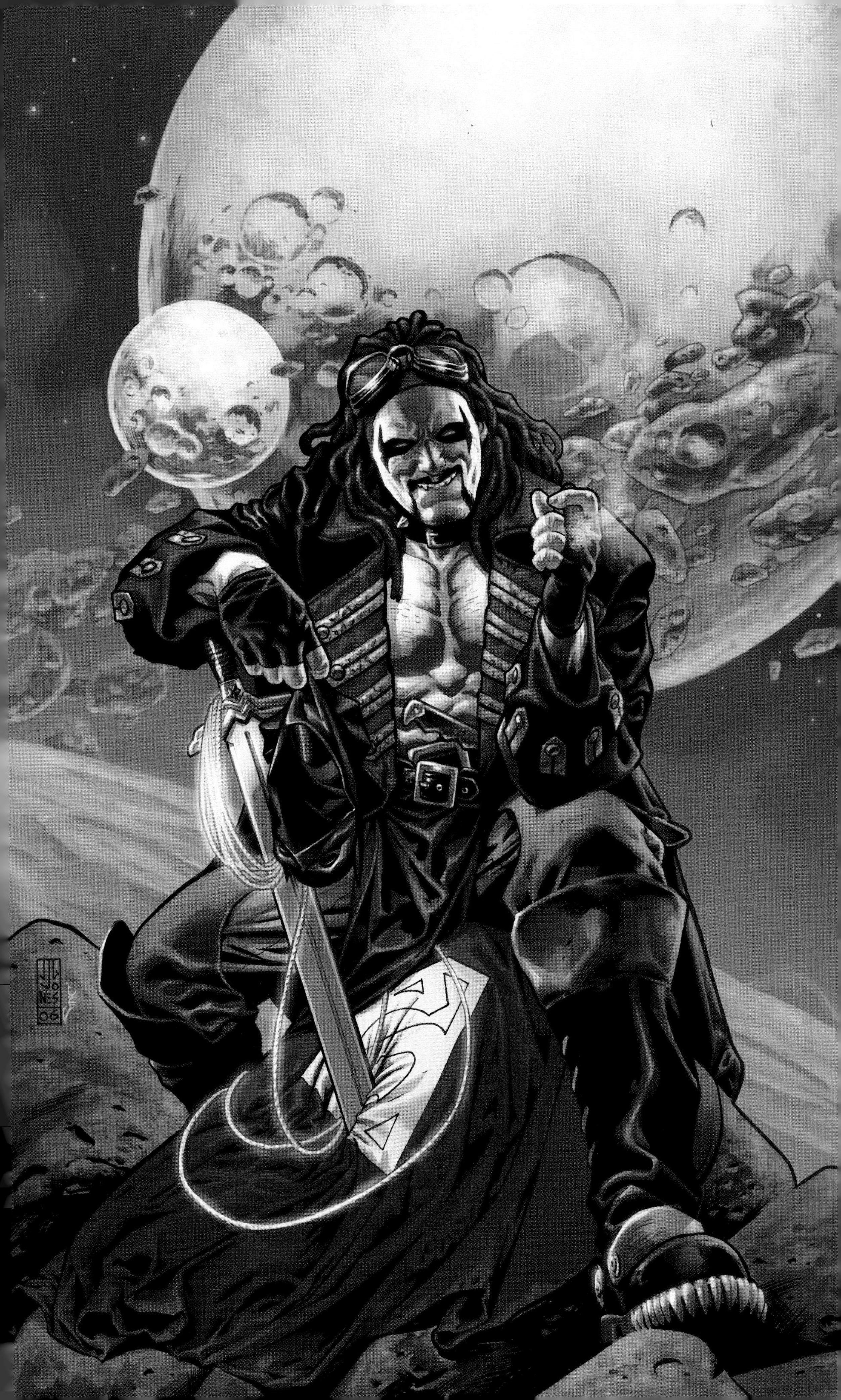

18

spooky
sky

Pyramid
in back

Det. →
chimp
&
shadow-
pact
in
rear

Ralph
stands
behind
glowing
Dr. Fate
Helm in
sand

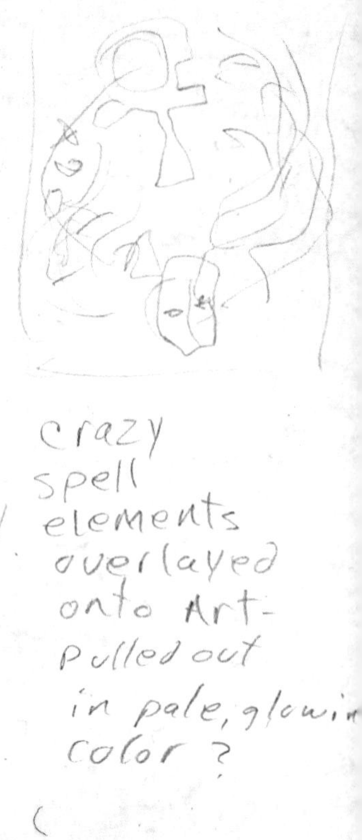

crazy
spell
elements
overlayed
onto Art-
Pulled out
in pale, glowing
color?

## WEEK EIGHTEEN

I gave this cover an old pulp magazine look, complete with hand-lettered title. I love the lurid look of those cheap paperbacks from the '30s and '40s and wanted to give it a try when the proper moment turned up. This was just what the doctor ordered.

Alex enhanced the dime novel feel by keeping the coloring bright and garish. He also added faux scratches and distress marks on the surface. Cool, huh?

18

Lurid
TALES
of TERROR

5:20
on the
clock

CALLING
DR. FATE!

MEET
FATE

Blue or
Green

18

Yellow

Yellow

CALLING
DR FATE

Red

Phoney Tears & Yellowing
edges

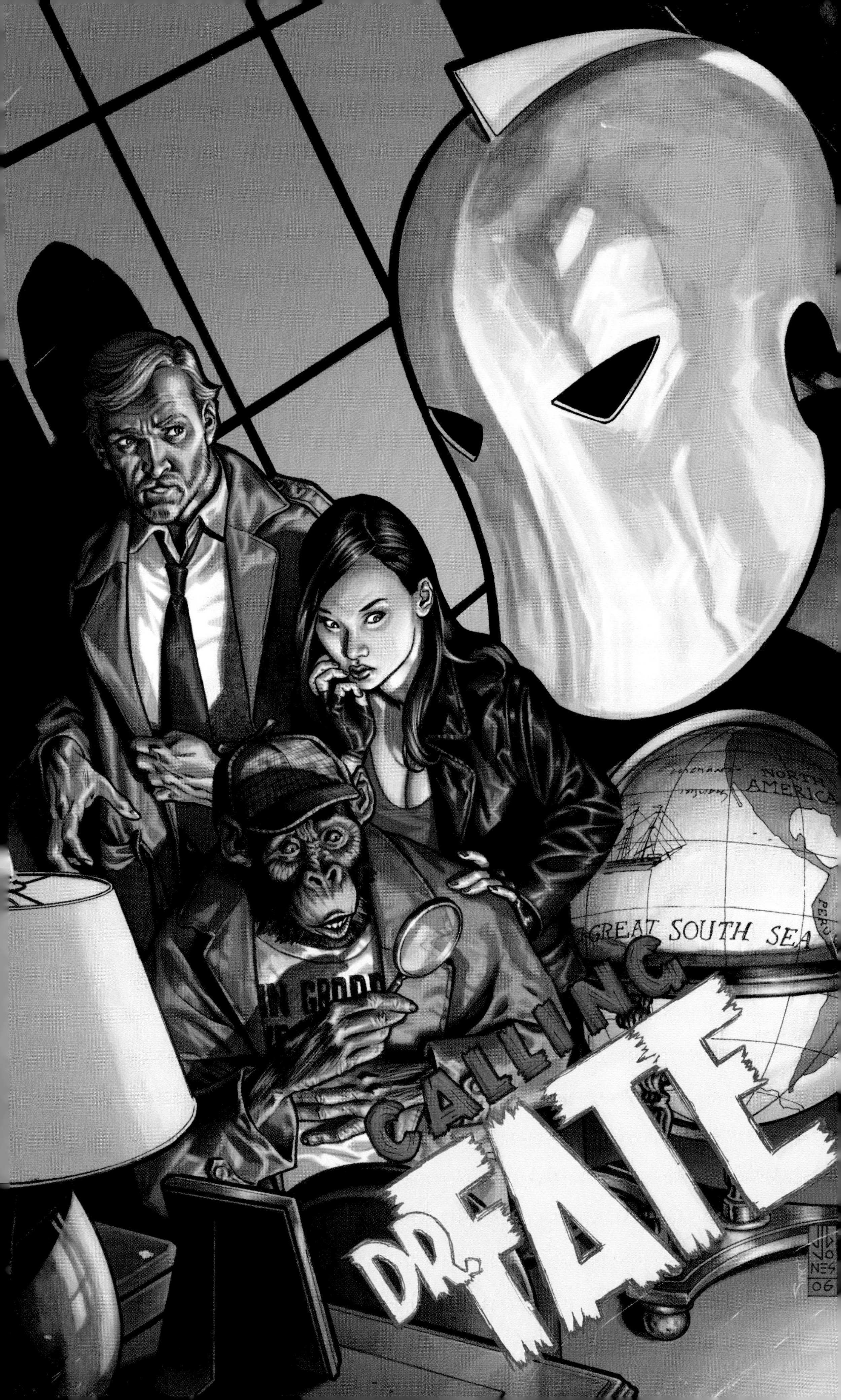
NORTH AMERICA
GREAT SOUTH SEA
PERU
CALLING
DR. FATE

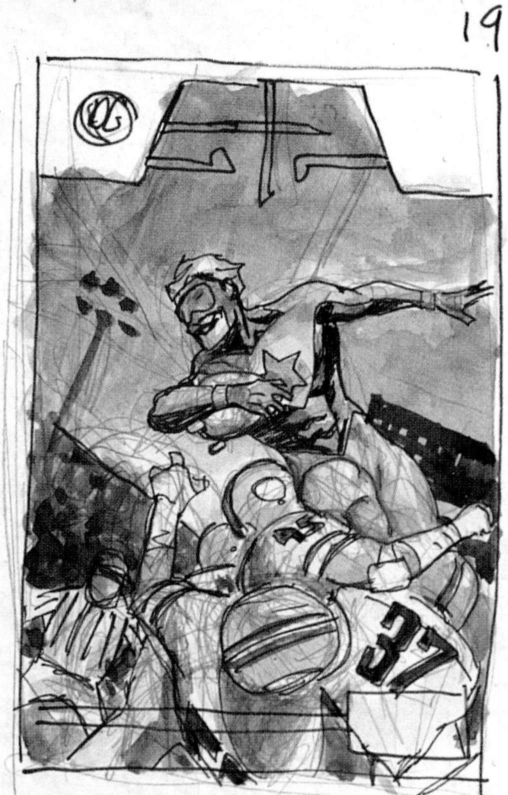

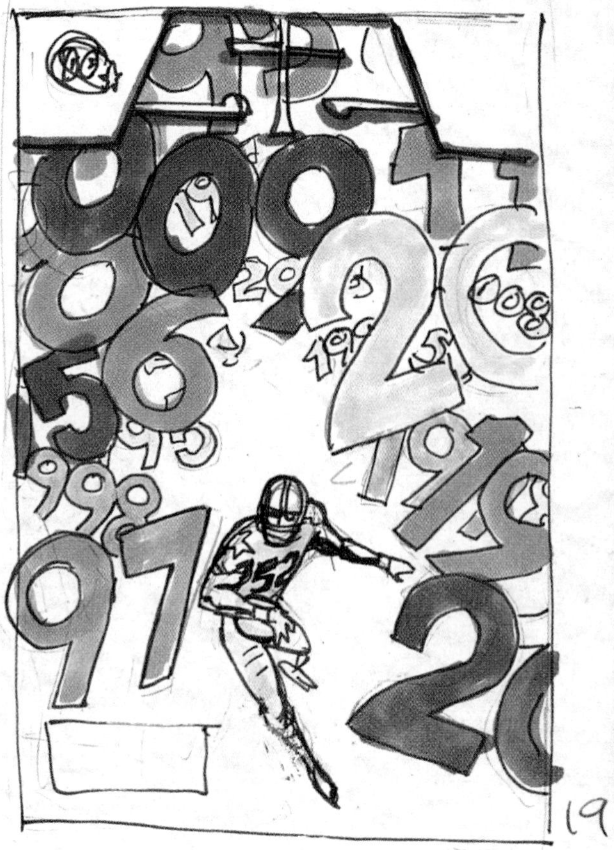

## WEEK NINETEEN

OK. We all know that Booster Gold was a football star before traveling back in time to the present and using his trusty robot sidekick's encyclopedic knowledge of events to fight crime and win acclaim. The fact that Skeets is shaped like a football as well made this just too good to pass up.

Steve Wacker nixed the initial touchdown sketches in favor of something that emphasized the time travel element of the story. Good call, Steve. Go long.

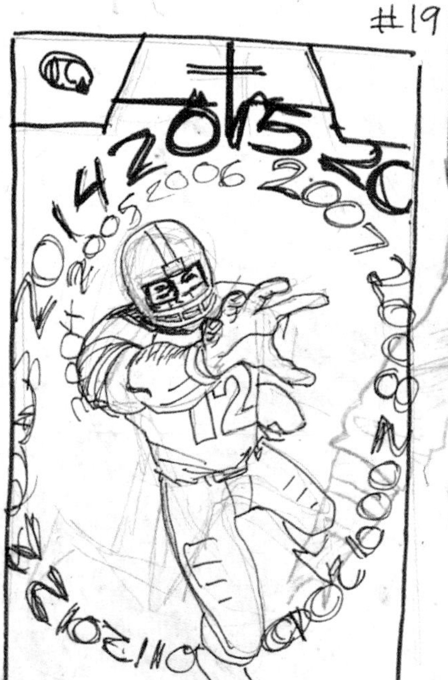

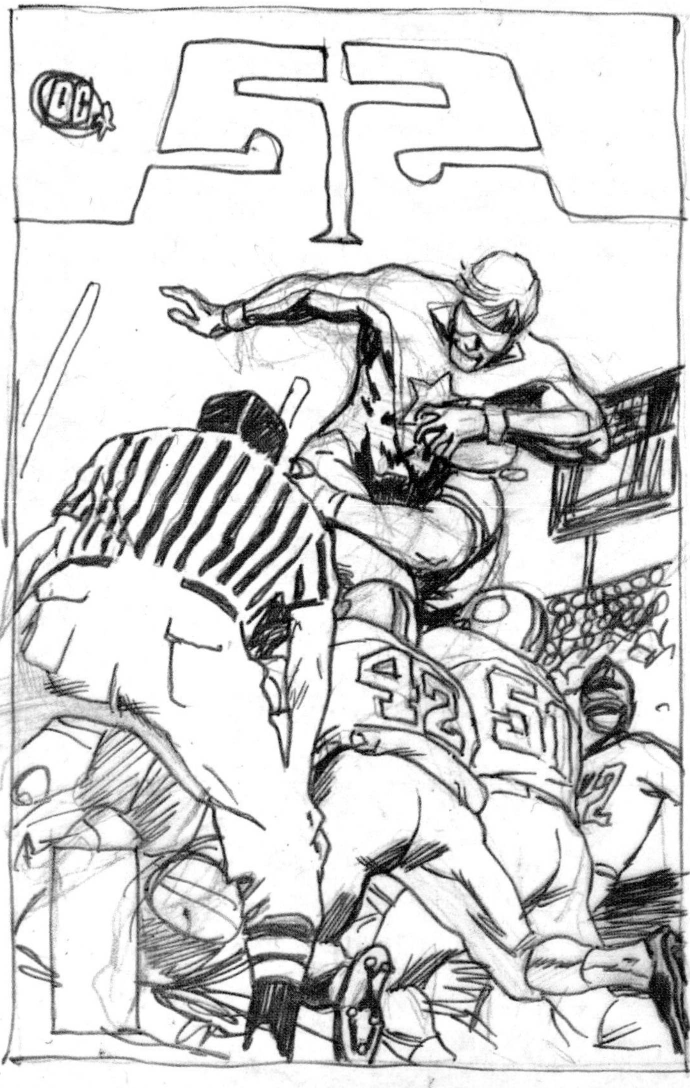

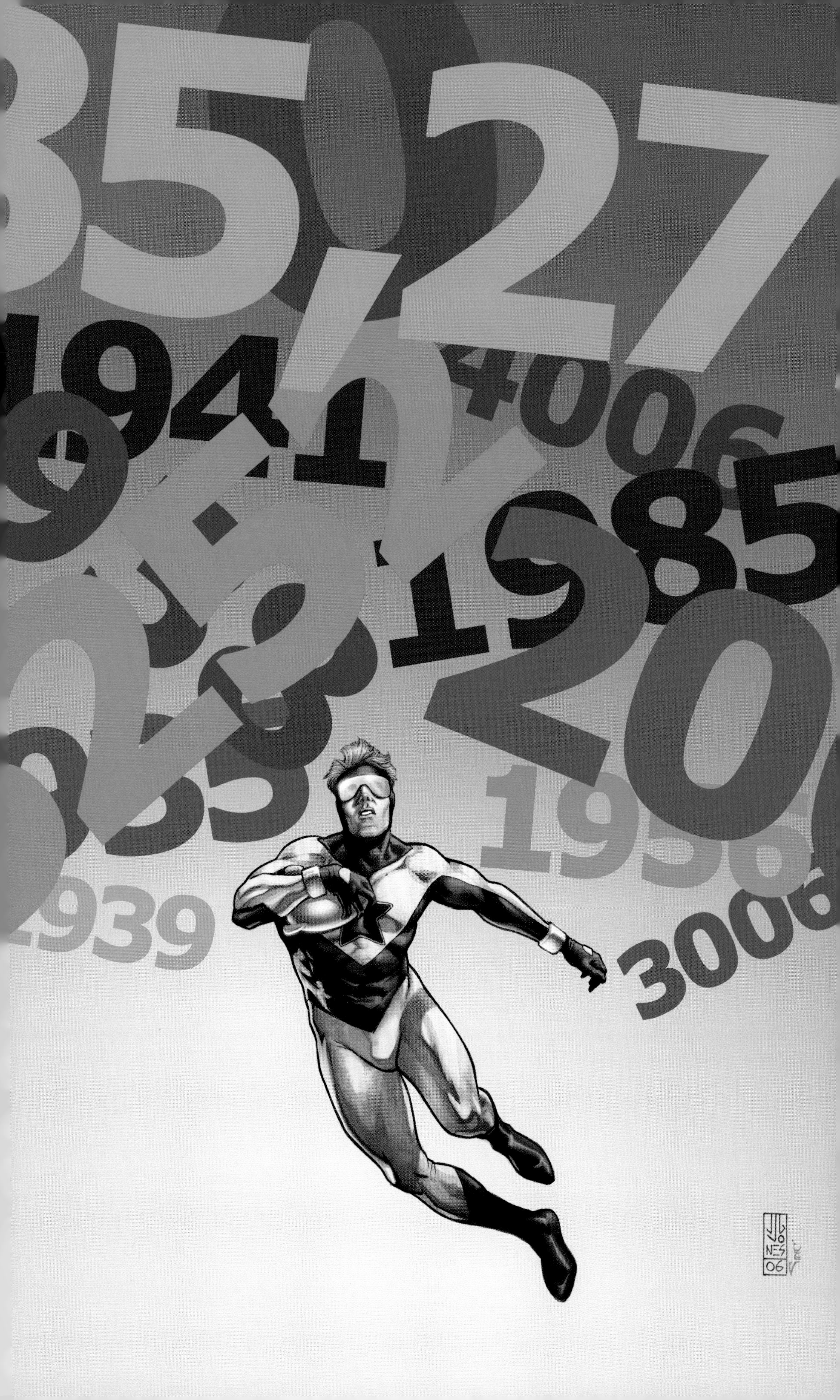
1941
1985

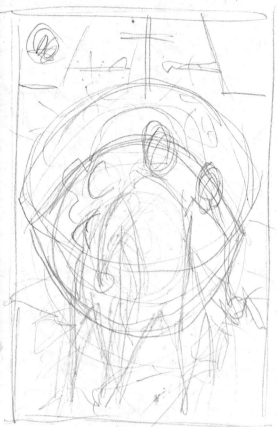

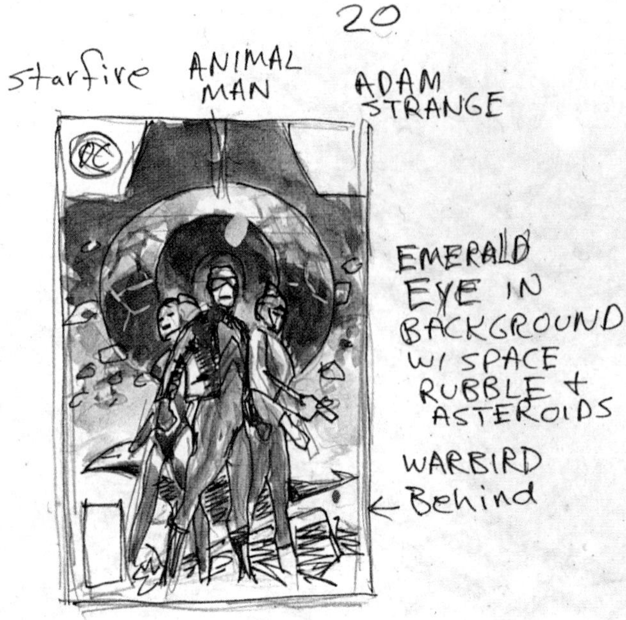

starfire ANIMAL MAN ADAM STRANGE

20

EMERALD EYE IN BACKGROUND W/ SPACE RUBBLE + ASTEROIDS

WARBIRD ← Behind

## WEEK TWENTY

Our intrepid spacefarers finally get the movie poster treatment. I don't really like to do covers like this too often, with the heroes just standing around posing for the camera, but the fans seem to love them. The Emerald Eye of Ekron dominates the background, as it will soon dominate their fate.

I felt that this was one of my weaker images, but Alex Sinclair bailed me out once again with his masterly color work.

USE Action poses instead

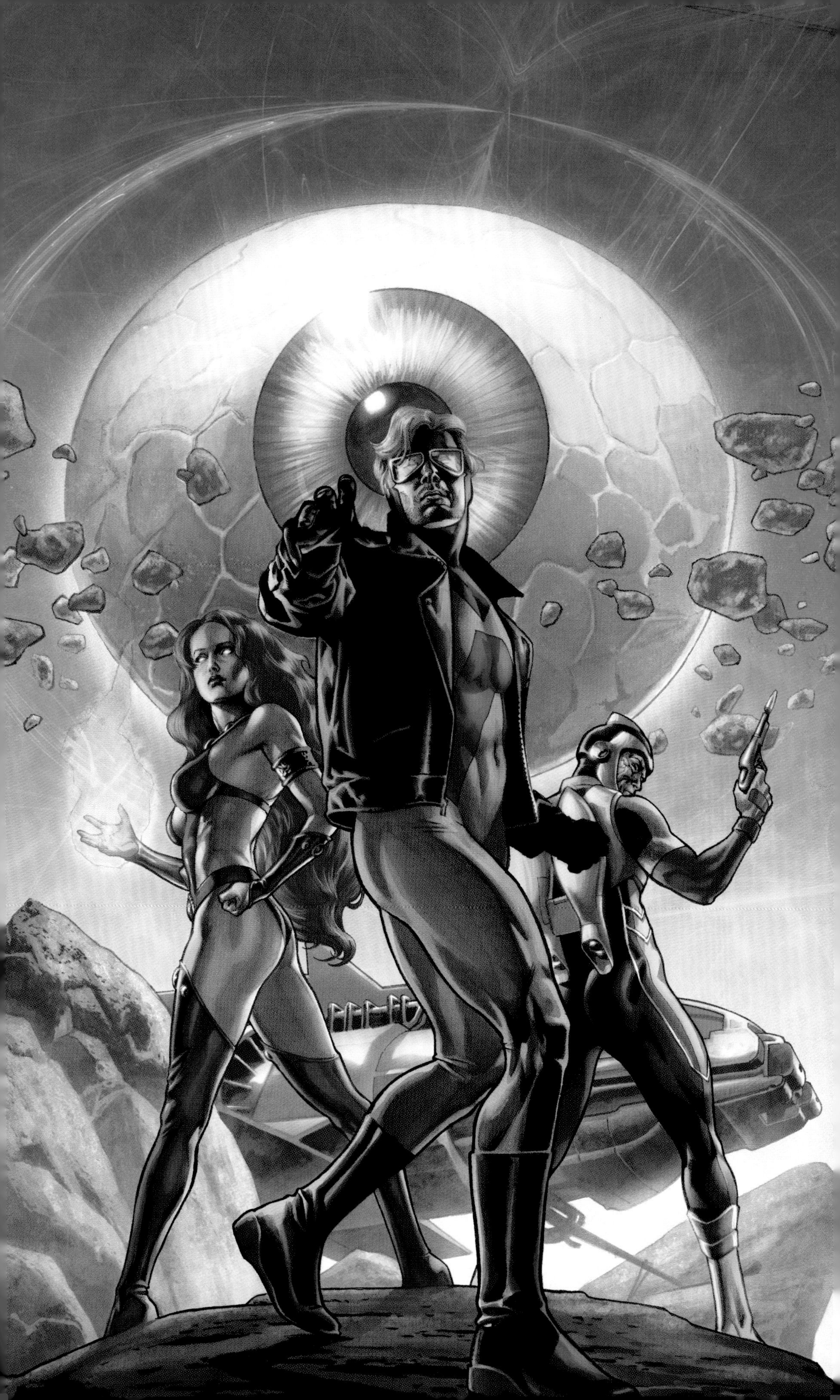

21

Infinity, Inc.
Shadows
become
the
Teen
Titans

21

INFINITY,
INC.
SHATTERING
FOREGROUND
PANEL——

TEEN
TITANS
ON BROKEN
SHARDS

## WEEK TWENTY-ONE

How do you get two superhero teams onto one cover without calling in George Pérez? The shadow gimmick in the first sketch only works well with a limited number of characters, and I was way over my limit here. Another solution was to have the replacement team shattering the image of the first team like a pane of glass. Works for me.

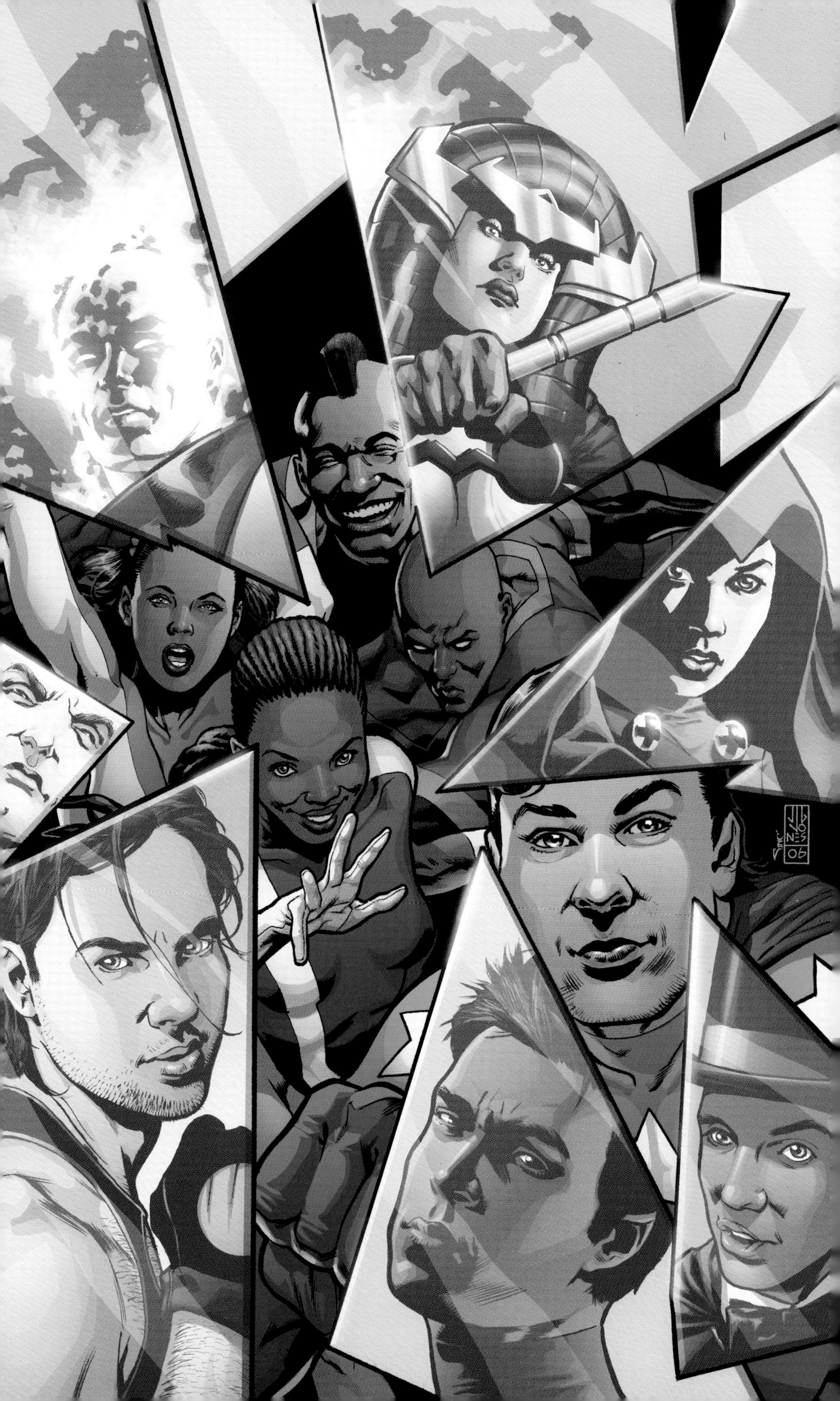

22

Dr. Magnus
Running
AWAY FROM
GIANT ROBOT

22

GRAPHIC
POSTER
STYLE

RED
SILHOUETTE
OF GIANT
ROBOT

↑
Dr. Magnus
Running

## WEEK TWENTY-TWO

This is one of my favorite 52 covers. I love great design but don't consider myself a great designer, so it was very satisfying for me to pull off an image that works well from a graphic design standpoint.

I was looking at a lot of great old film posters from the '40s and '50s for inspiration, which led me to limit the palette to two colors plus the white of the page. This is also where I got the idea of using the Metal Men's symbols as graphic elements rather than drawing them in as figures.

The running Doc Magnus is reminiscent of Cary Grant running from the airplane in *North By Northwest*.

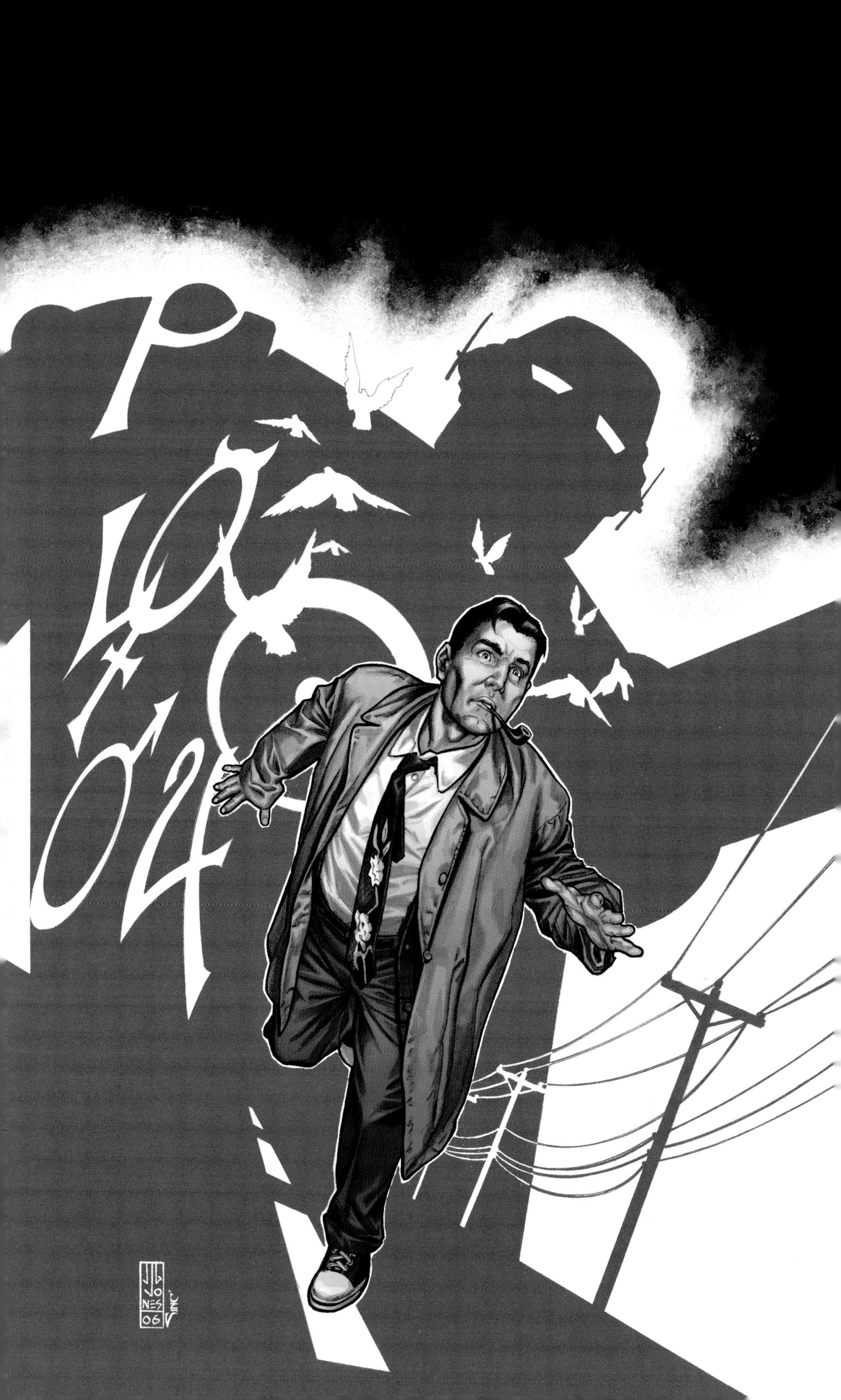
JG JONES 06

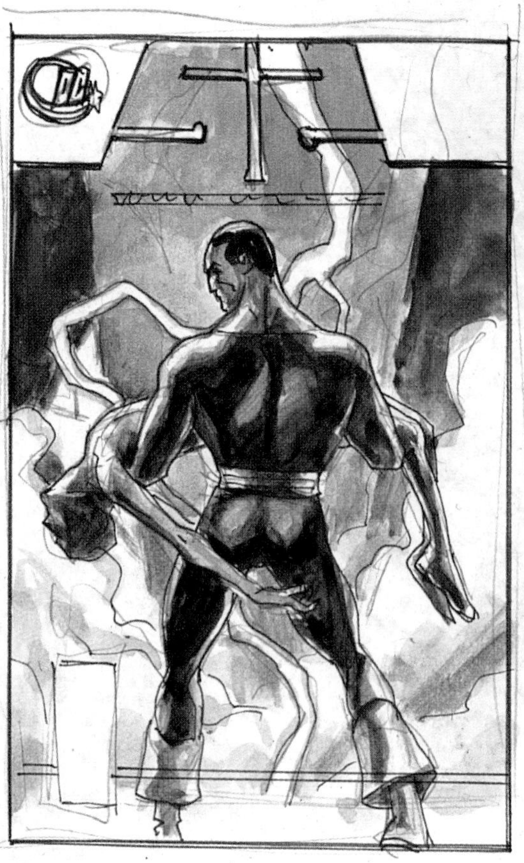

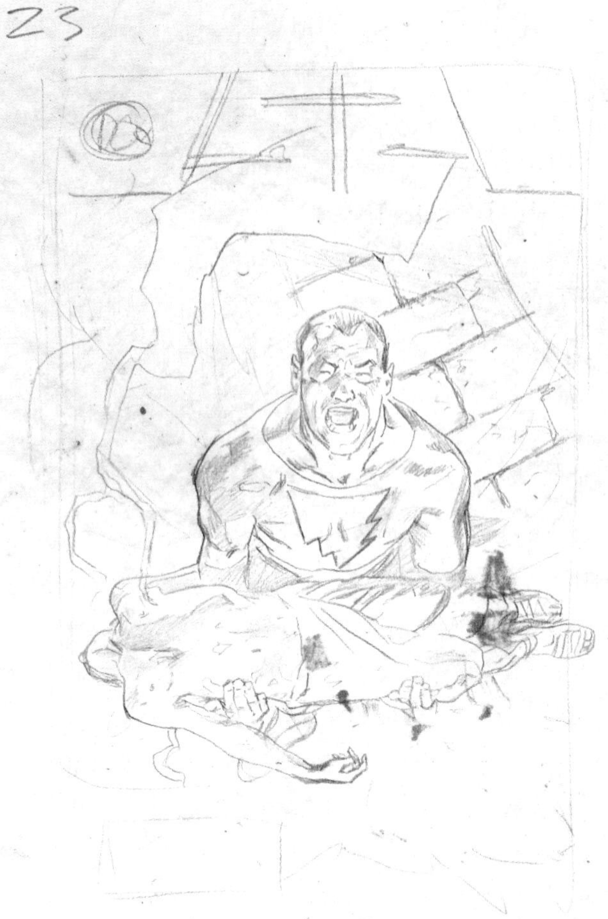
23

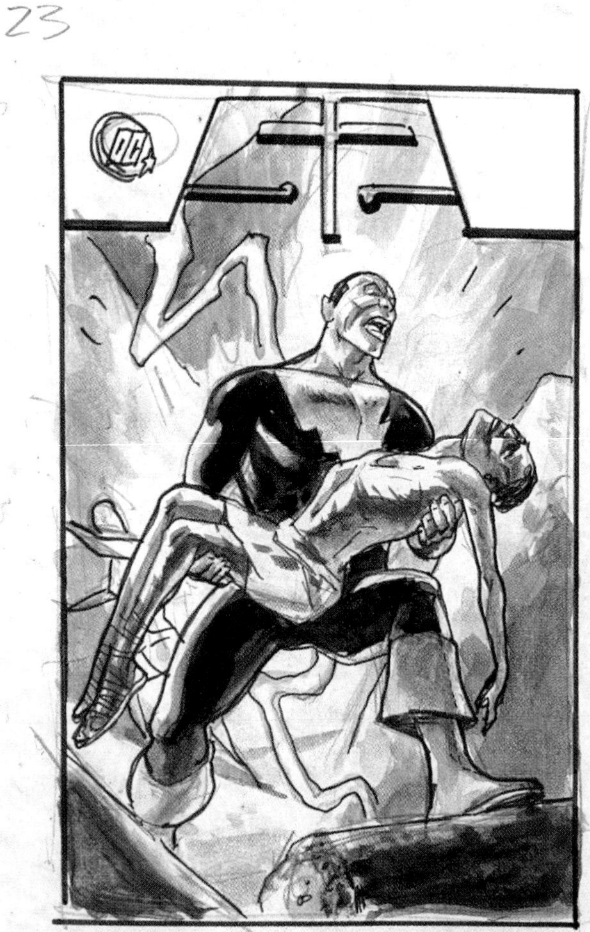
23

## WEEK TWENTY-THREE

Yeah, I know...we've seen this shot a million times before. The hero holds his dying comrade in his arms, head raised and screaming to the heavens, "Nooooooooo!" Hackneyed, right?

Only, this time, Black Adam is calling down the lightning that will imbue the dying boy with an amazing measure of Adam's own strength.

I went with the down-shot for the final version, and Alex's color work is just superb.

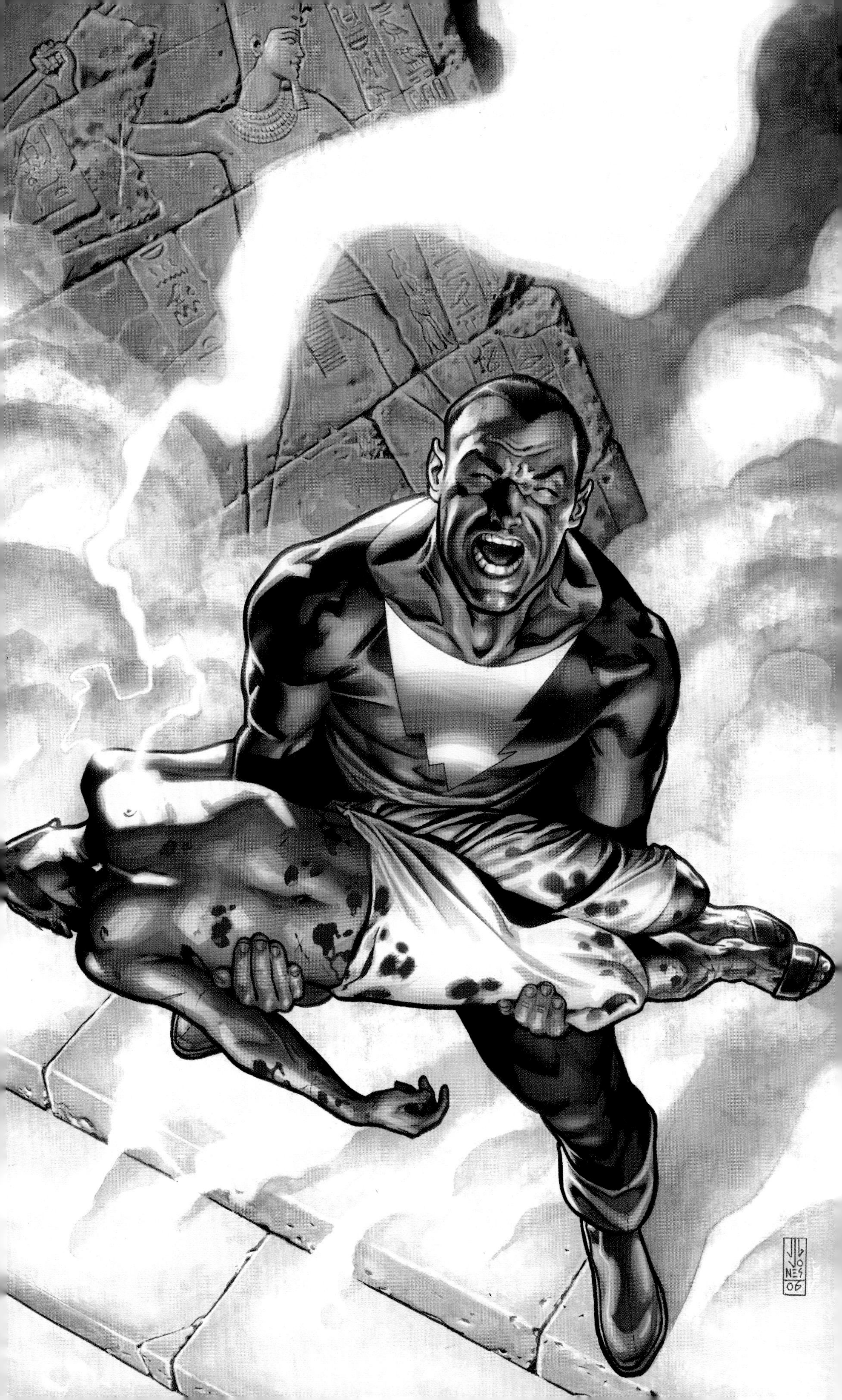

WE WANT
YOU
TO JOIN THE JLA

JUSTICE LEAGUE

FIRESTORM
FIREHAWK
BULLETEER
SUPERCHIEF
AMBUSH BUG

IN Battle with Pirates and
Futuristic Robowarriors
on zippy Skycycles

## WEEK TWENTY-FOUR

This is a riff on the old Uncle Sam recruiting poster, obviously. But that's not the odd thing about this cover.

What's odd is Firestorm. He's a guy who walks around with his head on fire. How does that work exactly? How does he avoid setting his curtains aflame or lie down for a nap without burning down his apartment building? He would be good to have around on a cold night in hobo village, though.

Ambush Bug's shirt reads, "THIS SHIRT'S A CLUE." Steve Wacker threw that in as a tongue-in-cheek response to the rumors that every cover held a hidden clue to solving the final mystery of 52.

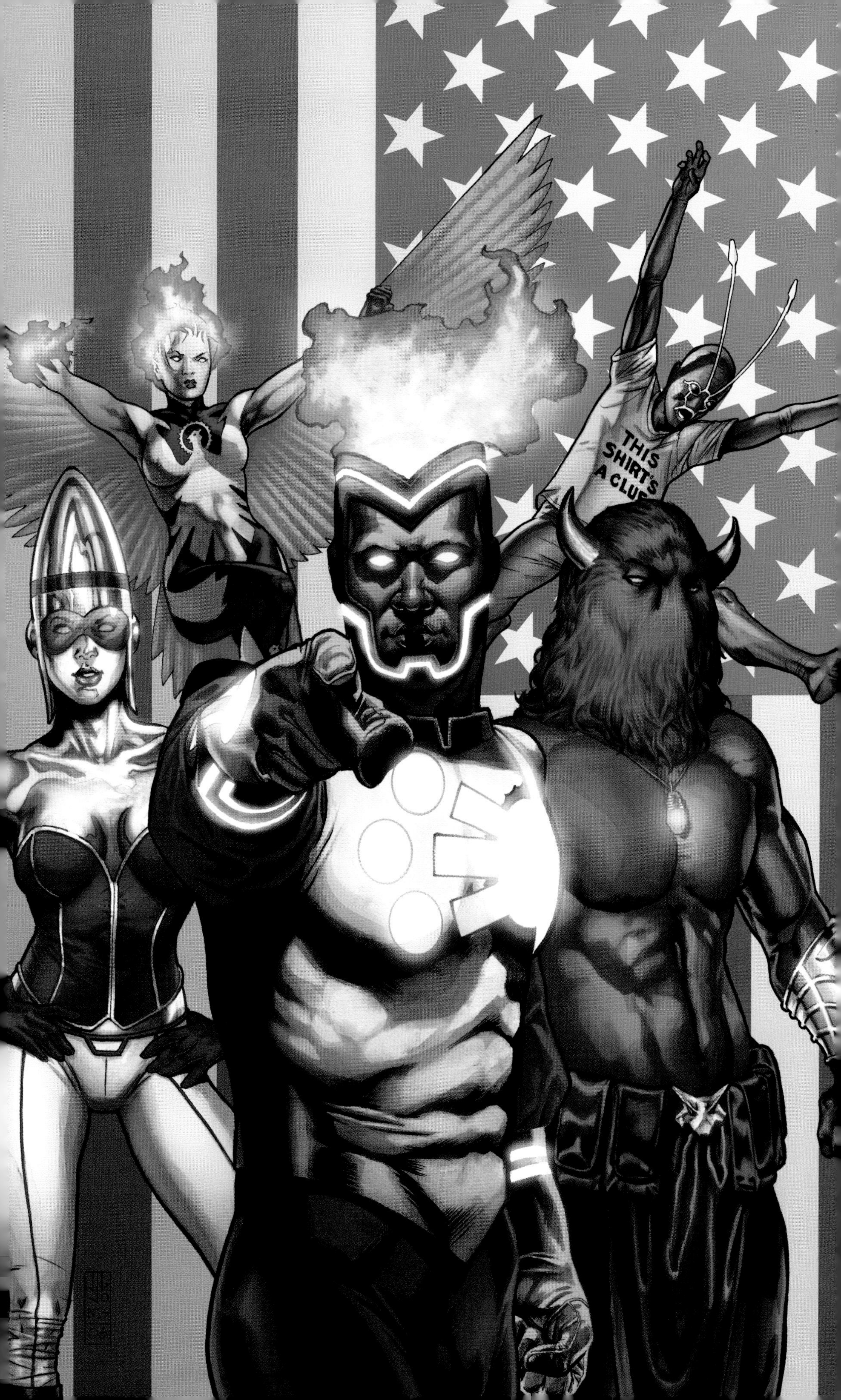
THIS
SHIRT's
A CLU

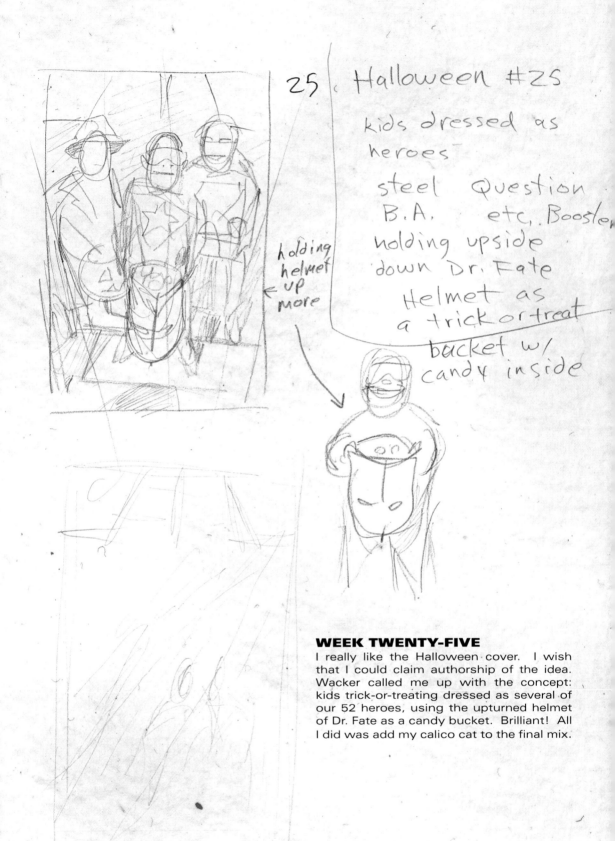

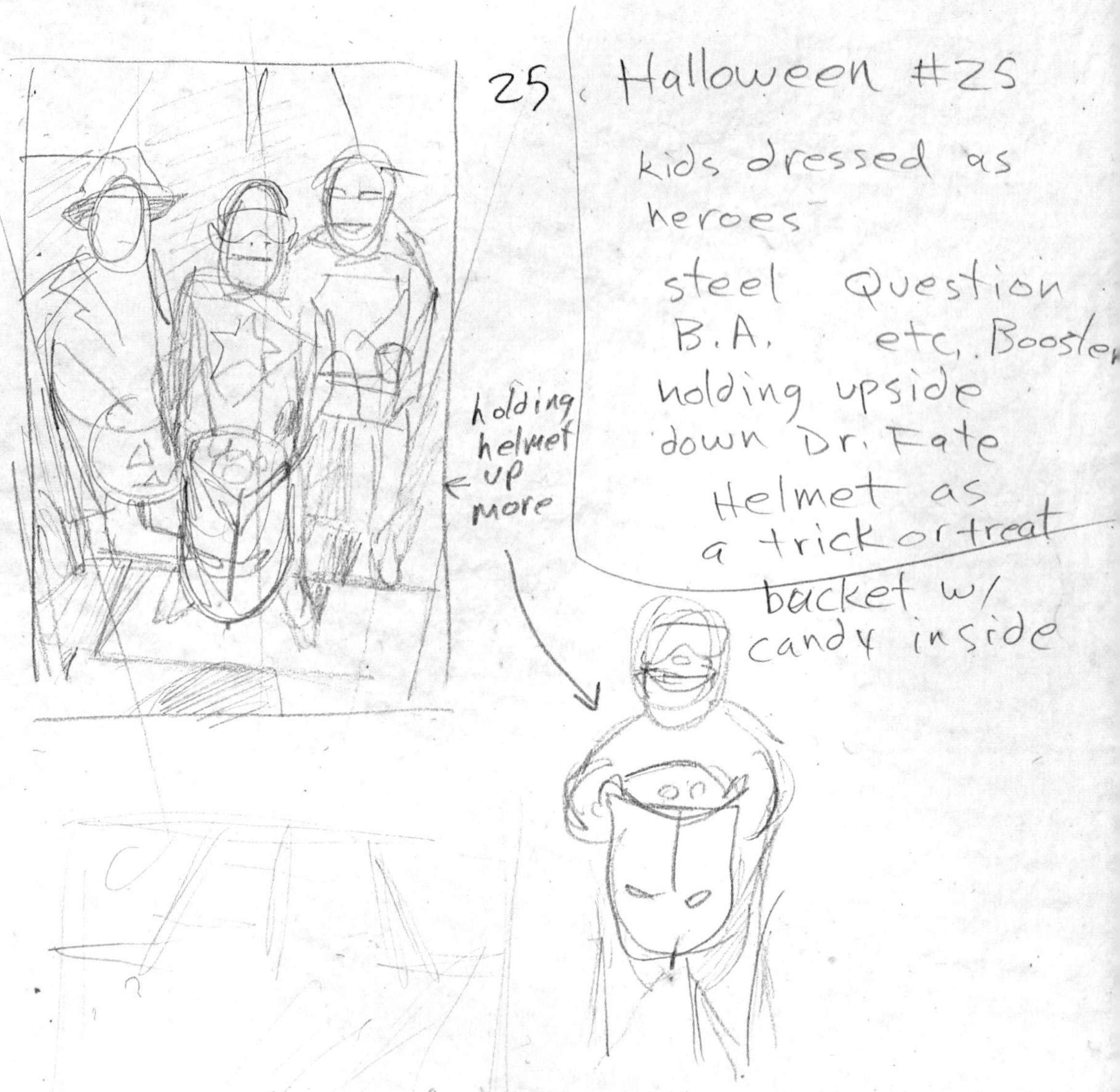
25. Halloween #25
kids dressed as heroes
steel Question
B.A. etc. Booster
holding upside down Dr. Fate Helmet as a trick or treat bucket w/ candy inside
holding helmet up more

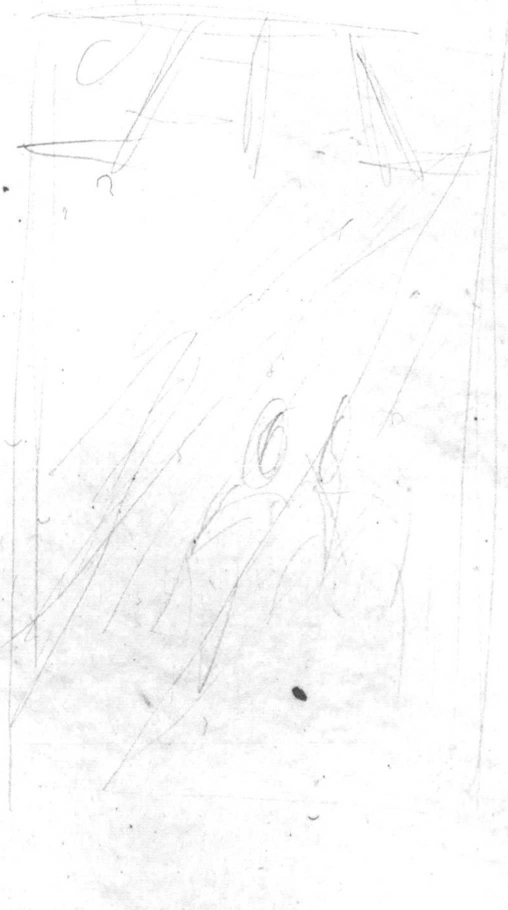

**WEEK TWENTY-FIVE**

I really like the Halloween cover. I wish that I could claim authorship of the idea. Wacker called me up with the concept: kids trick-or-treating dressed as several of our 52 heroes, using the upturned helmet of Dr. Fate as a candy bucket. Brilliant! All I did was add my calico cat to the final mix.

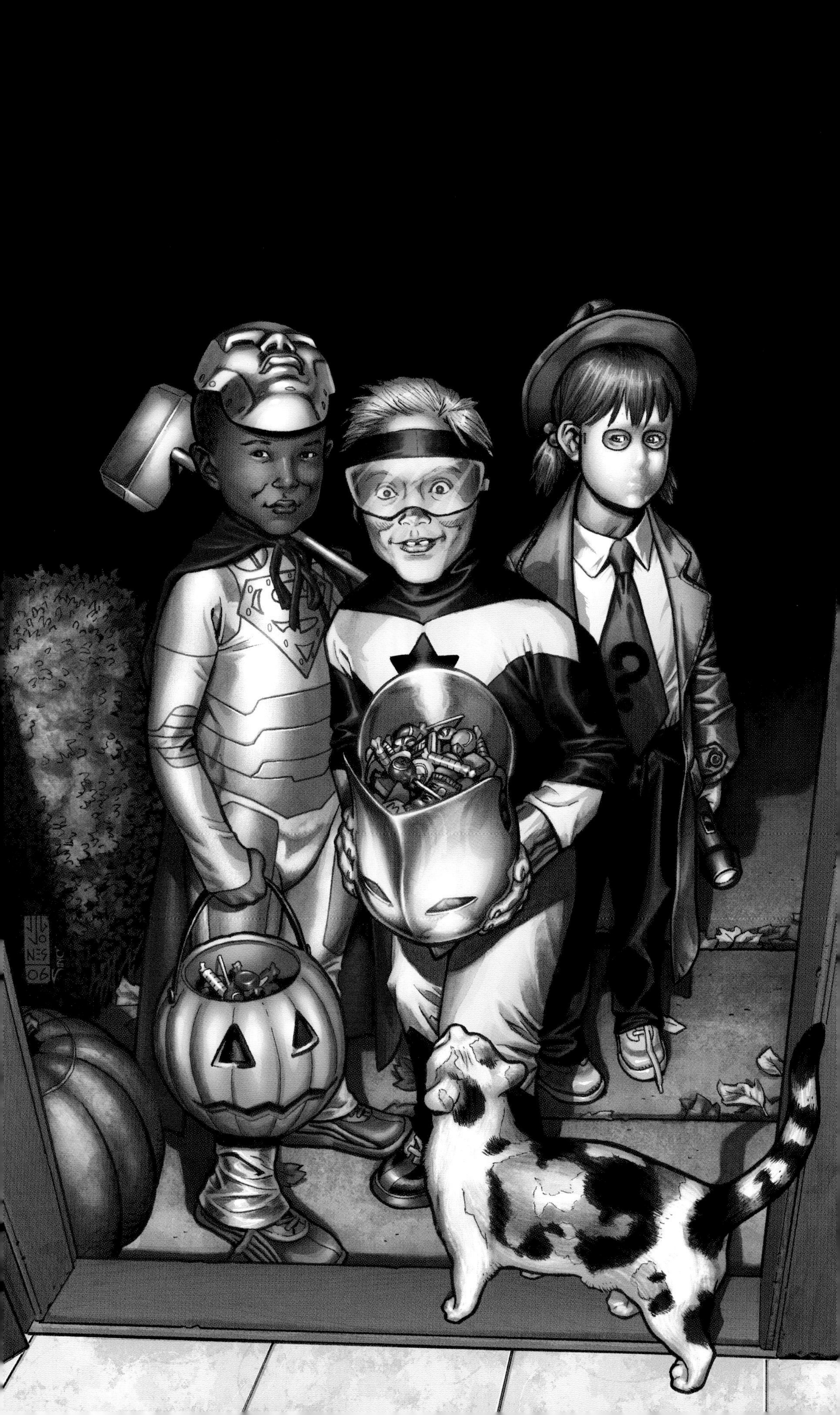

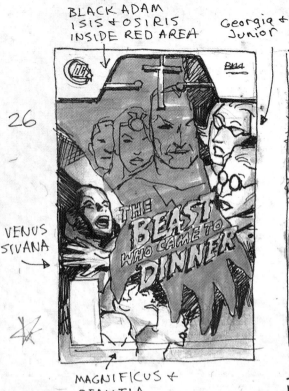

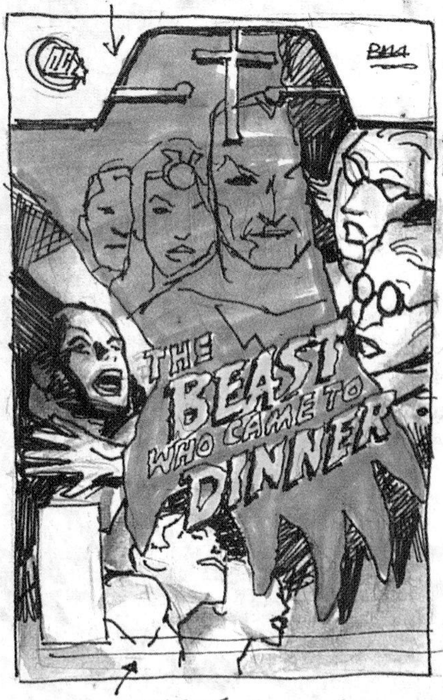
BLACK ADAM
ISIS + OSIRIS
INSIDE RED AREA
Georgia + Junior
26
VENUS SIVANA
MAGNIFICUS + BEAUTIA
THE BEAST WHO CAME TO DINNER

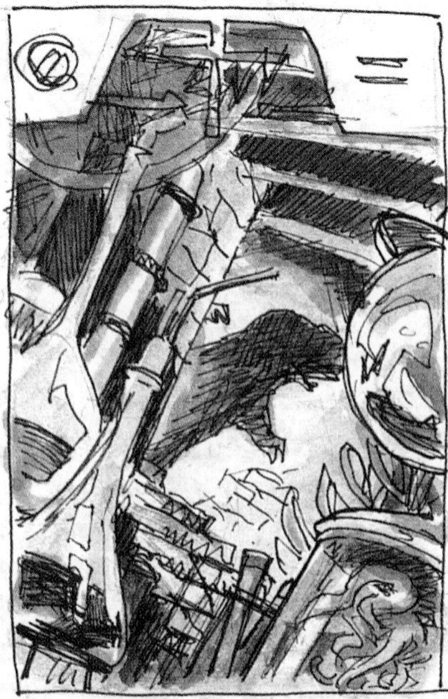
26
SHADOW OF SOBEK ON WALL (SCARY)
SIVANA Basement LAB
STEPS TO FIRST FLOOR

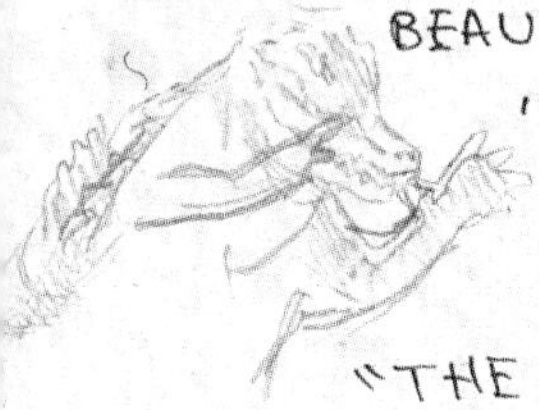

'40s MOVIE POSTER STYLE
"THE BEAST WHO CAME TO DINNER"

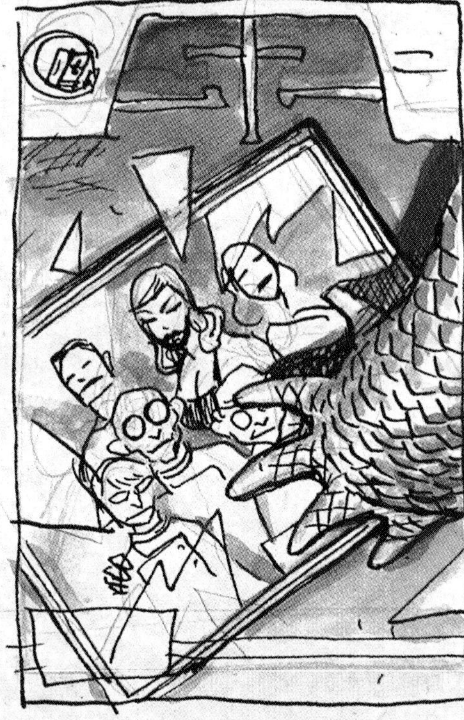
SMASHED Photo of Sivana family
Croc hand

## WEEK TWENTY-SIX

Another personal favorite, this was once again drawing inspiration from horror film posters of the '30s and '40s. THE BEAST WHO CAME TO DINNER refers not only to the crocodile, Sobek, but to the dangerous Black Adam as well. I like that ambiguity as well as the fun design and the hand lettering.

The coloring was the key to pulling this one off, and I worked closely with Alex to get the perfect hissing shades of green contrasted with the red of the graphic claw.

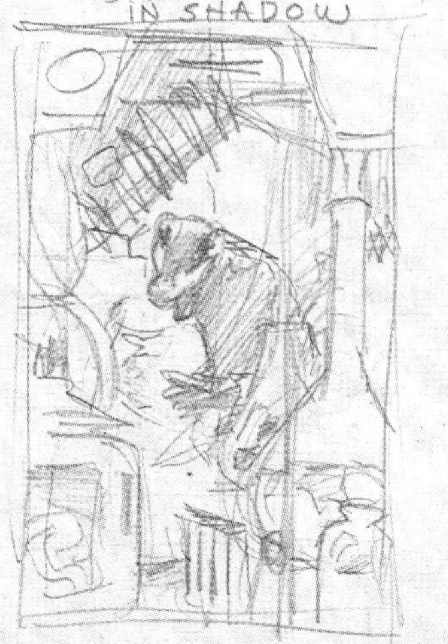
SOBEK IN LAB-
BACKLIT + MOSTLY
IN SHADOW

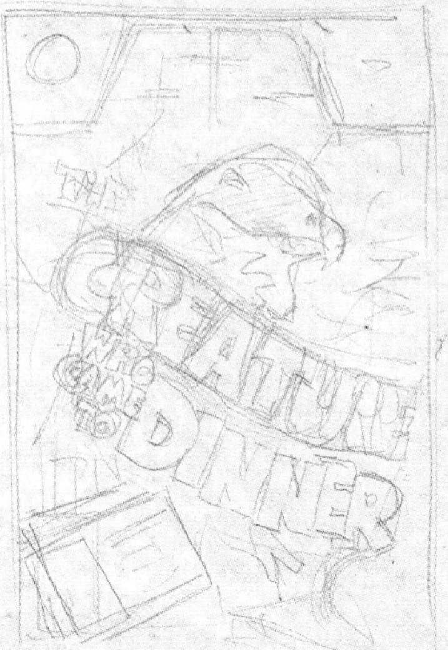
THE
CREATURE
WHO CAME TO
DINNER

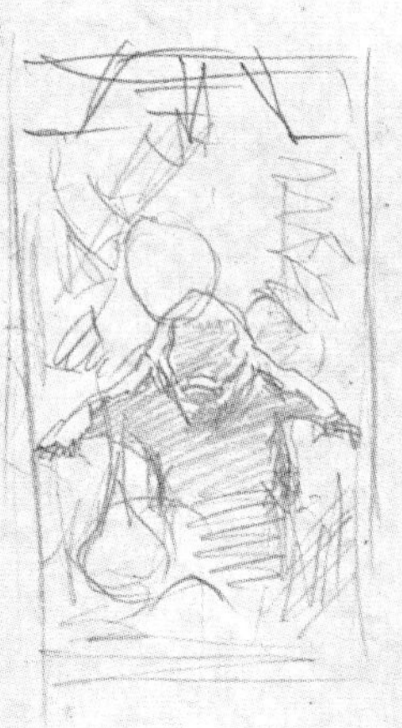

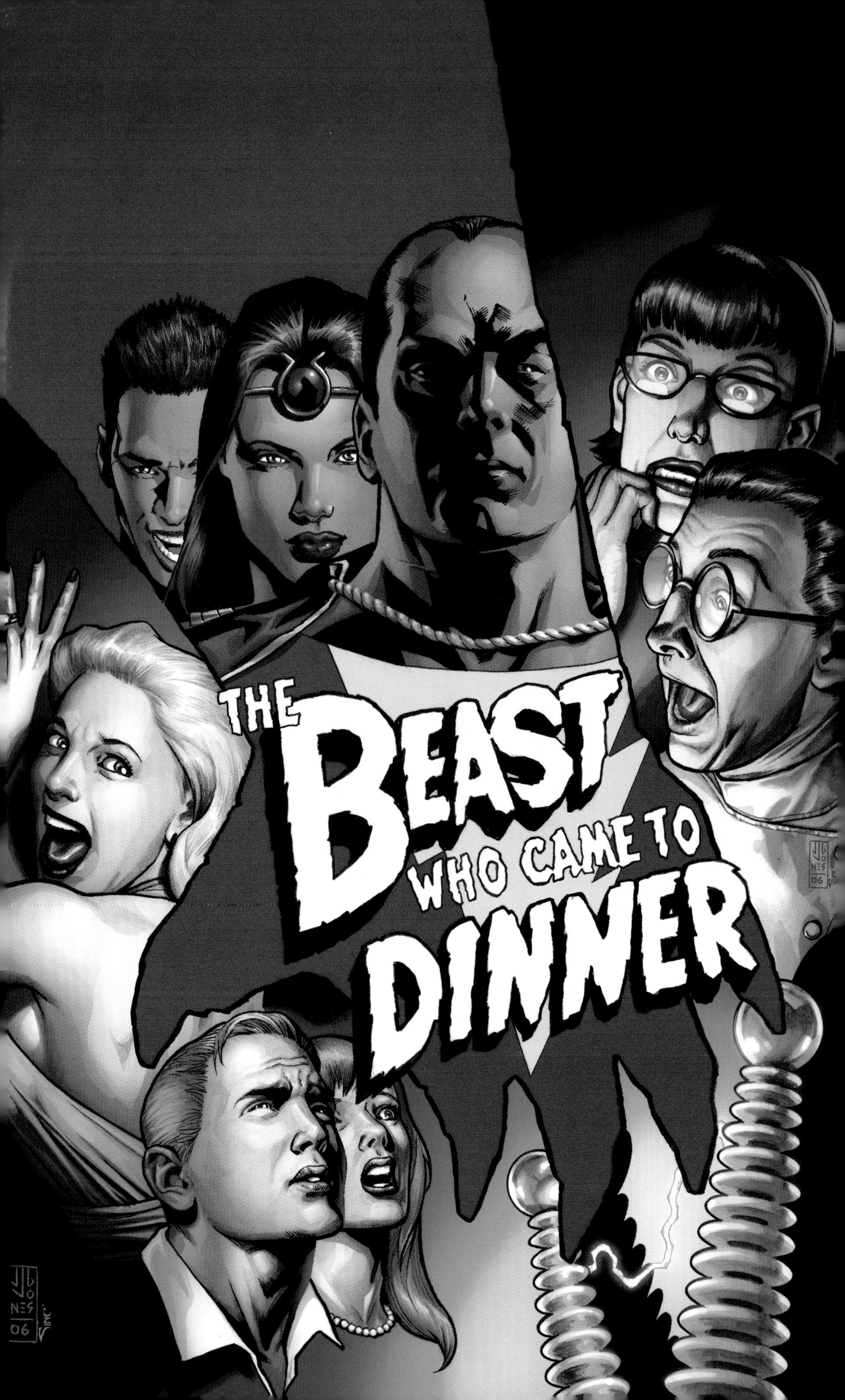
THE
BEAST
WHO CAME TO
DINNER

# UNUSED COVER CONCEPTS

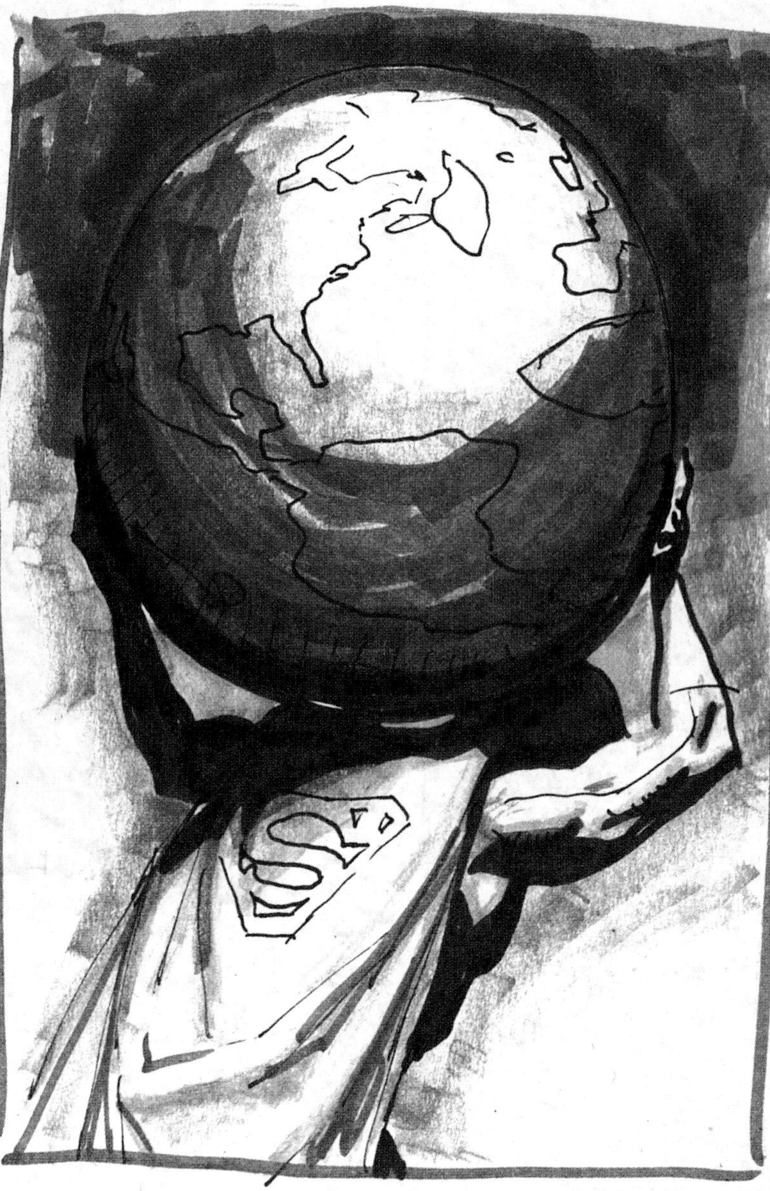

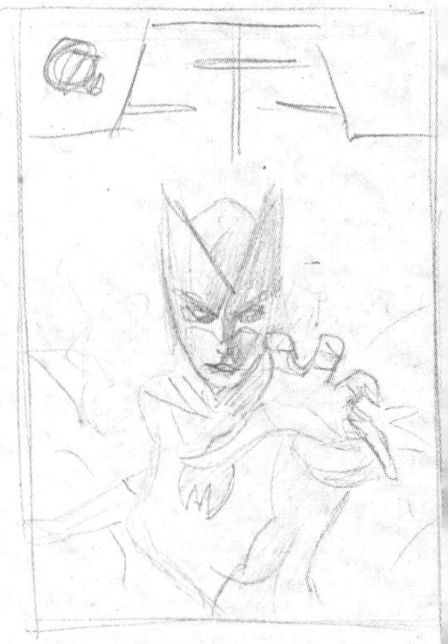

Super Nova costome with Superman's Cape

Booster as Superman- Trying to Support the world in Supe's absence

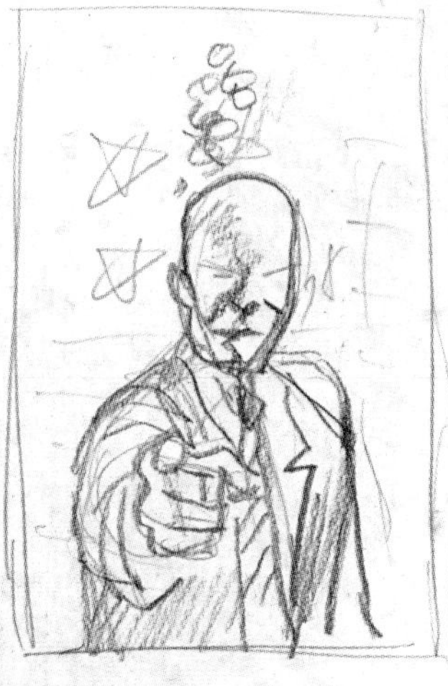

4th July Cover- Luthor "I WANT YOU" UNCLE SAM Poster

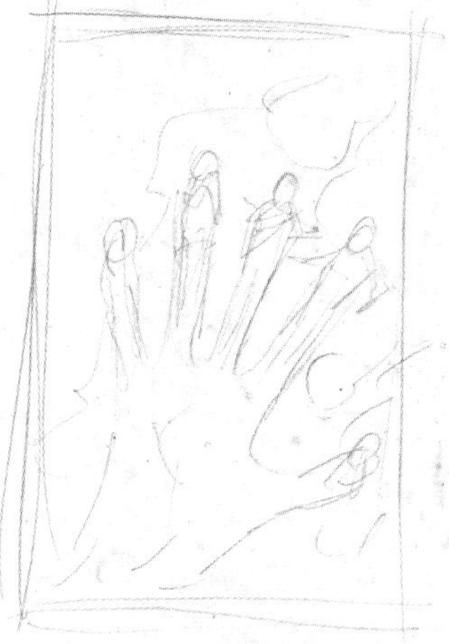

Faust's hand with characters as fingers

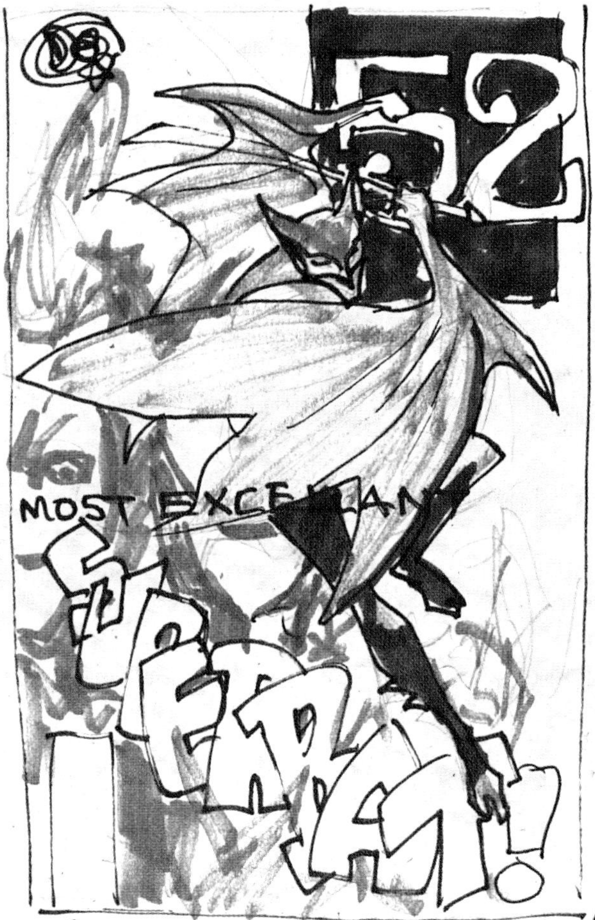
52
MOST EXCEL
MANGA STYLE
Most Excellent SUPER-BAT! IN ENGLISH AND IN CHINESE (Mandarin or Cantonese?)
Layered imagery like a hip manga cover

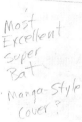

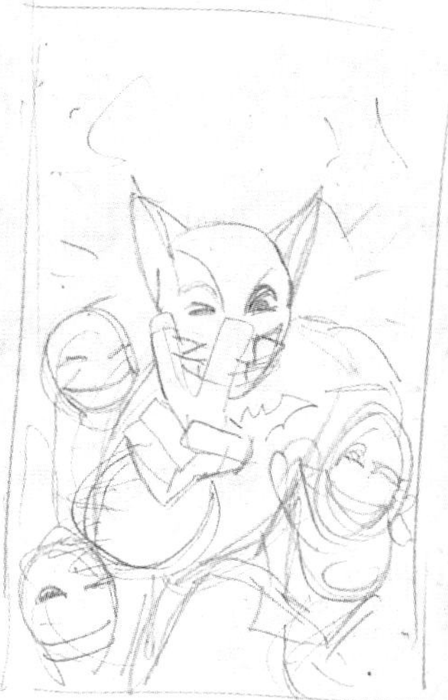
Most Excellent Super Bat
Manga-Style Cover?

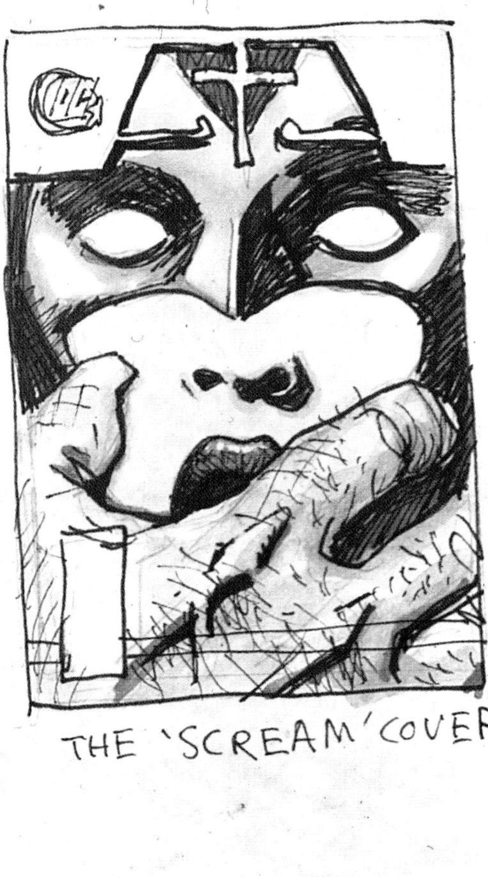
THE 'SCREAM' COVER

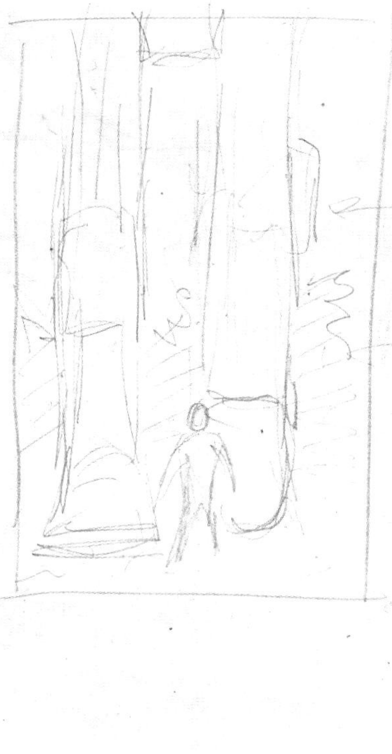
Robot Island
Giant Robot Legs
Jungle
Beach

## WEEK TWENTY-SEVEN

Alex had a lot to do with the success of this cover, since using both Eclipso and The Spectre together meant that the theme would have to be one of light and shadow.

There is this great moment in the story where we come upon Eclipso frozen in permanent orbit around a distant sun. That image just stuck in my head, and I wanted to use it.

In the first few sketches, all of the elements are parallel to the picture plane, which was very iconic and worked fine. But at the last minute, I chose to skew the camera to the side and twist the composition, which made it much more dynamic.

Spectre

#27

eclipso floating in space

I ♡ 52

WEEKLY? YEAH, RIGHT!

Planet with sun behind - light breaking over rim

Different Composition - same elements

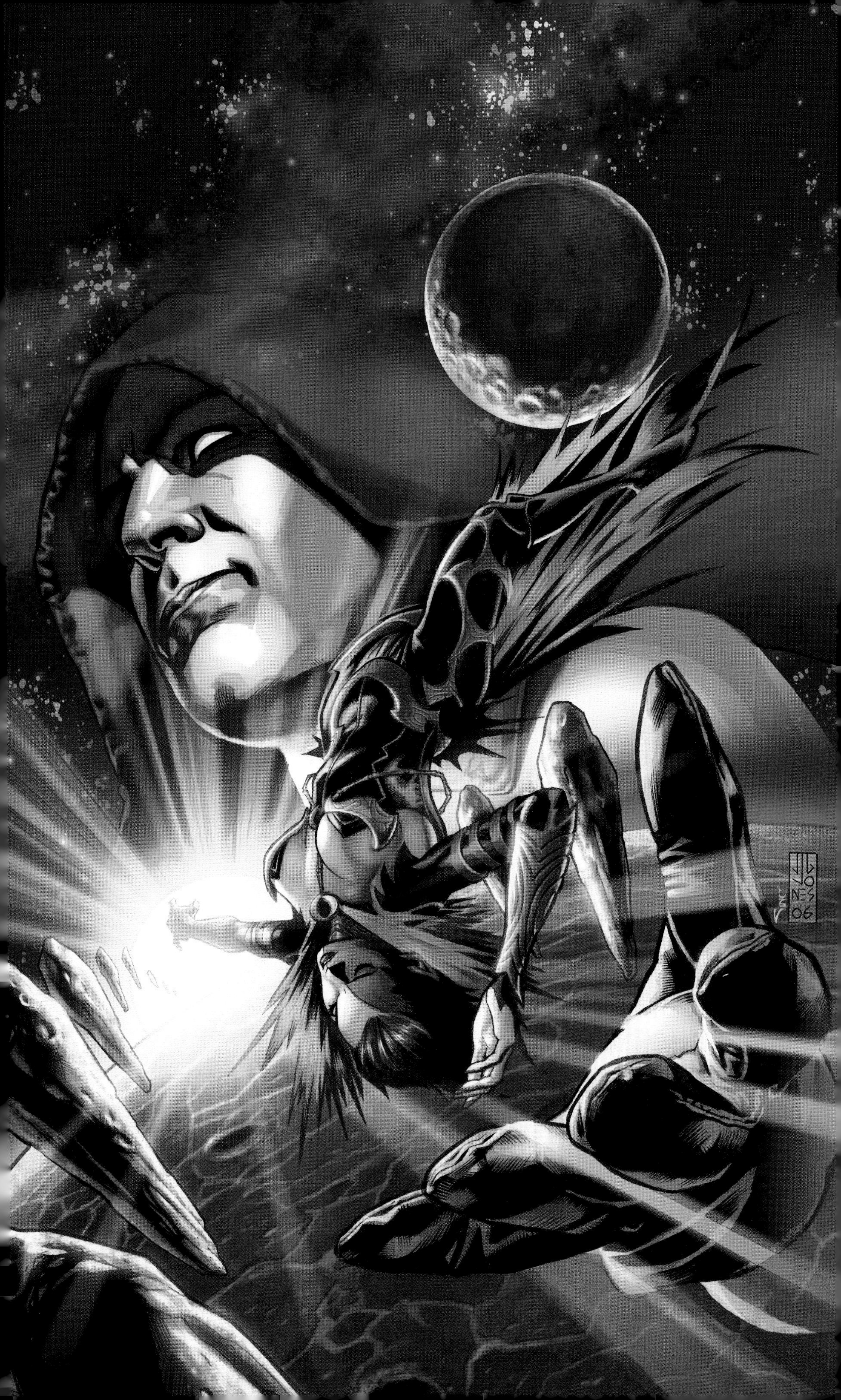

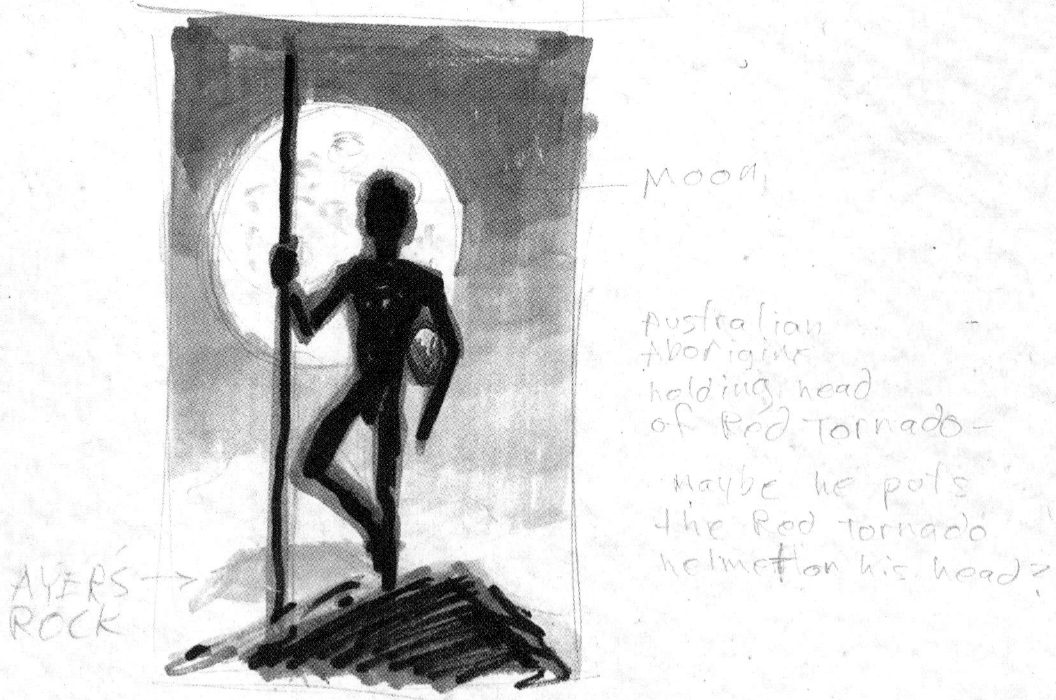
Moon
Australian Aborigine holding head of Red Tornado —
Maybe he puts the Red Tornado helmet on his head?
AYERS ROCK

## WEEK TWENTY-EIGHT

I probably drew forty or fifty cover designs in the first 52 plotting session, and we were able to use about ten of those for final covers. This is one of those that was sketched up early, and was also one of the first covers that was actually finished for the series, although it took a while before we found the right week to actually use it.

I like this one OK, but if I were to do it over again, I would stick closer to the original sketch, eliminating almost all of the color except for the red of Tornado's robot head.

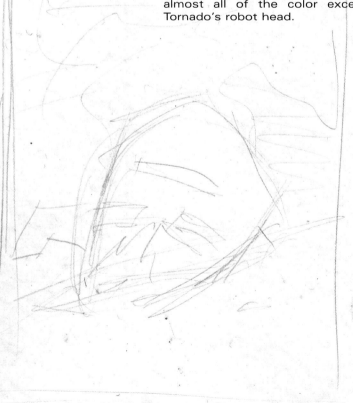

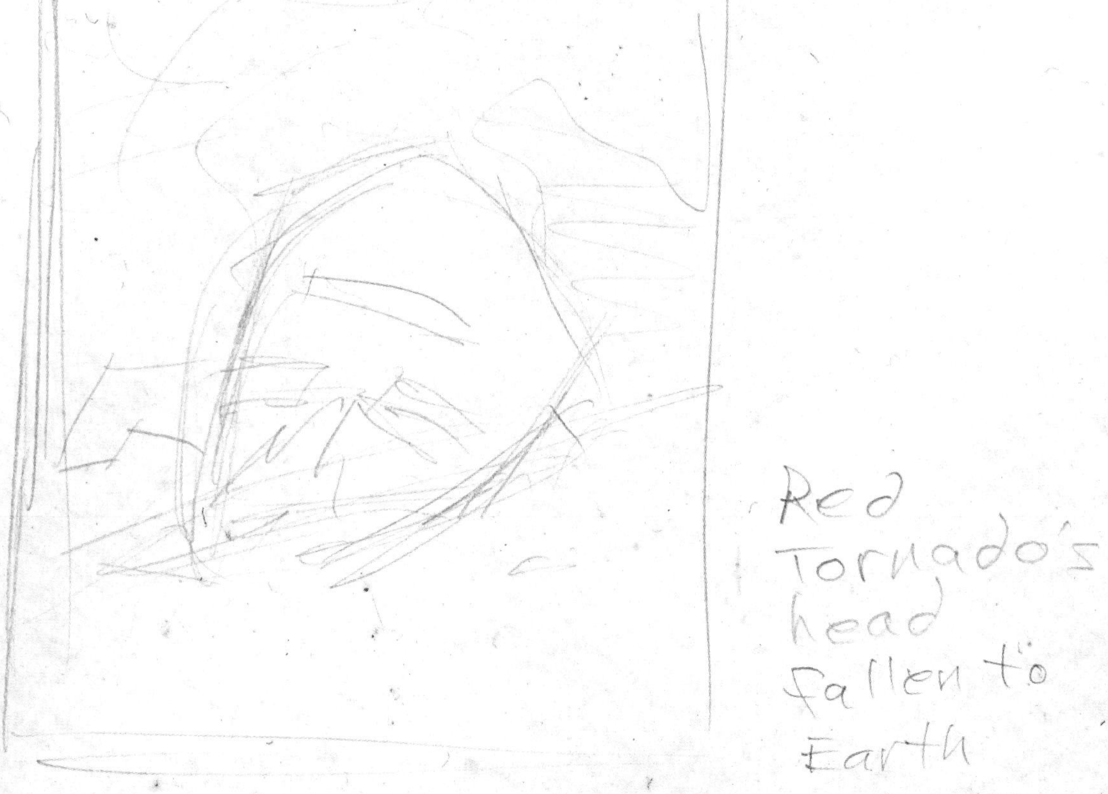
Red Tornado's head fallen to Earth

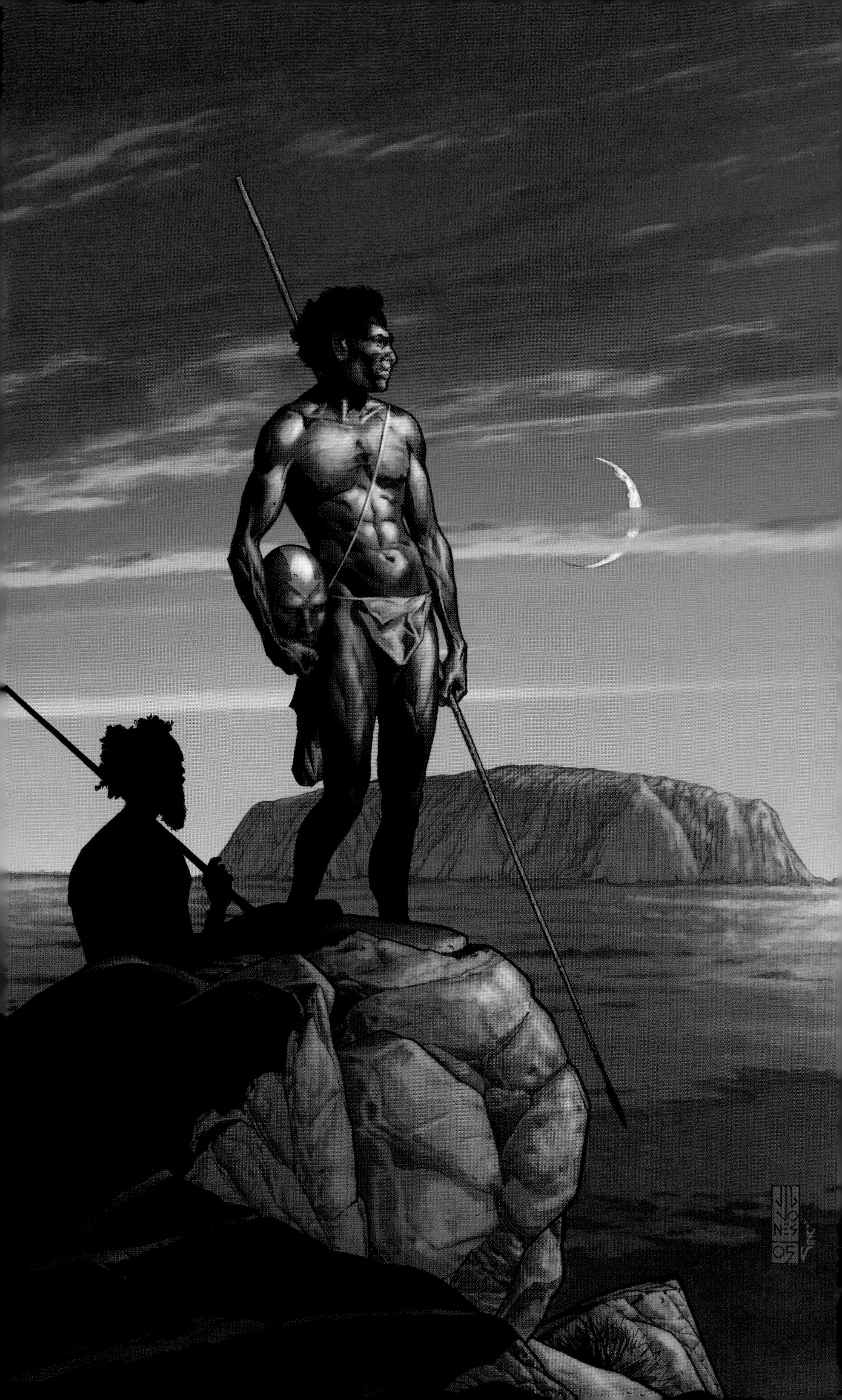

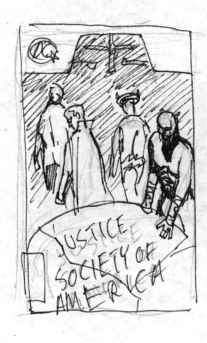

USTICE
SOCIETY OF
AMERICA
walking
away
from
JSA
Table

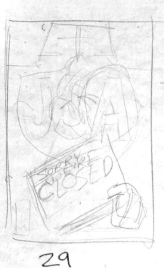

JSA
CLOSED
29

JSA
JSA
members
walk
away
wildcat's
hand
shut off
light

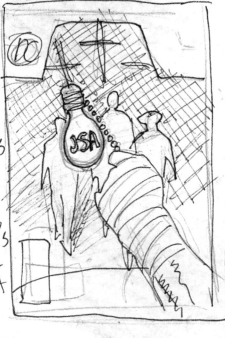

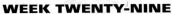

## WEEK TWENTY-NINE

Steve Wacker and I kicked a lot of options back and forth before settling on this disheartening image. I had been playing around with some kind of jokey ideas to show the disbanding of the JSA. One sketch had a "closed" sign on the door of the JSA brownstone. Another had Wildcat's hand shutting off a light bulb.

In the end, we decided the end of the JSA should be more somber, so I pared it down to just the essential elements. The darkened, unadorned room and long shadows tell the story as we watch the final members of the vaunted superhero team shuffle toward the open door.

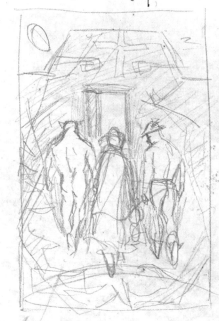

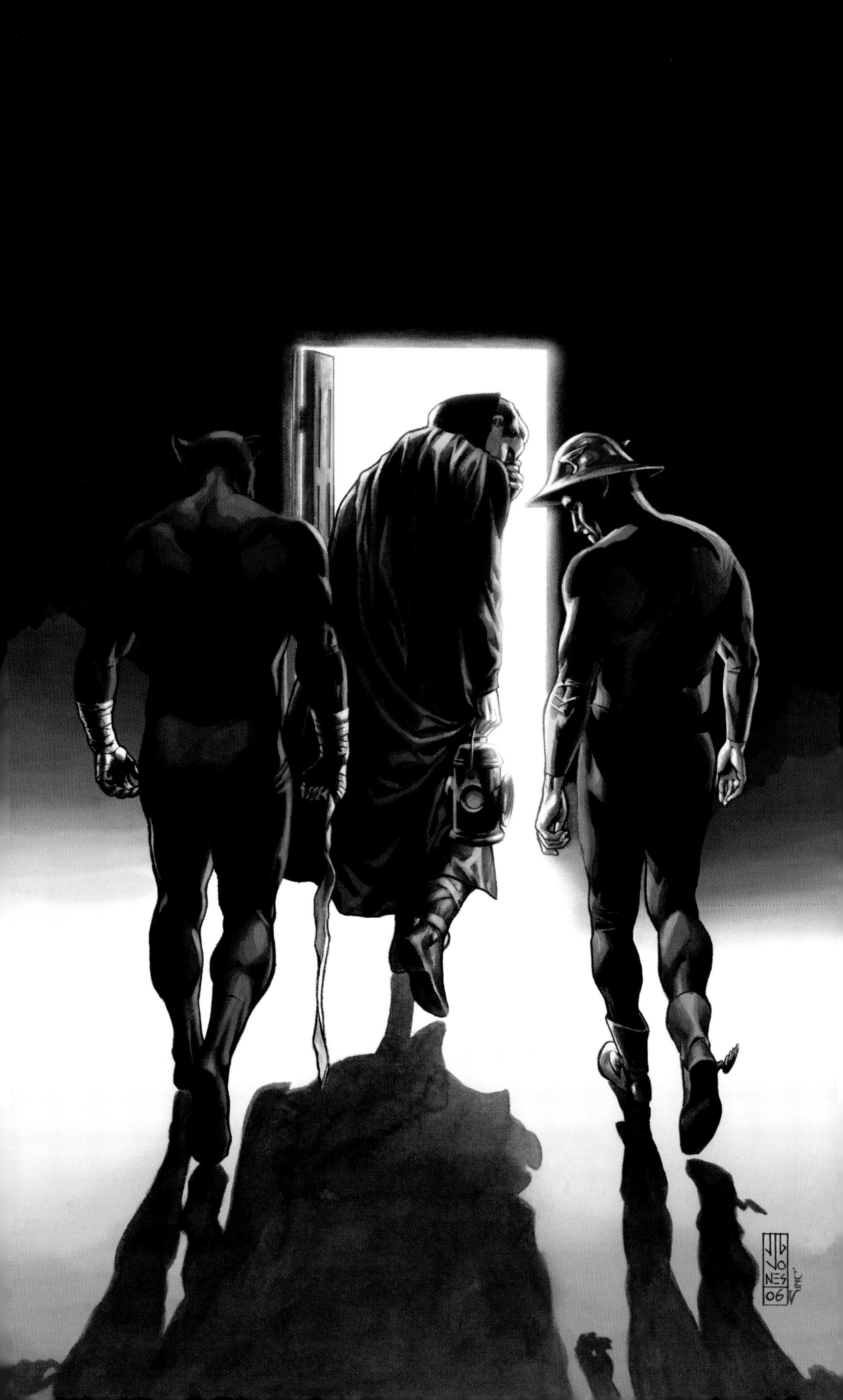

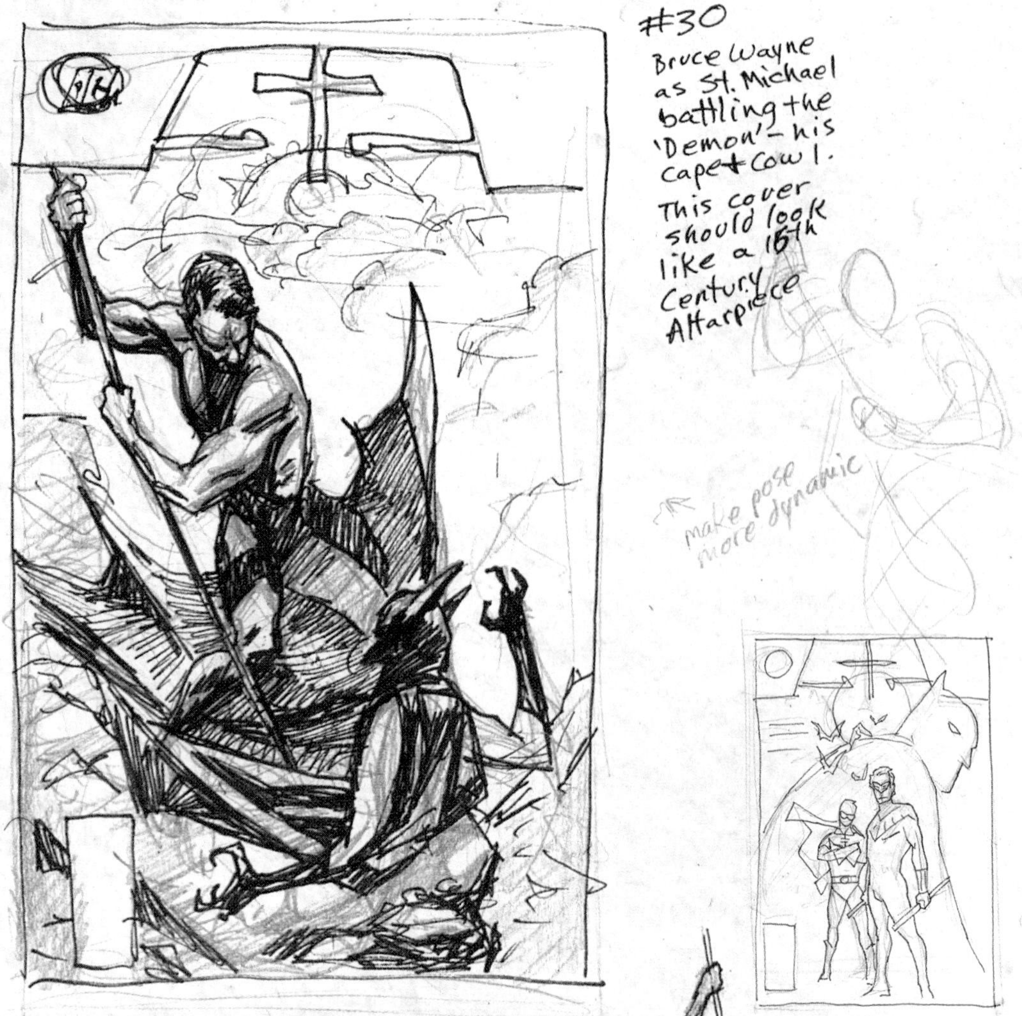
#30
Bruce Wayne as St. Michael battling the 'Demon' – his cape + cowl.
This cover should look like a 15th Century Altarpiece
make pose more dynamic

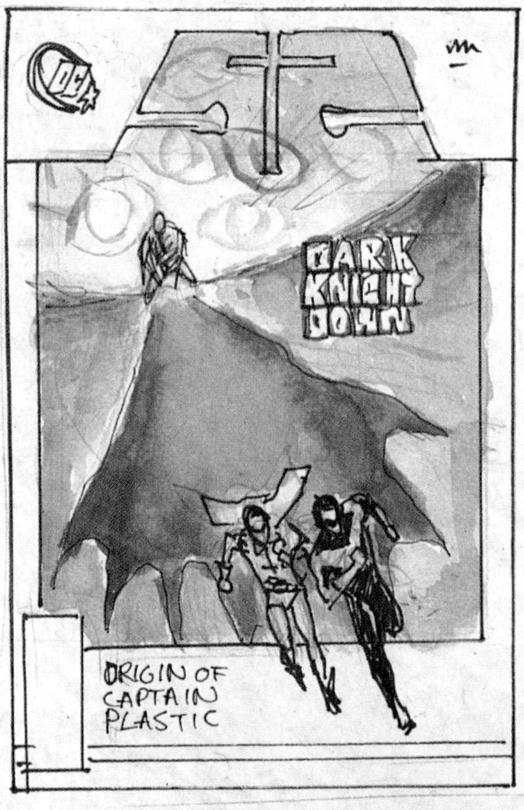
DARK KNIGHT DOWN
ORIGIN OF CAPTAIN PLASTIC

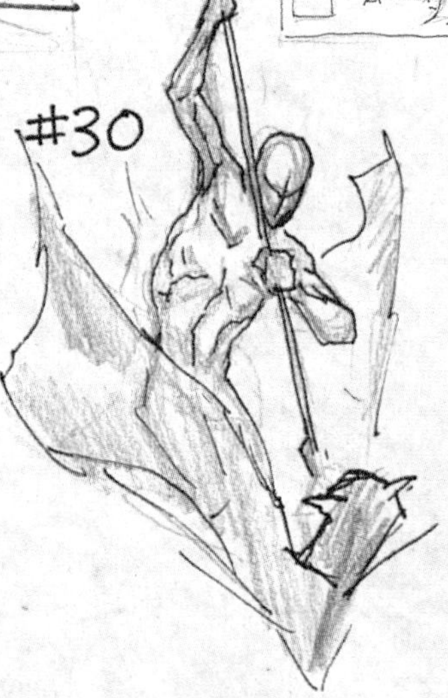
#30

## WEEK THIRTY

The cover for issue 30 came together in fits and starts. I did a number of sketches for it and actually got halfway through an initial version before abandoning it. It just was *not* addressing the core of the story.

So I went back to square one: how to depict Bruce Wayne's struggle with his Batman persona. I borrowed the iconography of St. Michael defeating Satan from some 14th and 15th century altarpiece paintings, and the whole thing came together.

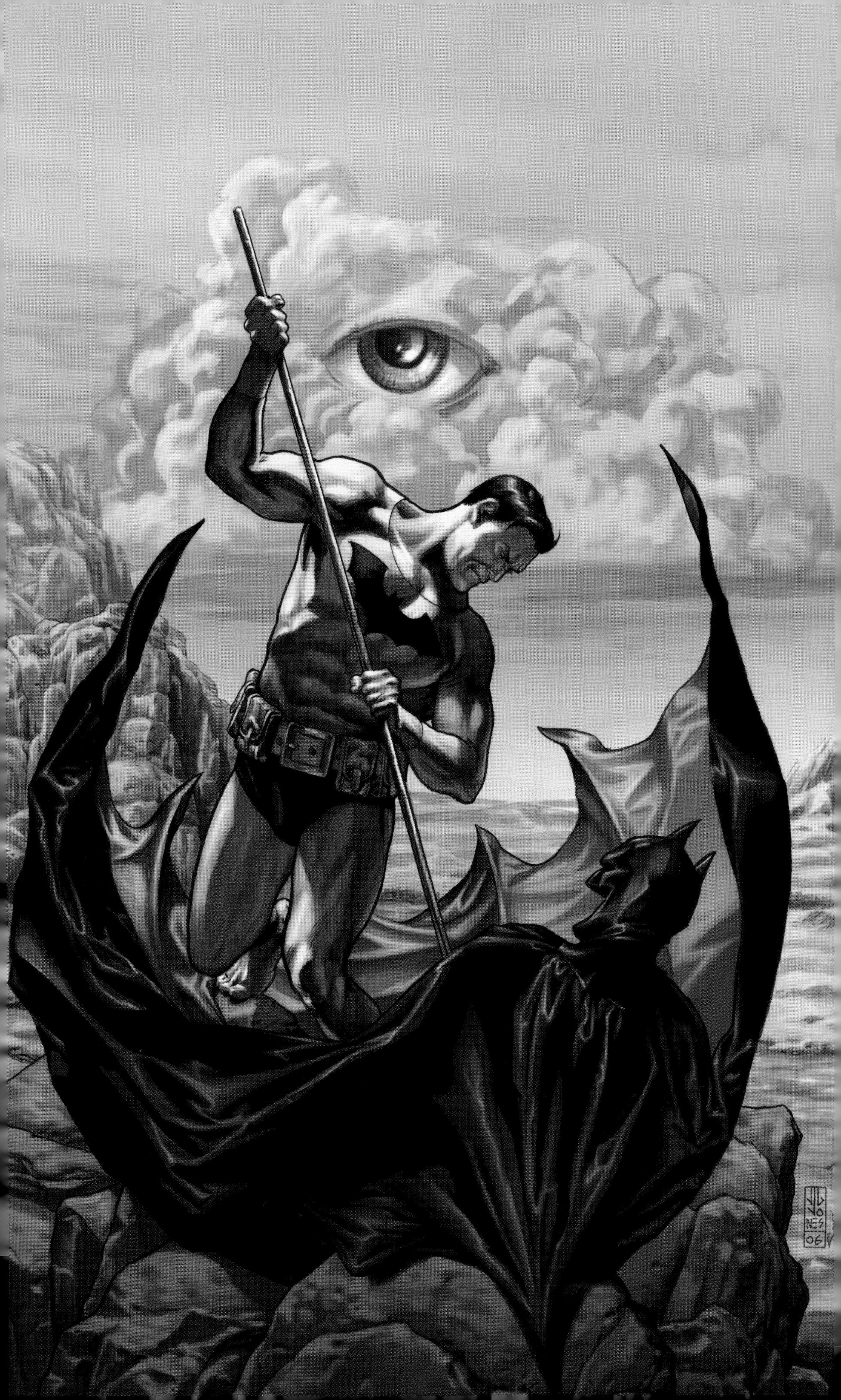

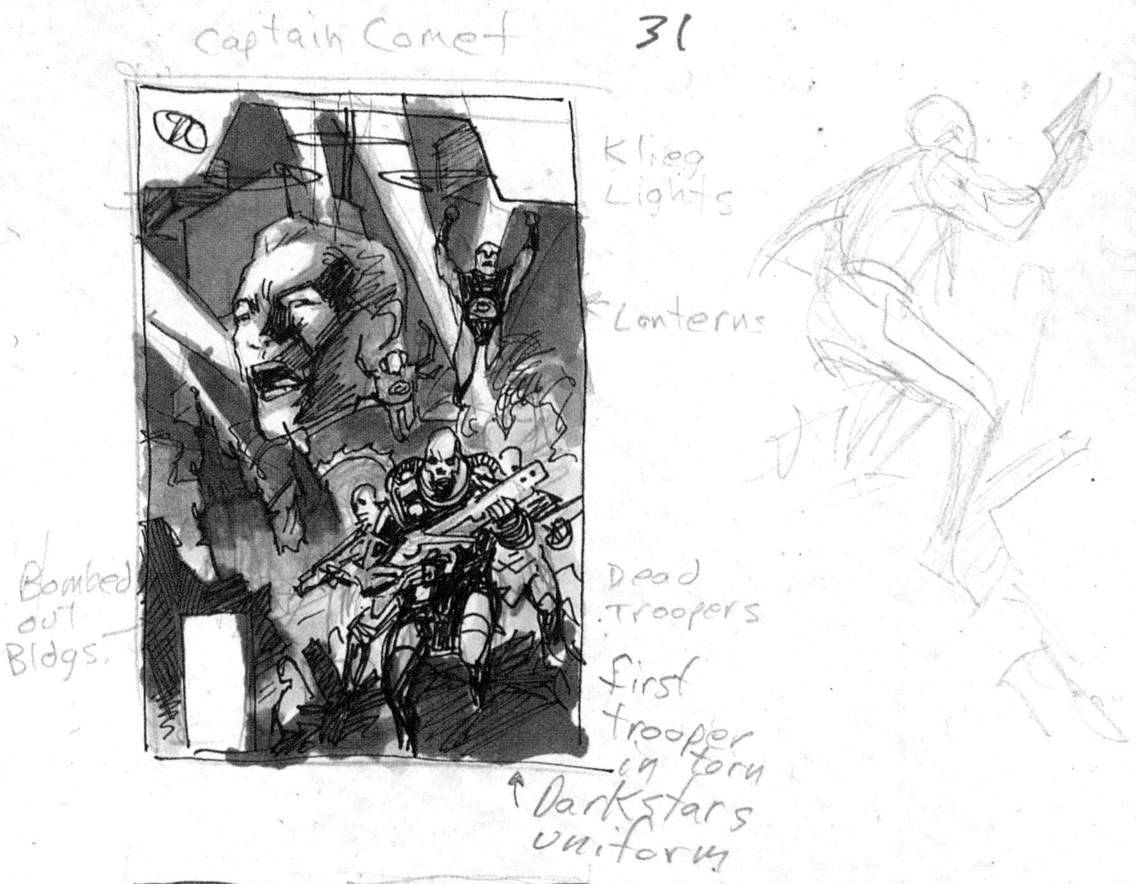
Captain Comet
31
Klieg Lights
Lanterns
Bombed out Bldgs.
Dead Troopers
first trooper in torn Darkstars uniform

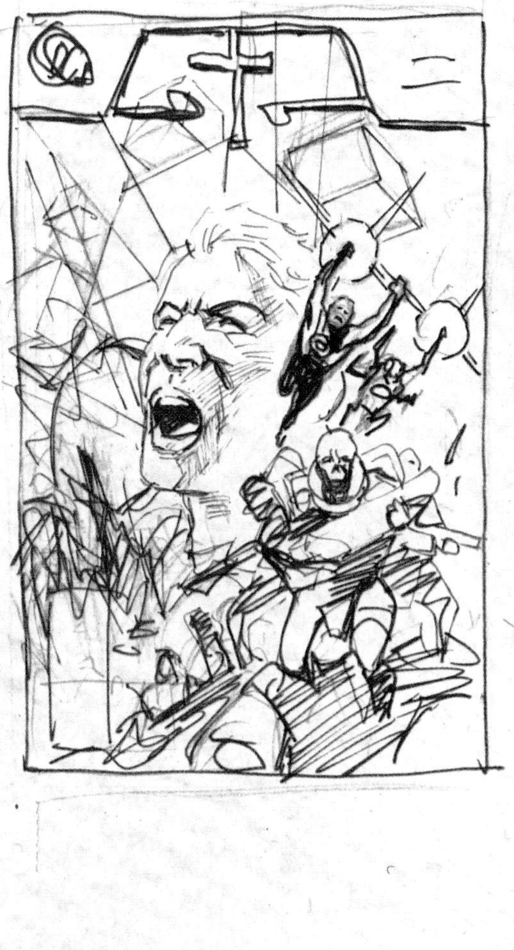

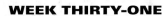

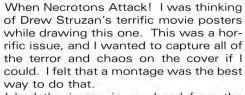

## WEEK THIRTY-ONE

When Necrotons Attack! I was thinking of Drew Struzan's terrific movie posters while drawing this one. This was a horrific issue, and I wanted to capture all of the terror and chaos on the cover if I could. I felt that a montage was the best way to do that.

I had the image in my head from the start, and just had to fine-tune the drawing and the poses. It's a very busy picture with so much going on that I had Alex limit the color palette to just red and gray, which helped to focus the eye and set the proper mood.

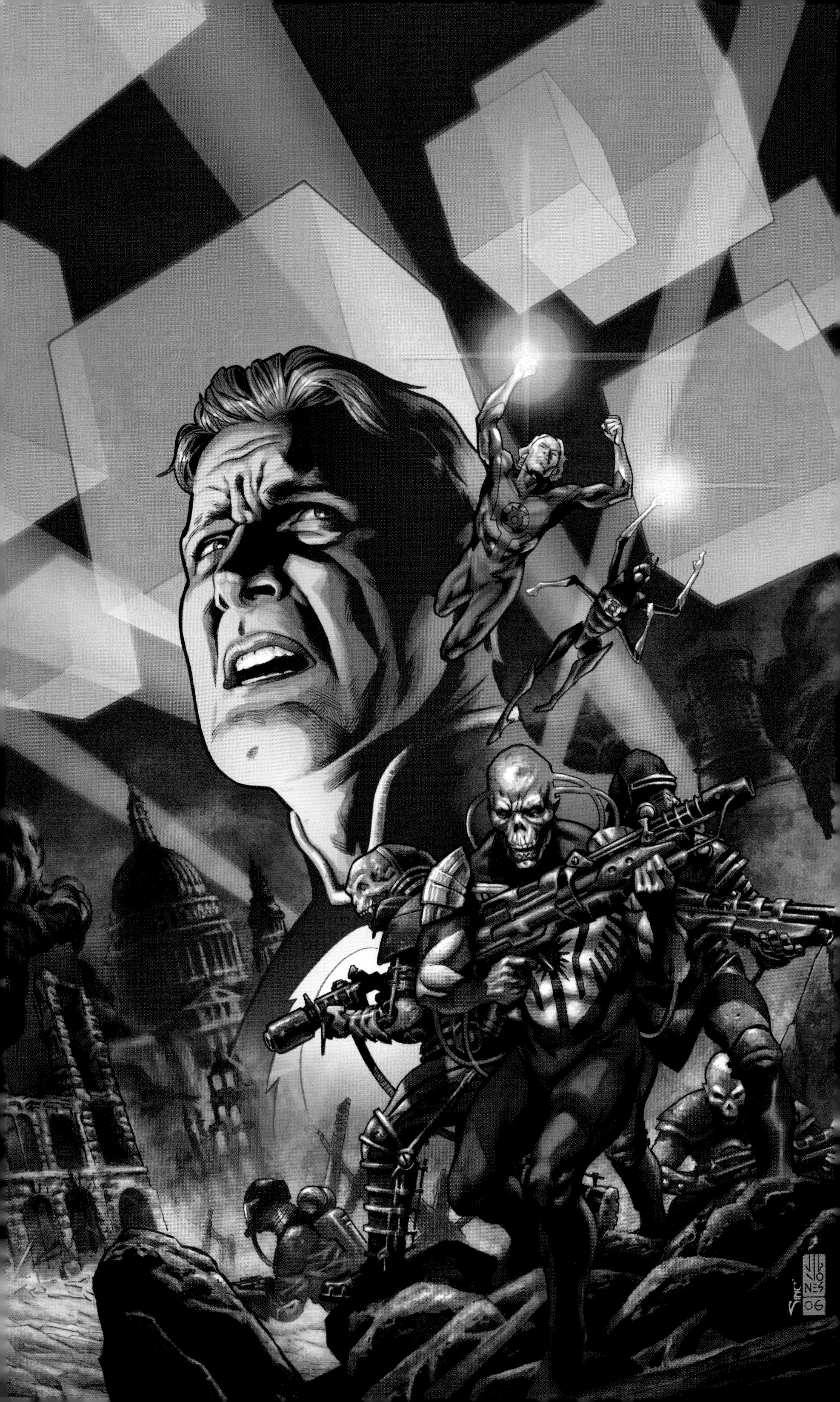

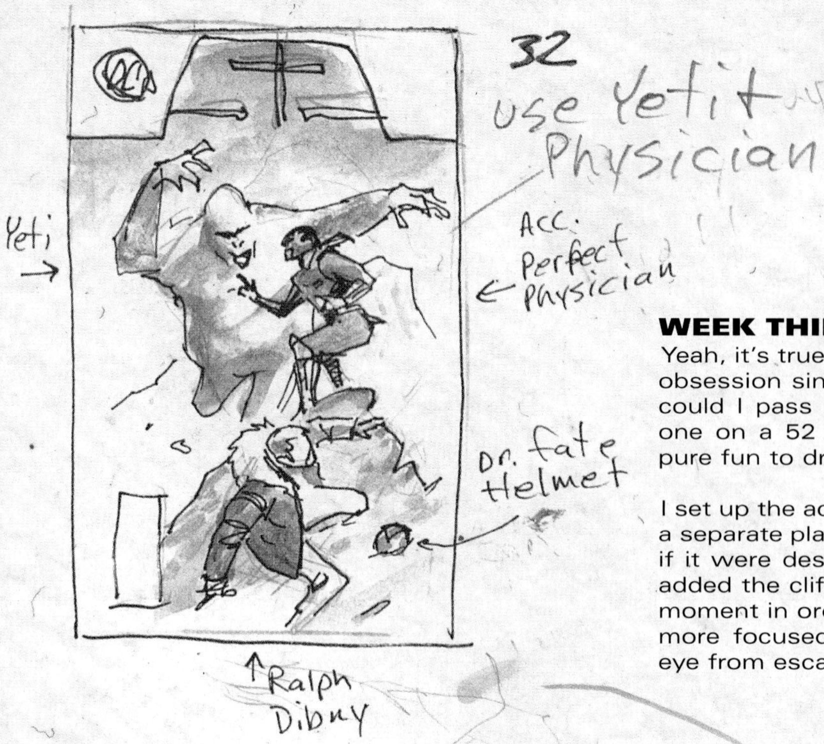
32
use Yeti
Physician
Acc.
Perfect
Physician
Yeti
Dr. fate
Helmet
Ralph
Dibny

## WEEK THIRTY-TWO

Yeah, it's true...I've had a Bigfoot and Yeti obsession since early childhood, so how could I pass up an opportunity to draw one on a 52 cover? This one was just pure fun to draw.

I set up the action with each character on a separate plane, one behind the other, as if it were designed for the stage. I only added the cliffs as a backdrop at the last moment in order to make the action even more focused and to keep the viewer's eye from escaping from the composition.

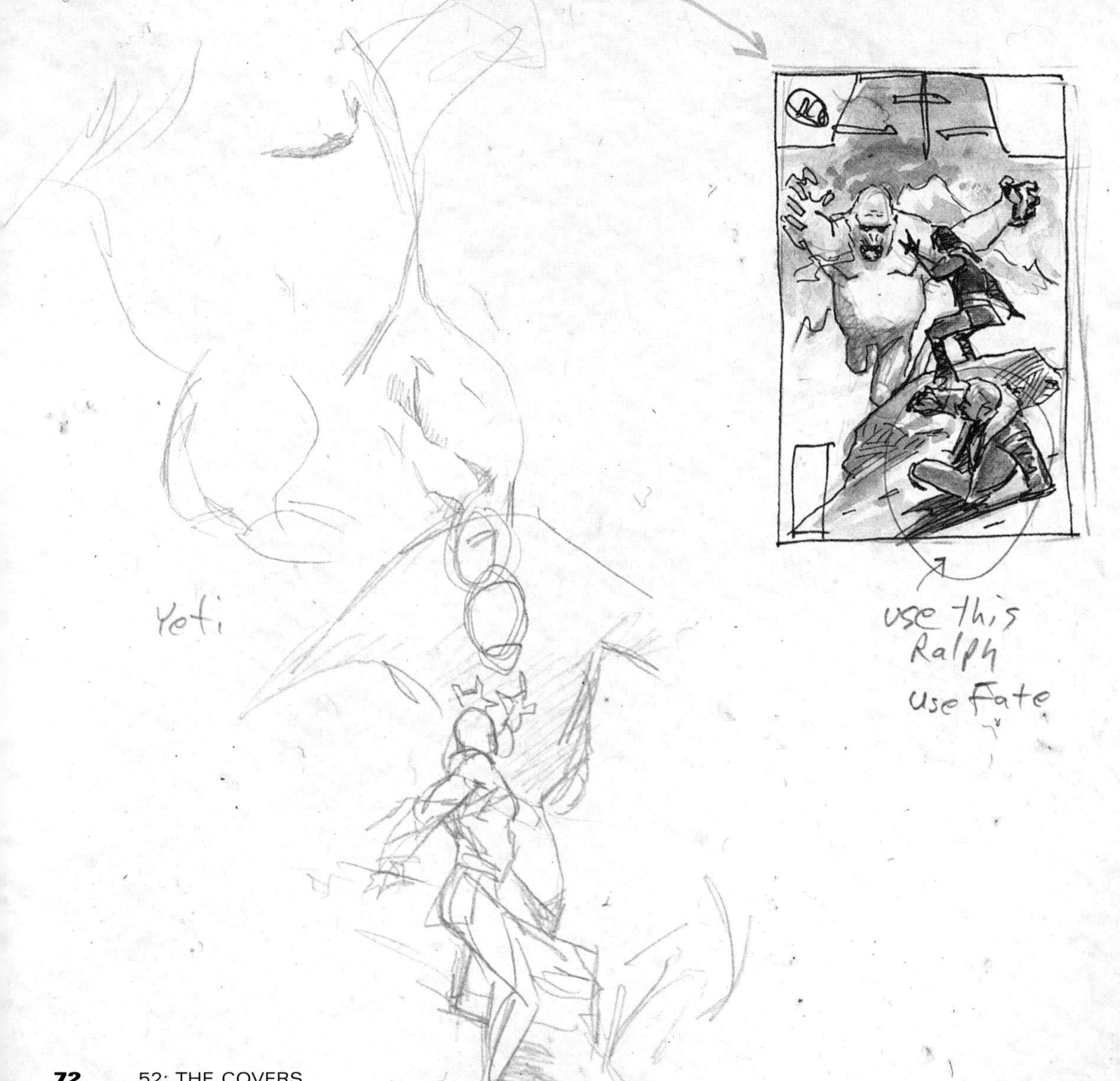
Yeti
use this
Ralph
use Fate

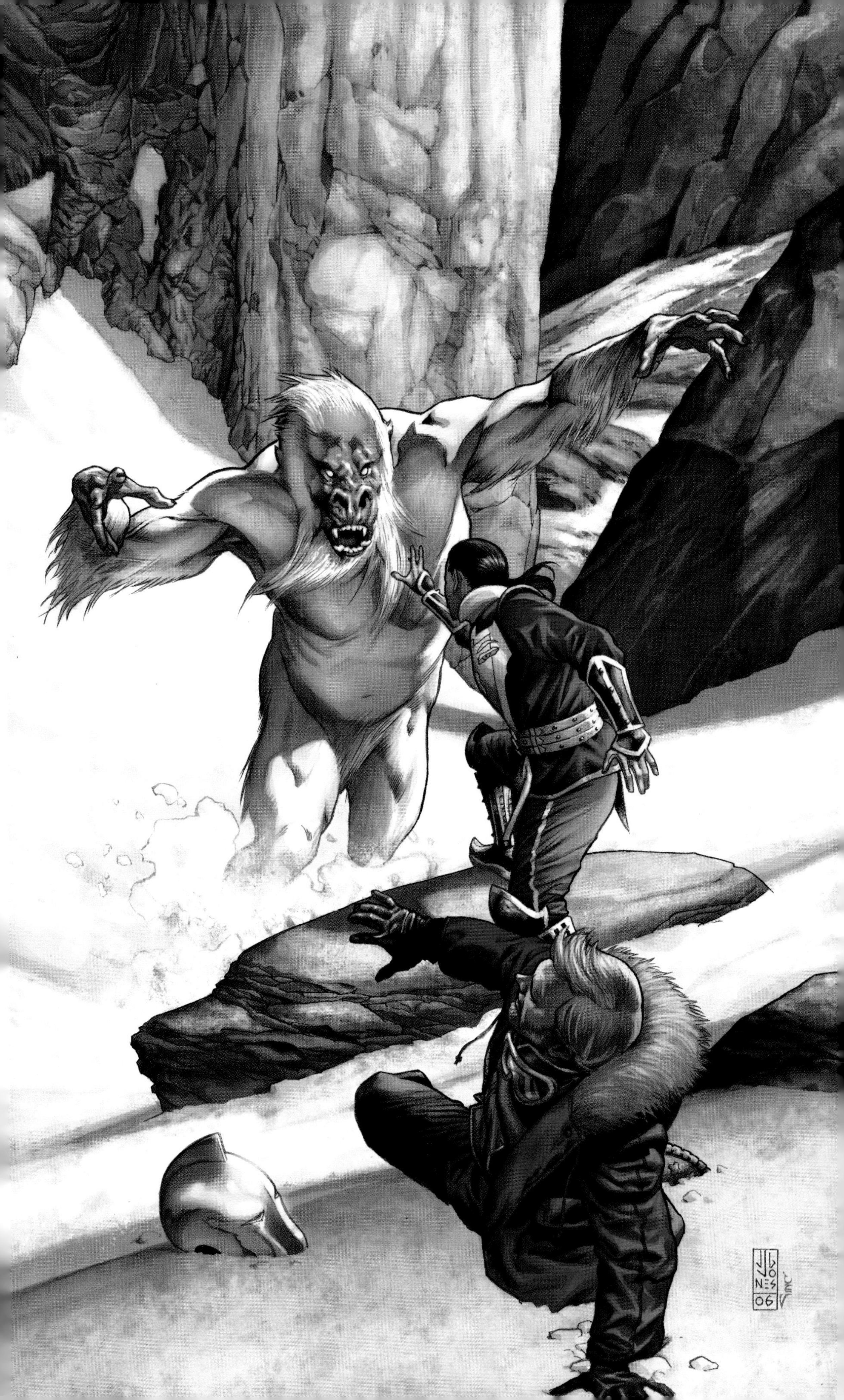

Falling
snow

Batwoman
Holding
Gift
Box

Night-
wing
Swings
Away

ICE SKATING RINK
Rockefeller Center
Type Plaza w/
Christmas Decorations

33

UPSHOT-
BATWOMAN HOLDING
PRESENT-NIGHTWING
WEARING SANTA HAT

## THIRTY-THREE

Pin up the stockings and cue the Vince Guaraldi tunes. It's the holiday season in old Gotham town.

I went with the down shot to depict this little moment for several reasons. This shot allows me to set the scene because we can see all of the holiday decorations around the skating rink, which sets the mood and establishes the time of year quickly and easily. It immediately explains the wrapped gift in Batwoman's hands, and allows me to do a bit of action as well by having Nightwing falling away. This gives the whole thing a bit of kinetic energy, which was lacking in the more static poses of the first sketch.

All the story elements come together and make the image easy to read. Plus, I didn't have to draw that stupid Santa hat on Nightwing's head.

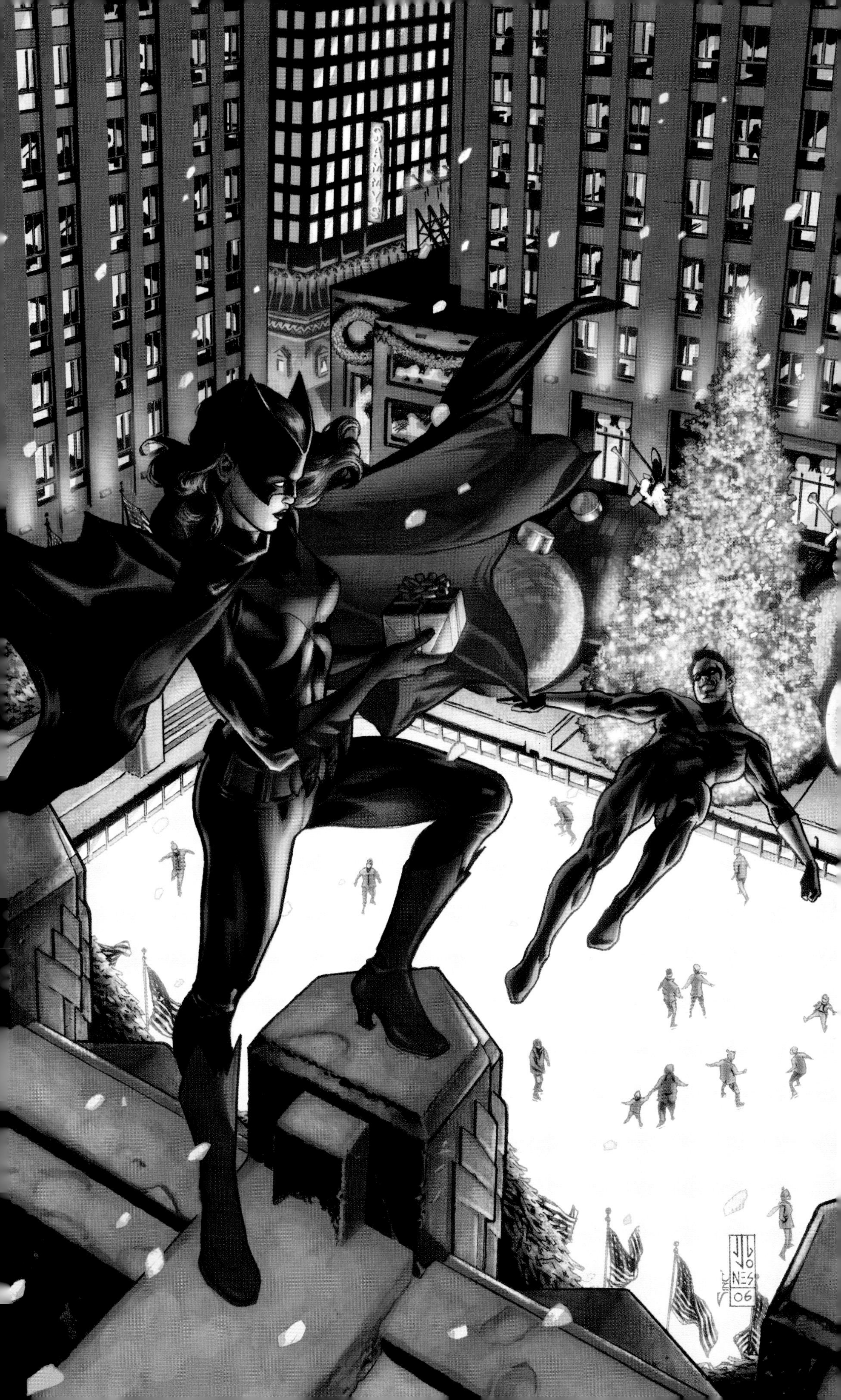
SAMMYS
JG JONES 06
SINC

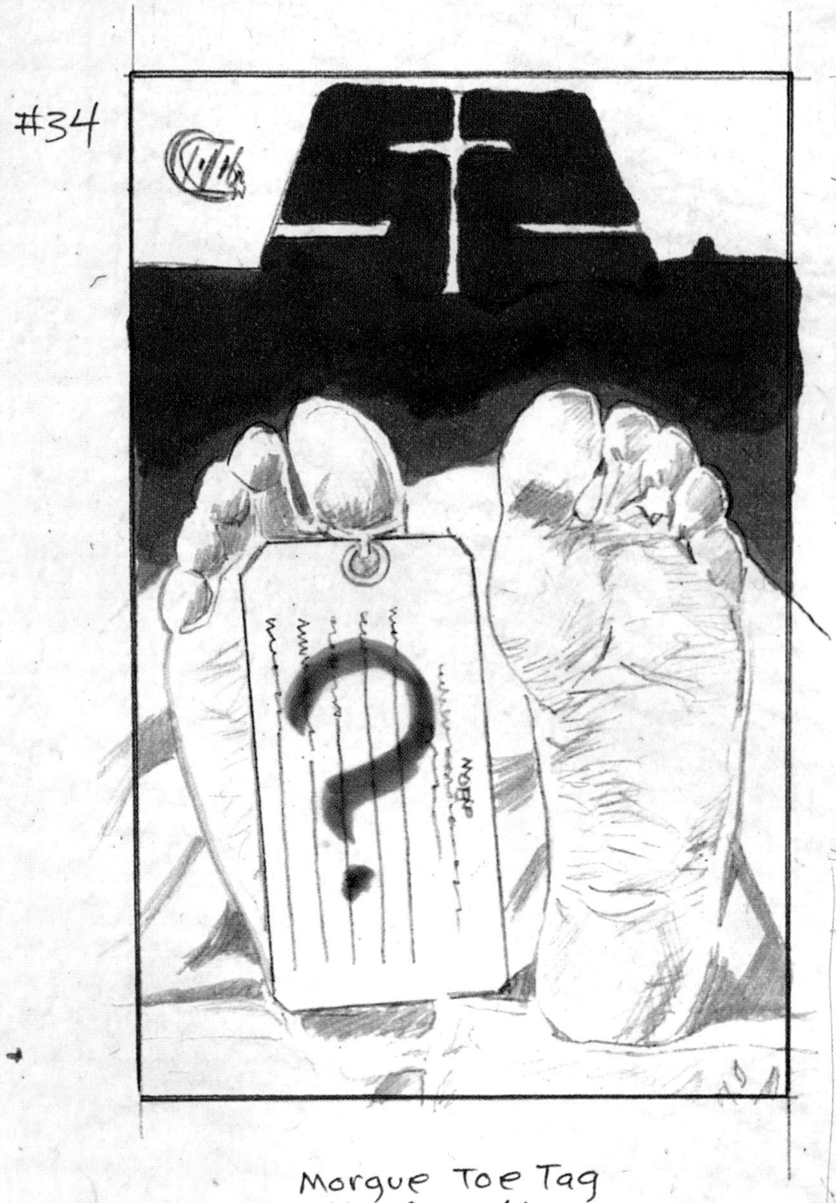
#34
52

Morgue Toe Tag
with Question
Mark

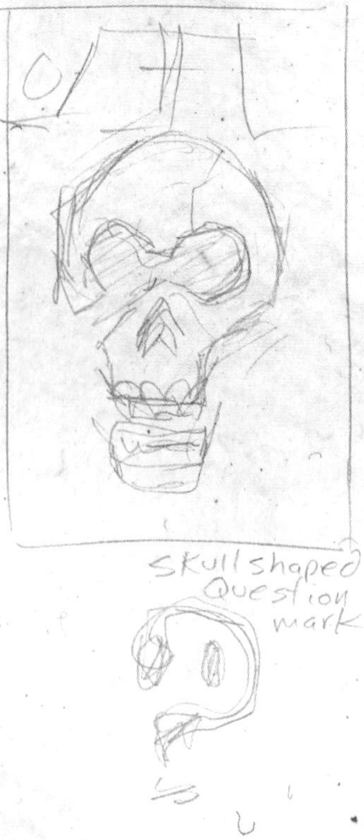

Skullshaped
Question
mark

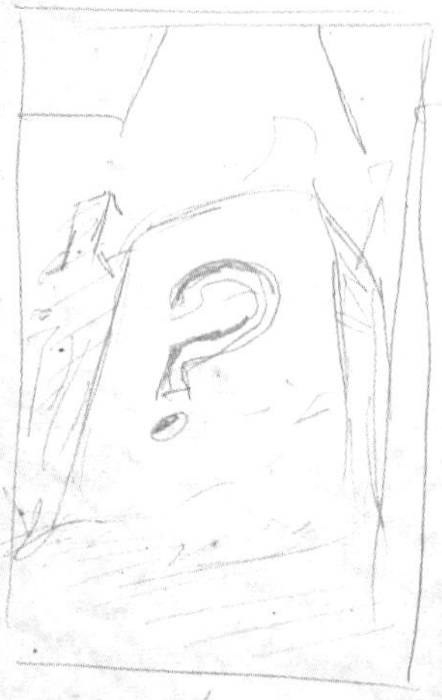

Question
Mark on
Gravestone

## WEEK THIRTY-FOUR

I like the ambiguous nature of this cover. The toe tag with the question mark can be read a number of ways. Is the body a John Doe? Who has died? Is this The Question's body? Is he really dead?

It's a simple, stark image and I wanted to limit the color so that the red question mark would stand out. It made for an easy week for Alex Sinclair.

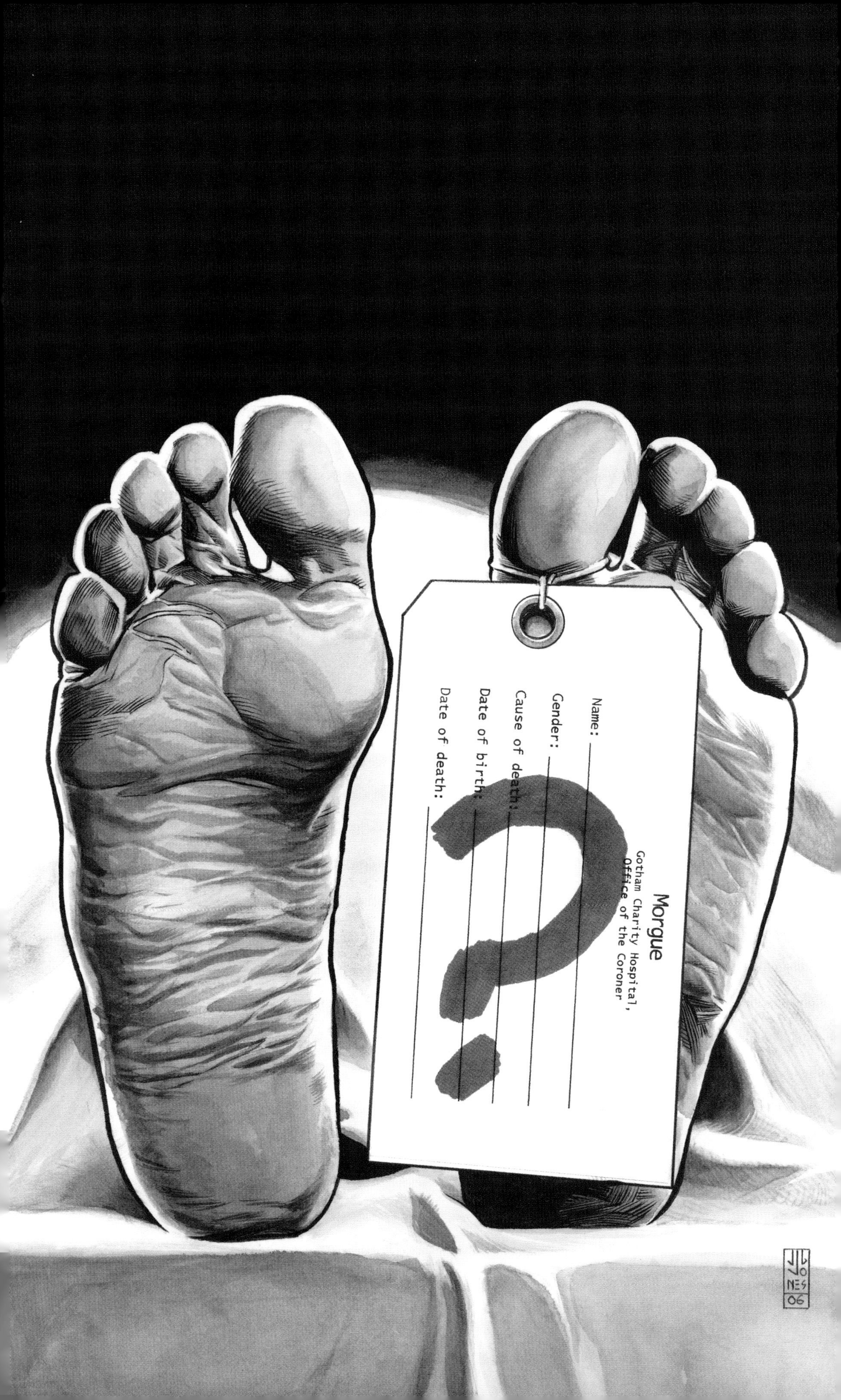

Morgue
Gotham Charity Hospital,
Office of the Coroner
Name:
Gender:
Cause of death:
Date of birth:
Date of death:
JG JONES 06

#35

NIGHT
SKY

CLOCK
SHOWS
12:00

Heroes
Falling-
Graphic
Version
with figures
parallel to

LUTHOR
WATCHING
HEROES
FALL FROM
THE SKY

## WEEK THIRTY-FIVE

Lex Luthor is not a nice guy. He would give a baby candy just so he could then take it away. That's just what the New Year's Eve cover depicts. Lex has been handing out super powers through his Everyman Project, and now, in a moment of pique, he has taken those powers away.

I had a number of sketches depicting heroes plummeting from the sky, but I had to bring Lex back into the equation as the author of the slaughter. He could hardly be more evil and callous, as he casually watches these people fall to their deaths.

HEROES
FALLING

BUILDING
WITH NEW
YEAR'S BALL
ON TOP

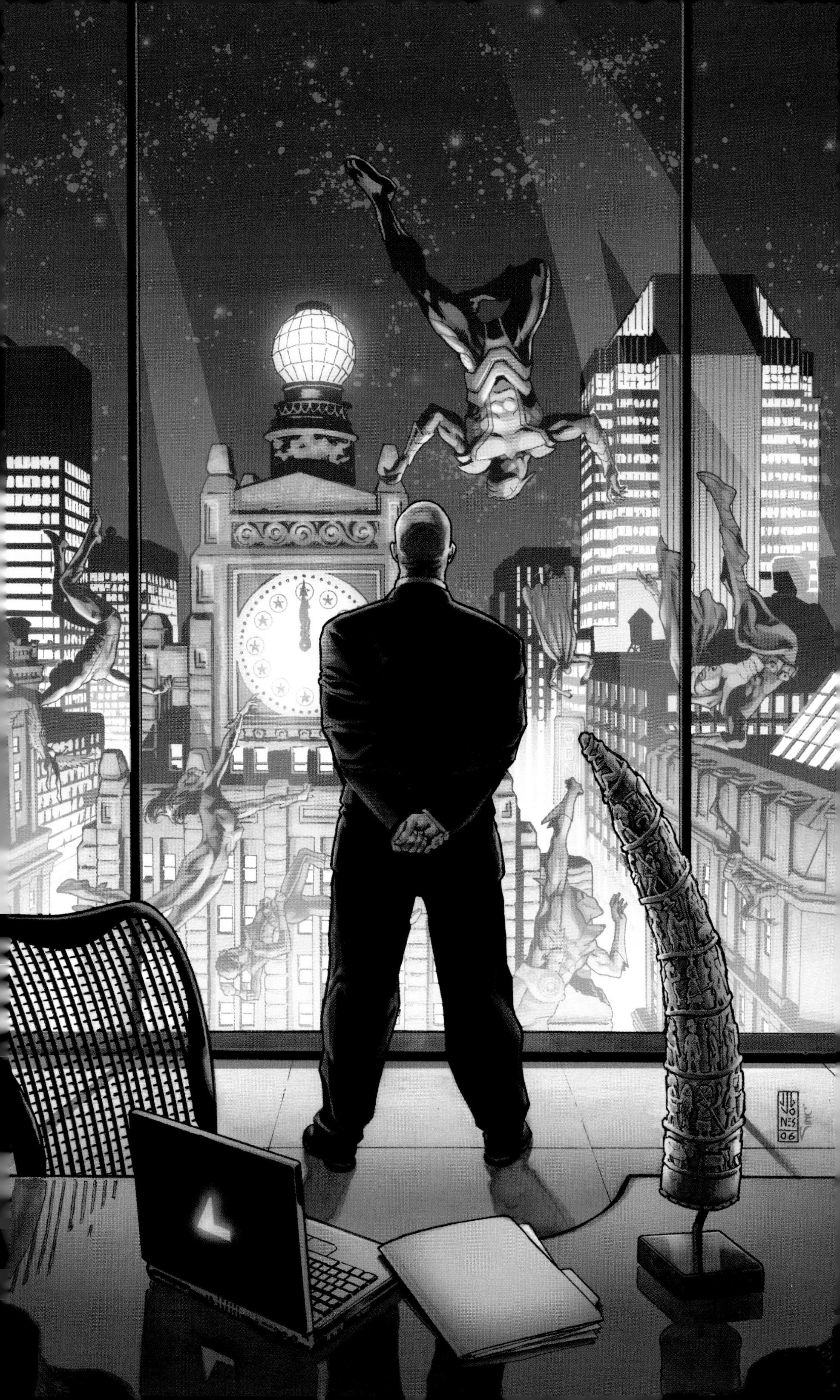

WHITE SKIN OF
LOBO CONTRASTS
WITH BLACK
NECROTONS
IN A WILD
MELEE

### WEEK THIRTY-SIX

A white-skinned Lobo battling an entire army of reanimated zombies in black armor was too good a moment to pass up. This is just the sort of thing that most of us got into comics to draw in the first place.

This was great fun, although it took me a while to draw all of those guys in black armor.

Lady Styx
reflected
in Lobo's
Red Eyes
(He's literally
seeing red)

Think Clint
Eastwood
getting good
and pissed

L. STYX
Holding
head of
Lobo

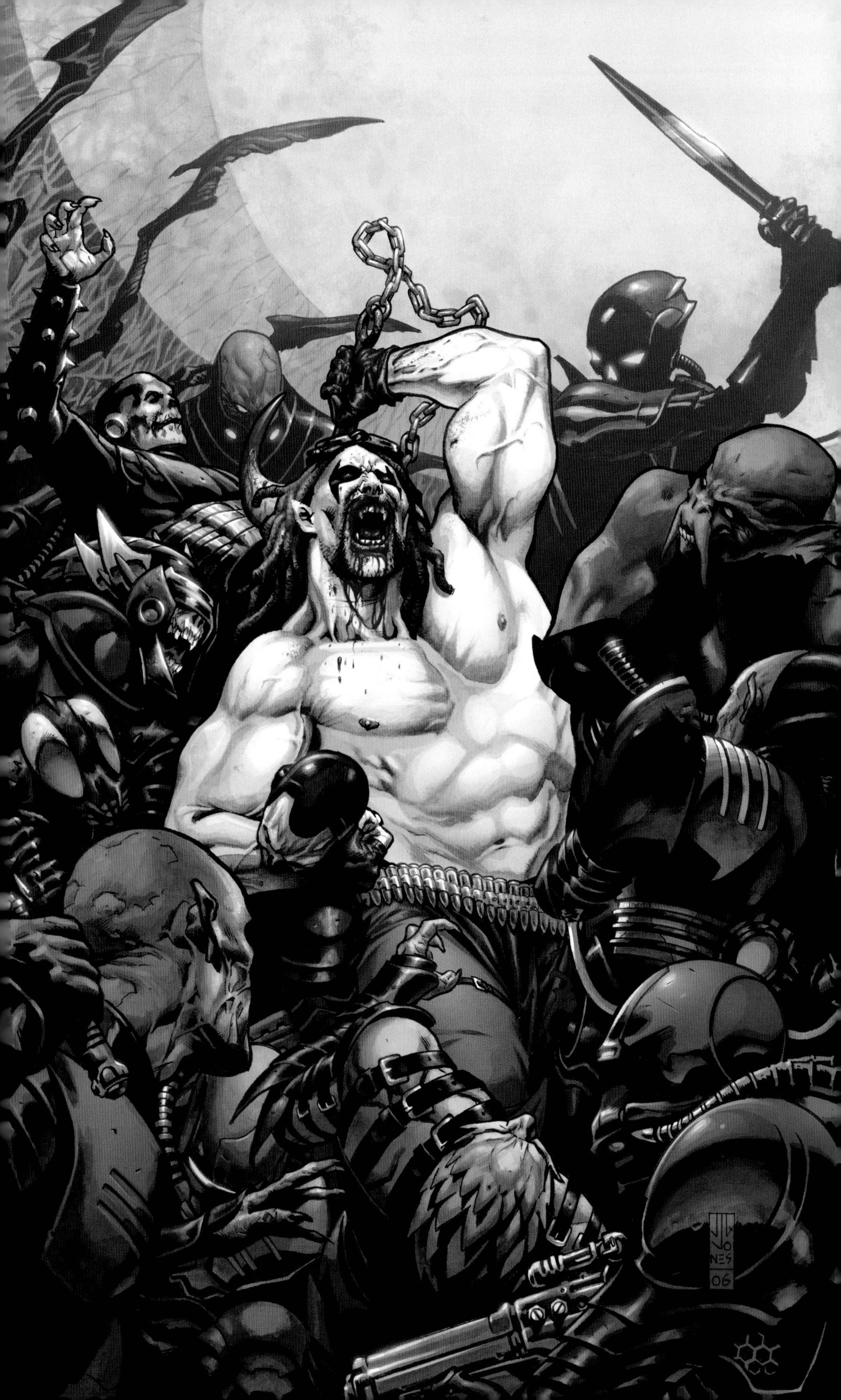

FIGURE REFLECTED IN SKEETS'S METALLIC SURFACE— IN GOLD SKIN, SUPERNOVA IS REFLECTED. IN BLUISH VISOR, BOOSTER GOLD IS REFLECTED.

FIGURE HOLDS THE BOTTLE CITY OF ~~K~~ANDOR

-Rip Hunter Holding Supernova cape + cowl weird science weapons around

Booster in his undies holding Kandor & facing skeets in Supe's fortress of solitude

### WEEK THIRTY-SEVEN

This cover was editor Mike Siglain's idea. I had been working up a really graphic concept cover with a shadow figure of Supernova, a time tunnel, and a numerical countdown. I wanted to find a way to introduce all of the essential story elements without giving away the issue's big secret: Supernova is really Booster Gold.

But Mike wanted to reveal the big secret right there on the cover, through the visual device of Booster reflected in Skeets's golden surface. I think it was my idea to split the figure so that each identity is exposed; Supernova in the golden surface, and Booster in Skeets's visor.

This was really successful only after Alex was done with his terrific color effects on those golden surfaces. Nicely done.

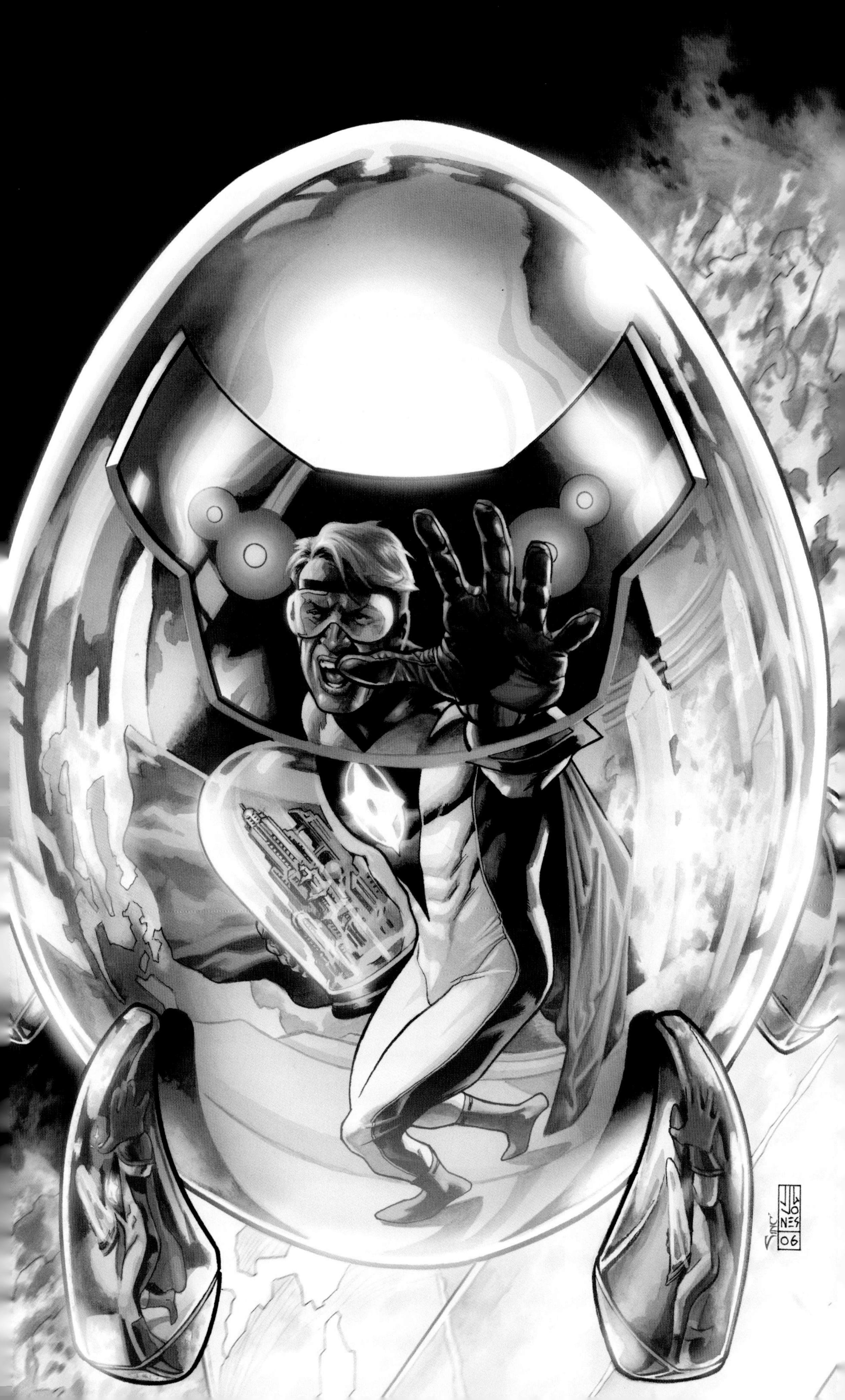

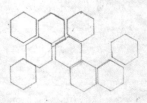

AZRUEZ-
Death in front- His
scythe cracking open the
globe
they are
standing
on-
ZORRM
Behind
him
Roggrq-
in back

38

Dark, scary, moody,
smoke and crackling
energy light coming
out of cracked glo
to under light Azrue

symbols overlay art
in reverse
Biohazard
symbol

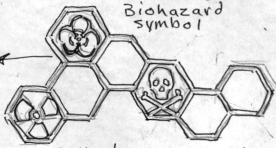

Fallout
symbol

Skull +
crossbones

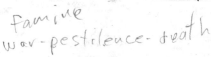

Famine
War-pestilence-death

**WEEK THIRTY-EIGHT**

These horrific gentlemen are three of the Four Horsemen of the Apocalypse, created by a cabal of mad scientists to destroy Black Adam. I place them figuratively atop the Earth with Death's scythe splitting open the globe. They look as if they have just emerged from the pits of Hell.

The overlying DNA molecule honeycomb has a hazard symbol for each Horseman as a final visual clue to the identity of each.

I think Alex enjoyed coloring this one. He expressed surprise that I had composed a cover in this way. That's a good thing...I think.

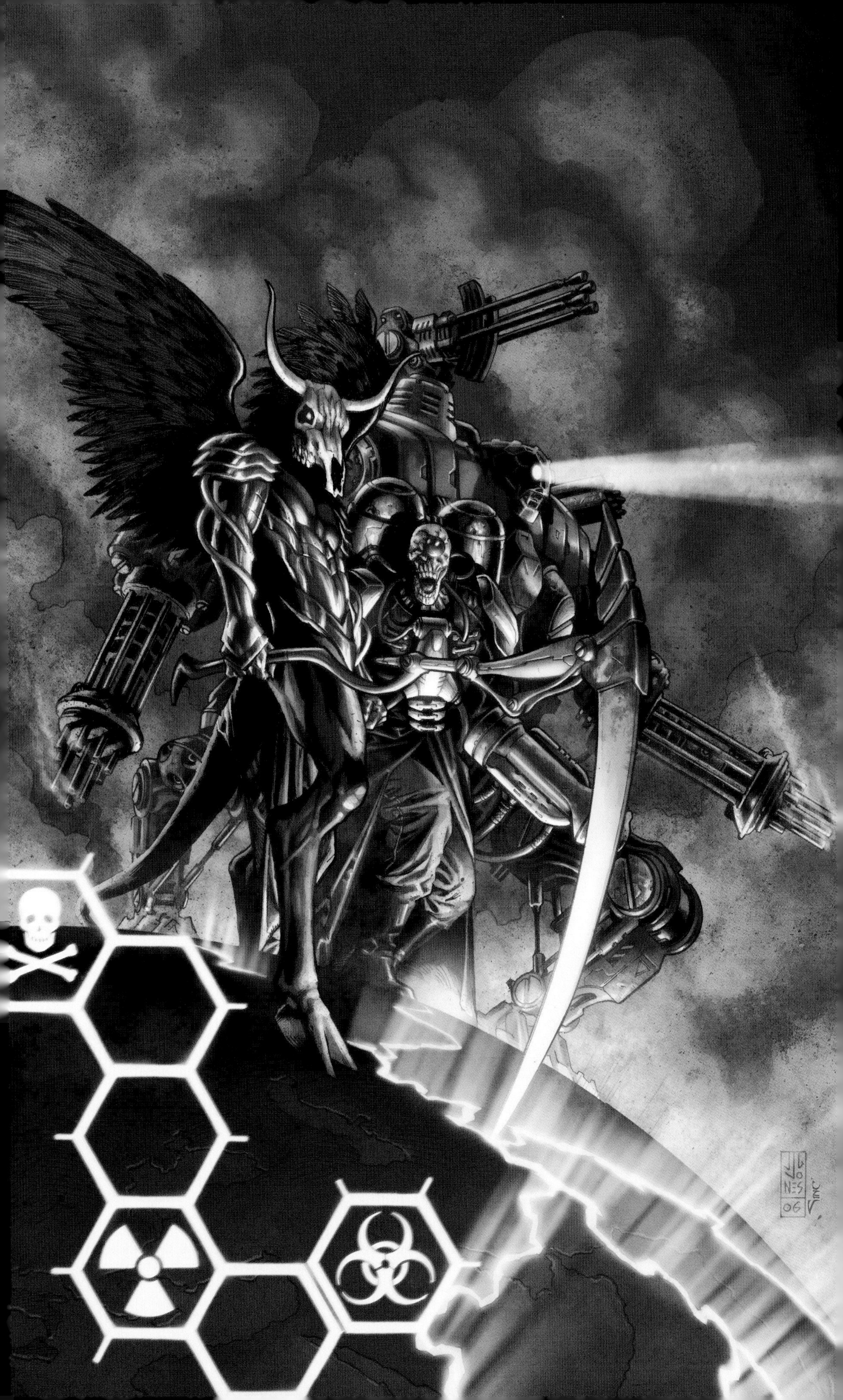

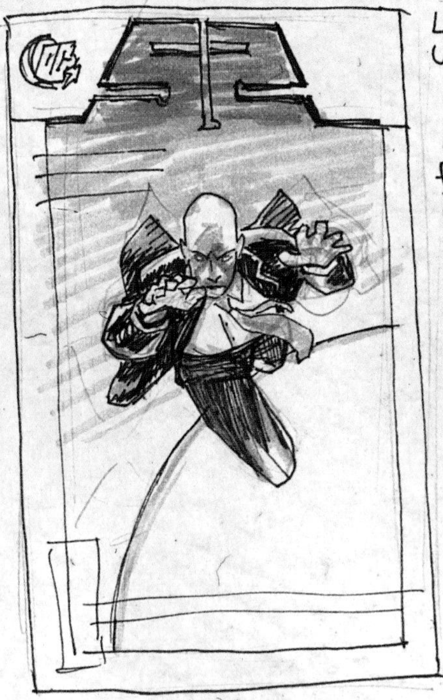
LUTHOR UNBOUND
Lex flying in his business suit - Eyes glowing red -
Either planet Earth in Background or downshot of Metropolis

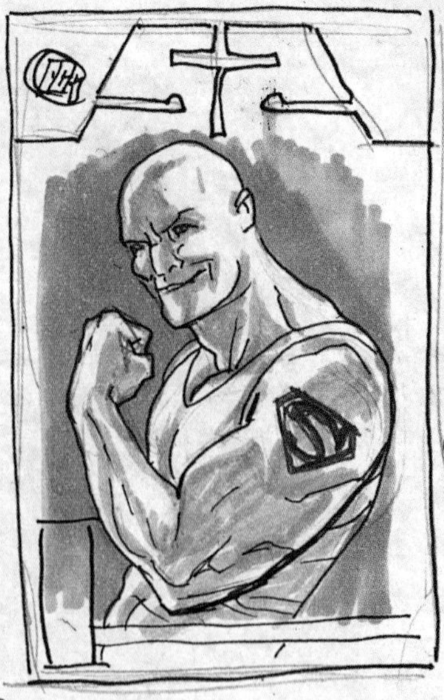
Luthor - Red Glowing eyes - bulked up. Superman tattoo (like Shaq's) on Shoulder. Evil Smirk.

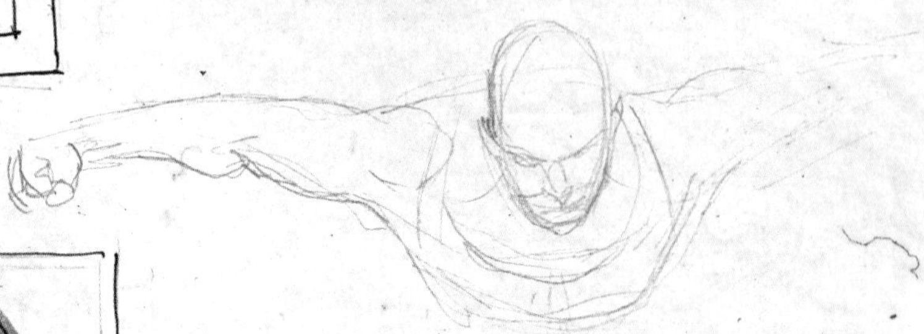

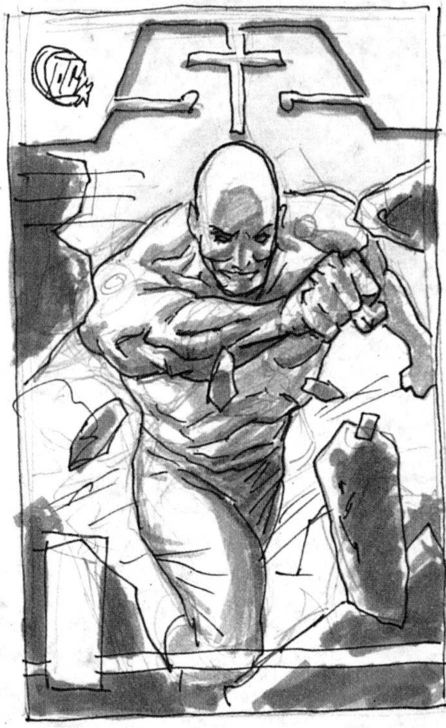
39
Super Powered Lex smashes Through wall -
Red glowing EYES

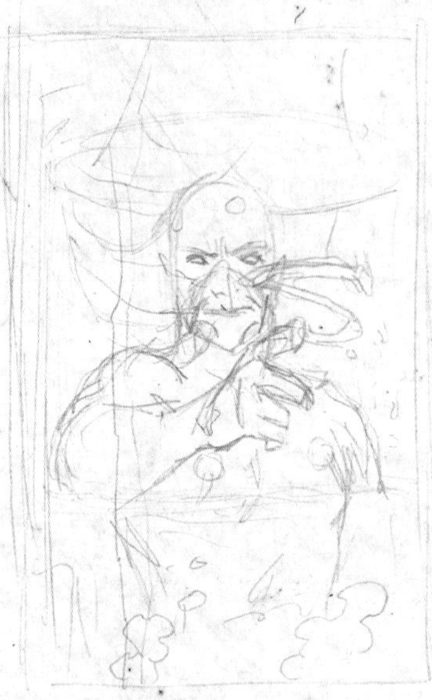

## WEEK THIRTY-NINE

Lex Luthor has achieved his goal and now possesses superpowers. This cover ended up as a pretty straightforward image. I wanted to do something more oblique and creative, but Mike Siglain insisted that the cover show Lex exhibiting his superpowers by breaking chains, flying, or something along those lines.

After doing a number of rejected sketches, I finally gave in and did the kind of cover Mike wanted. Deadlines have a way of forcing your hand sometimes, but in the end, this turned out to be the weakest cover of the entire series.

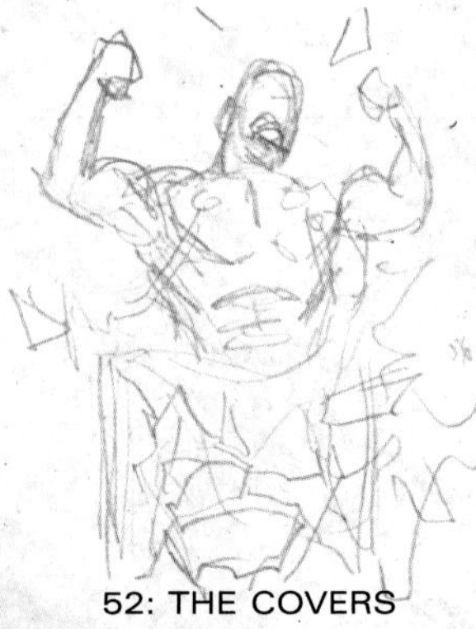

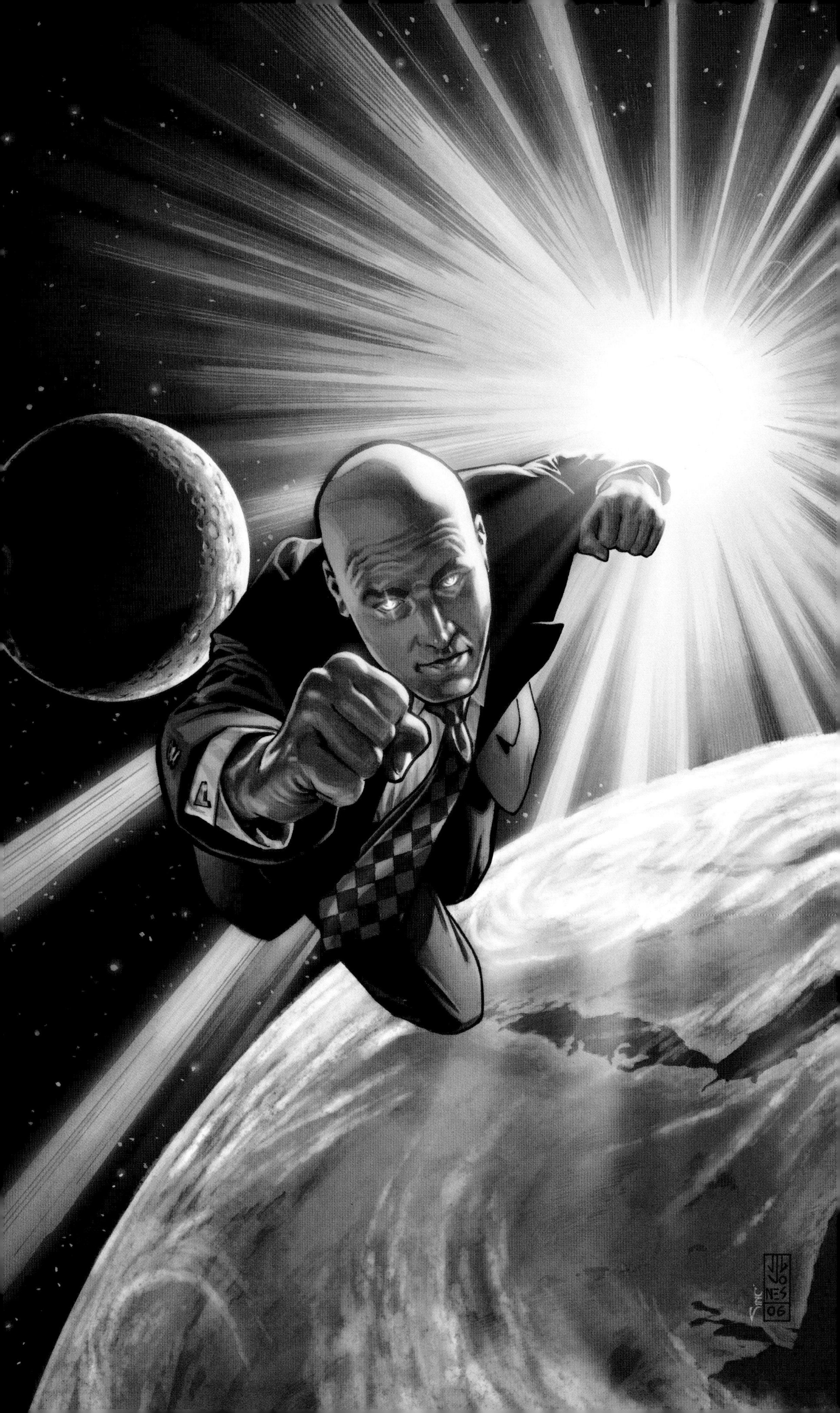

# 52 COLORS

by Alex Sinclair

Color artist Alex Sinclair breaks down the process of coloring a single **52** cover (in this case, the **52 Volume One** collection) in five not-so-easy steps!

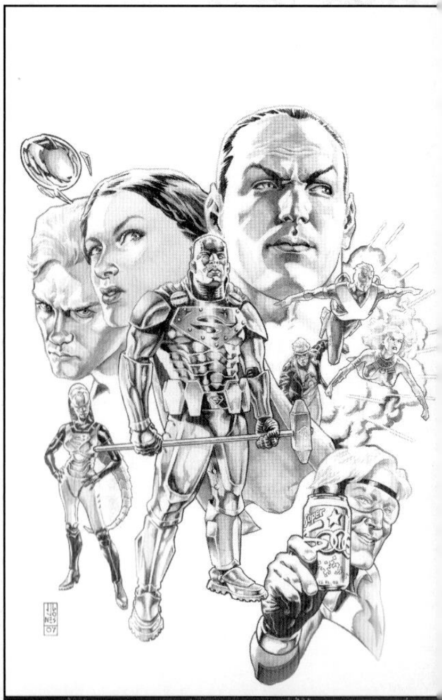

**B&W and Prep:**
"I always get a raw scan, notes and reference for each cover. For this one, J.G. sent me a JPEG of a Drew Struzan poster and asked that I give it that same feel. I usually prep each scan by establishing the white points and making sure the inks are a pure black throughout while making sure his washes remain true to the original. I also adjust the values on some of the art — here I've lightened the small figures on the upper right and Steel's legs."

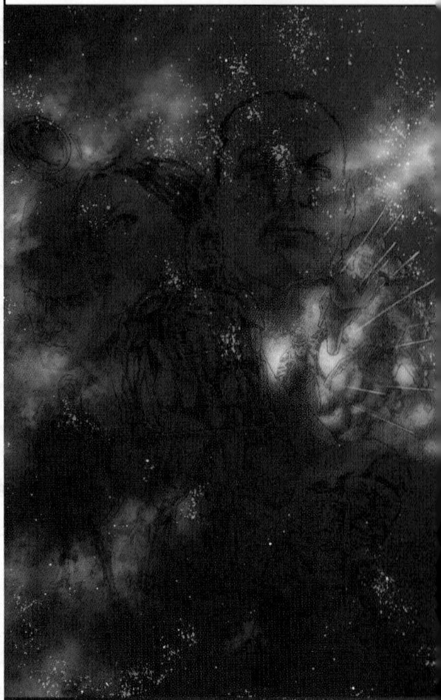

**Background:**
"Each **52** cover has a different approach, and for this one I basically had to paint and airbrush the background to get the right feel. Since some of the figures had to be semi-transparent, I painted through most of the figures."

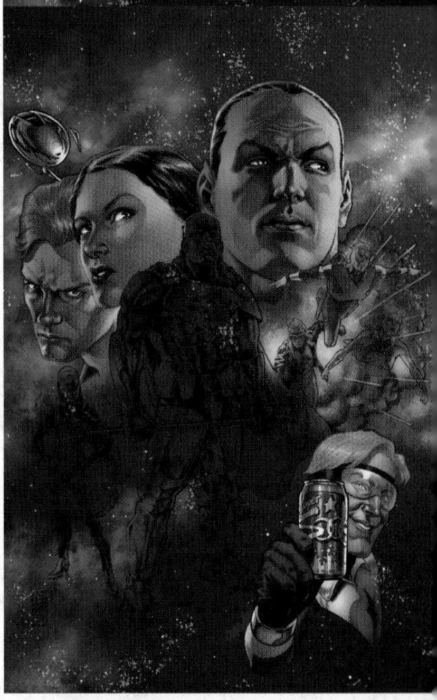

**Heads:**
"I bring the line art back in to render the headshots mirroring the cool to warm palette I used on the background. I use similar painting techniques here and also use subtle shape gradients to help give the heads some mass."

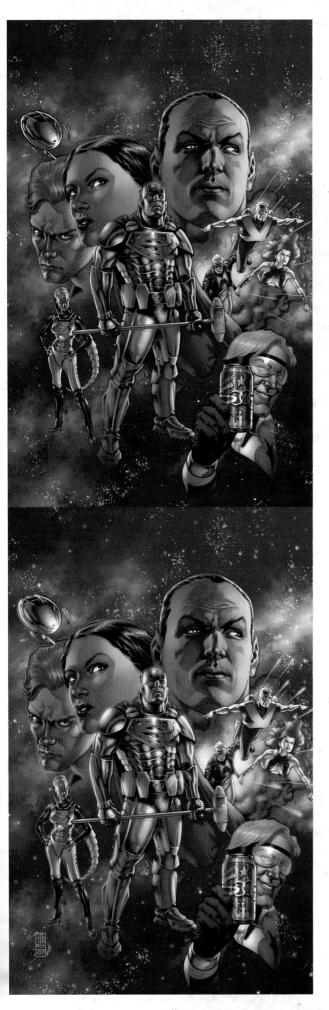

### Figures:

"Next I color the small figures of the piece. Struzan uses a lot of monochromatic palettes for figures like these, so I do the same. Steel is a different story. He is in the extreme foreground so his body has three different light sources — I use a natural light for the top/front and bring in the orange and blue from the background as reflective light. I also blend him into the background a little (another Struzan cheat)."

### Finish:

"I add highlights and slight glows from the explosion. I also adjust the values on a couple figures so the piece works a little better. Some glowing stars here and there and voilà...another **52** cover in the can...although this one's #53?!"

Steel
knocks
Giant 'L'
off
Bldg.

## WEEK FORTY

Time to wash away the bad taste left behind by the previous cover. The great thing about doing all 52 covers was that every week, I got to take a fresh shot at doing something fun.

The little sketch that became cover #40 was done in the second writers' summit meeting. The guys were discussing the final showdown between Steel and Lex Luthor high atop the Lexcorp Tower. Rather than have a shot of the two heavyweights fighting, I opted for the symbolism of Steel knocking the Lexcorp logo off the building. I like the simple, clean composition.

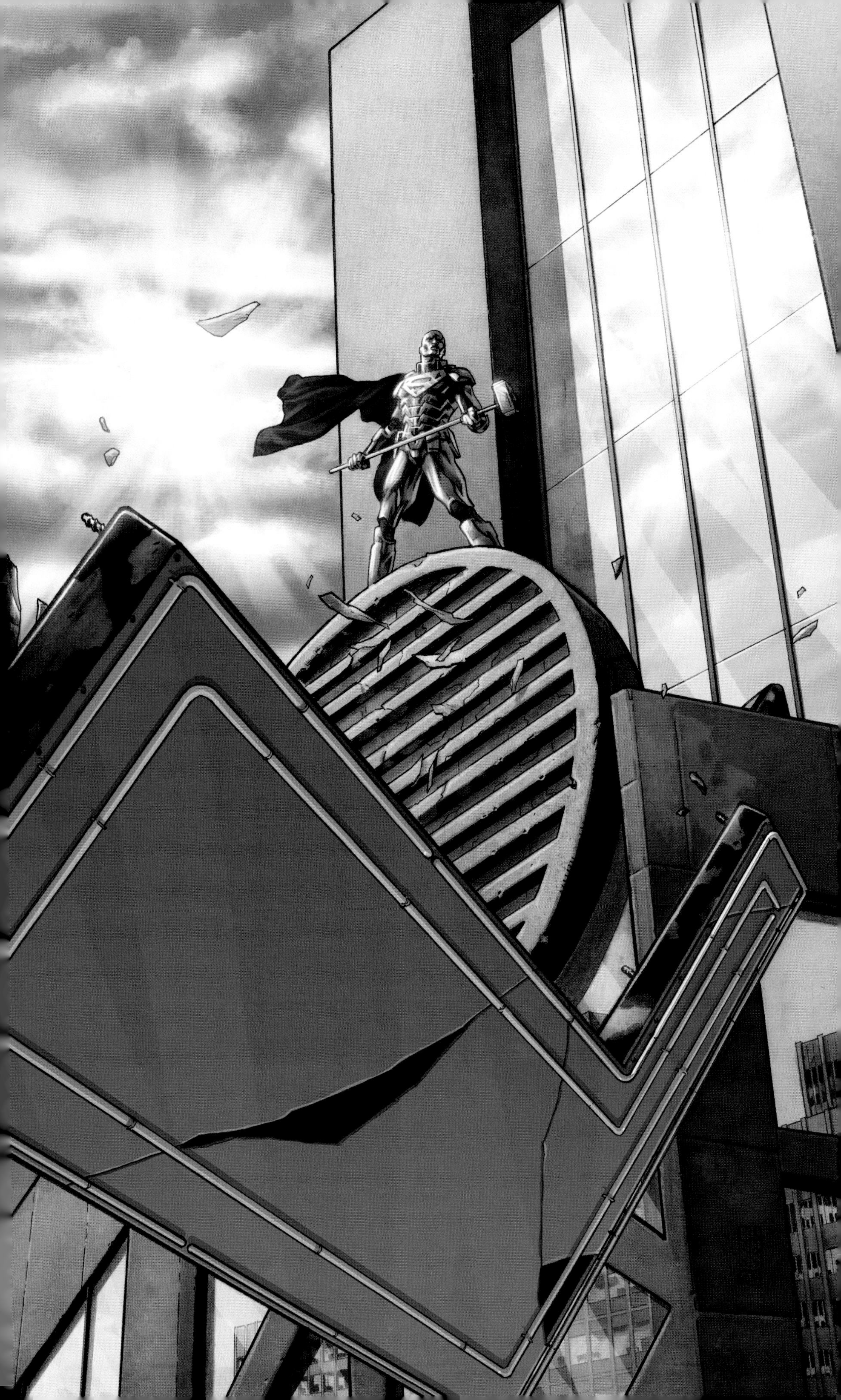

Add
Richard
Dragon

Ralph  Diana  A. Strange
Firestorm      41

Mogo

montoya's
Ponytail
shaped like
a Question
mark

Meditating
in Ice Cave

Mr. Moth

← SUN Dial

## WEEK FORTY-ONE

This is an odd cover that takes care of a number of bits of business from the various storylines all in one image. I needed something to anchor the scene, and Montoya in the ice cave worked well. I was thinking about the final scene from the classic film *The Lady From Shanghai*, which takes place in a carnival fun house — so I put her on the floor in the lotus position, contemplating the various scenes reflected in the faceted surfaces of the ice. There's a little hint about Montoya's ultimate fate here, as her ponytail takes the form of a question mark.

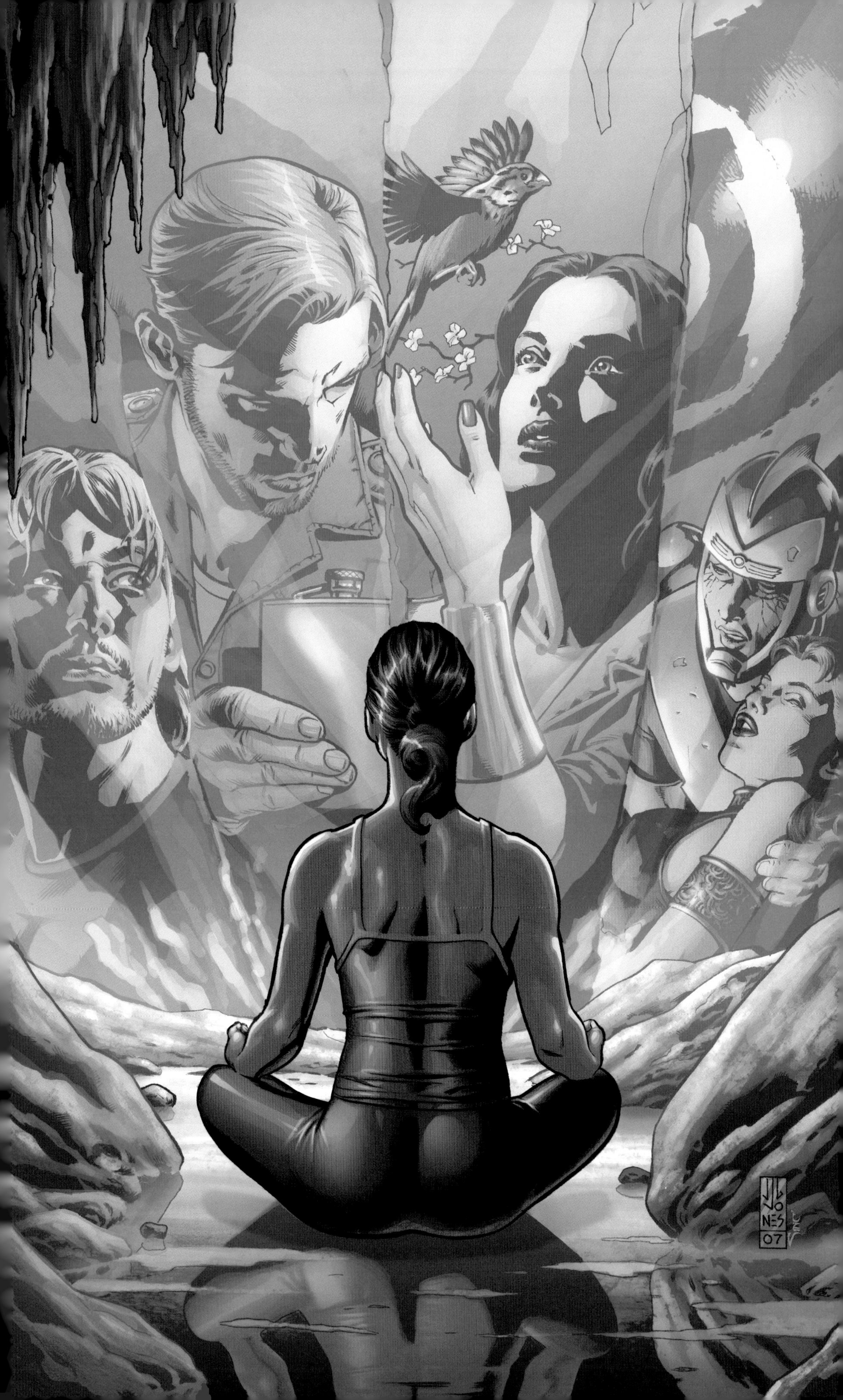

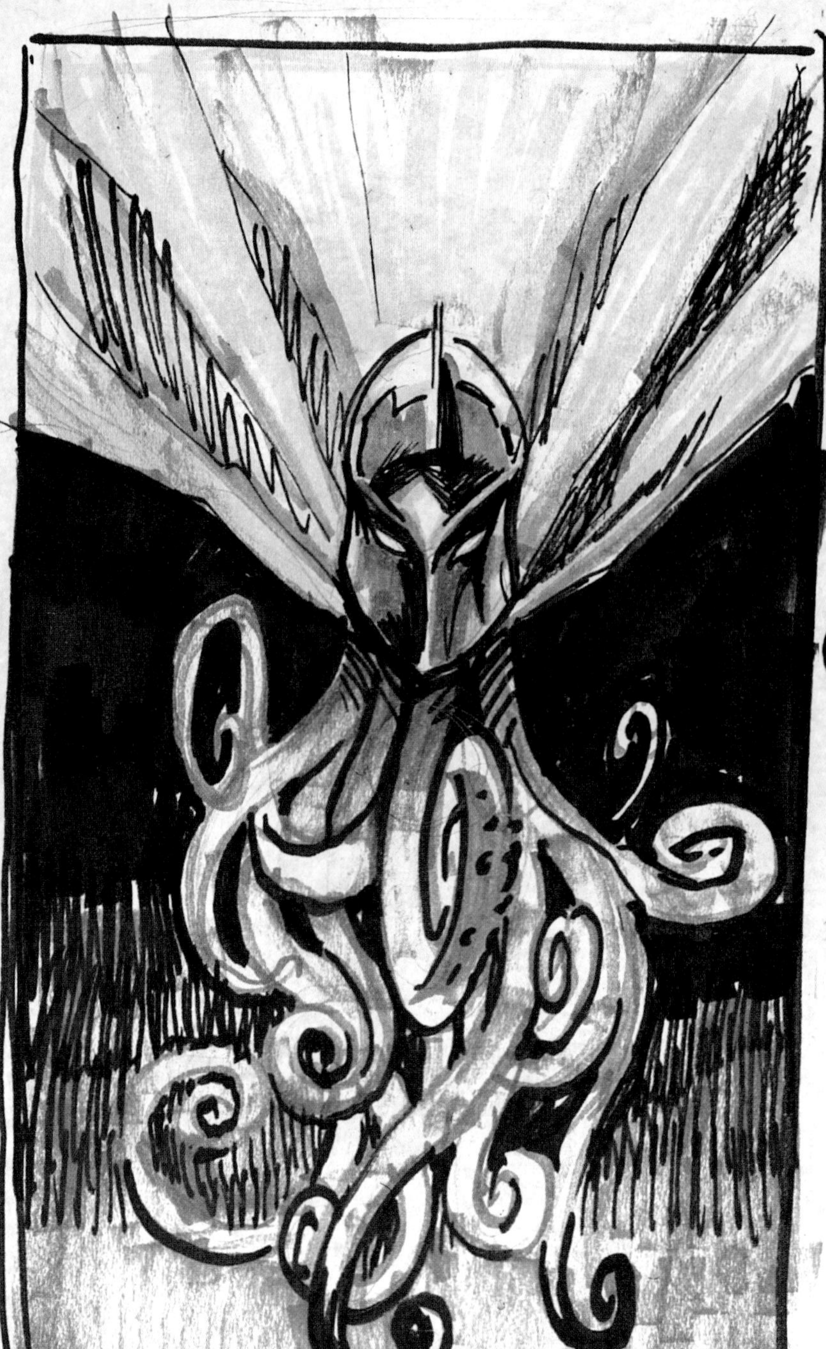

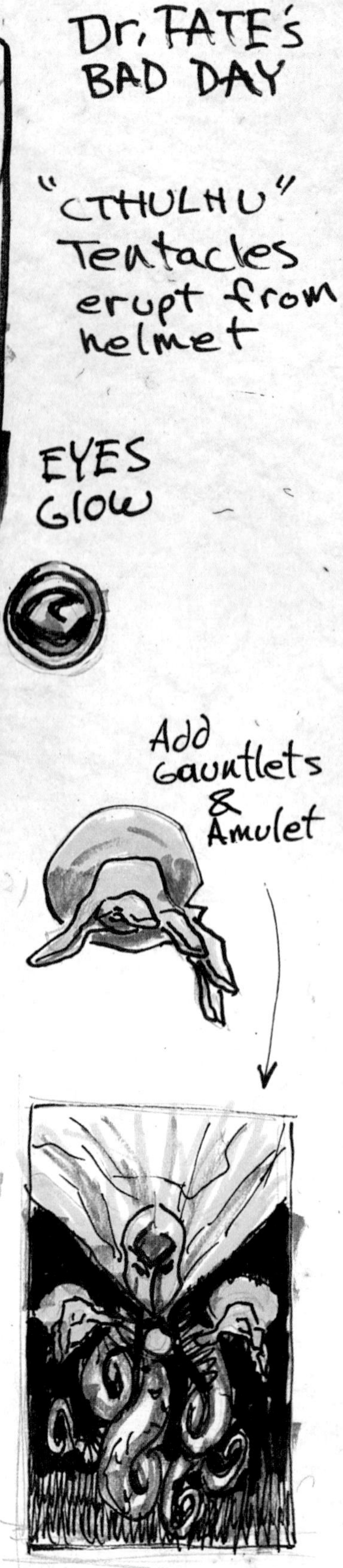
Dr. FATE's BAD DAY
"CTHULHU" Tentacles erupt from helmet
EYES Glow
Add Gauntlets & Amulet

**WEEK FORTY-TWO**

This cover was the second one that I drew, because the concept was sketched out in the early planning sessions. We were discussing the role of Fate's helmet, which is totally closed and never allows for any facial expression. Thus there is no way to ever read Fate's facial expressions or intent.

I had this idea of malignant evil pouring out of the helm in the form of Cthulhu-like tentacles. The writers loved the idea, so we kept the evil helmet in the story.

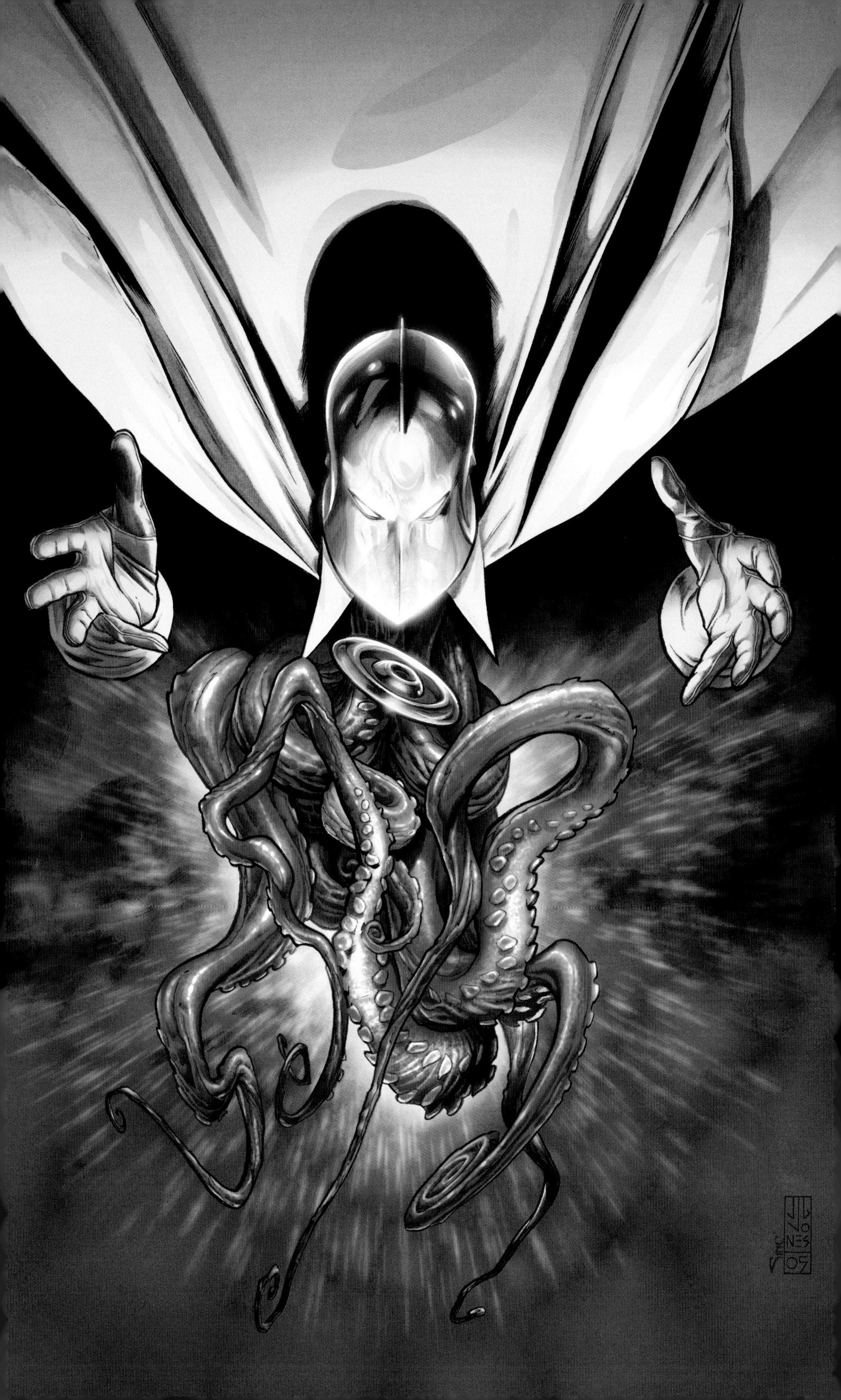

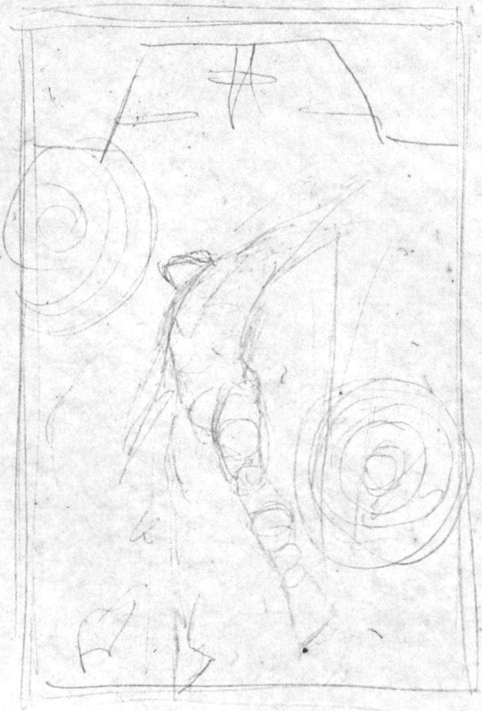

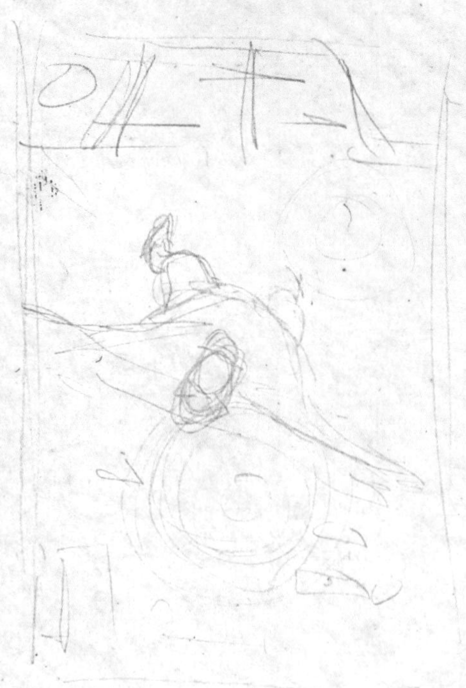

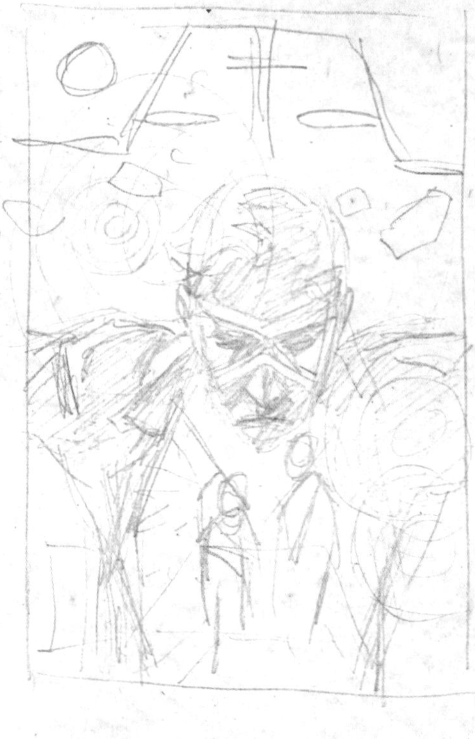

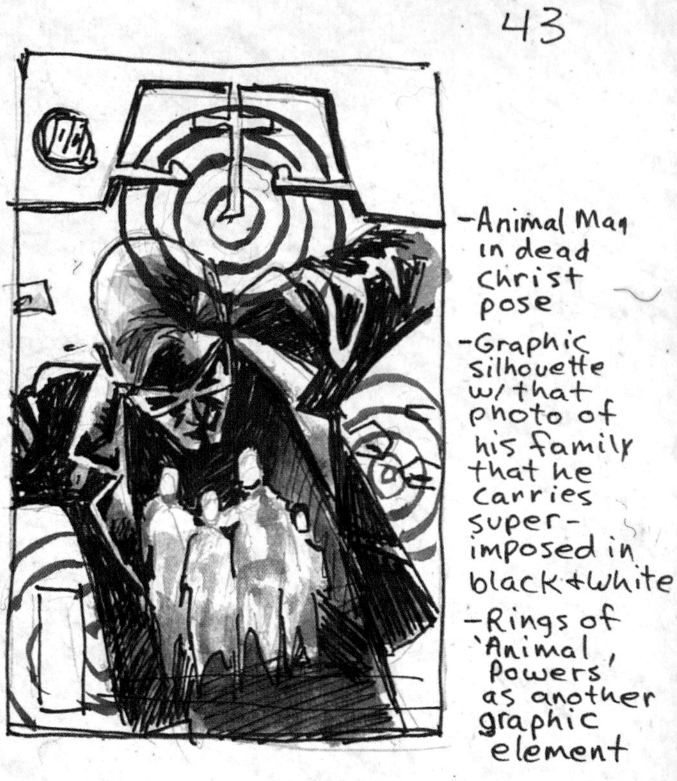
43
-Animal Man in dead Christ pose
-Graphic silhouette w/ that photo of his family that he carries super-imposed in black + white
-Rings of 'Animal Powers' as another graphic element

## WEEK FORTY-THREE

I chose the Animal Man storyline for #43 because it offered the best options for a really graphic treatment, and it also allowed me to avoid doing three Black Adam covers in a row.

The concentric circles that indicate the use of his animal powers offer a powerful visual element. I also tried to keep the rest of the composition simple and stark to focus on the figure of Animal Man and the photo of his family that he carries at all times.

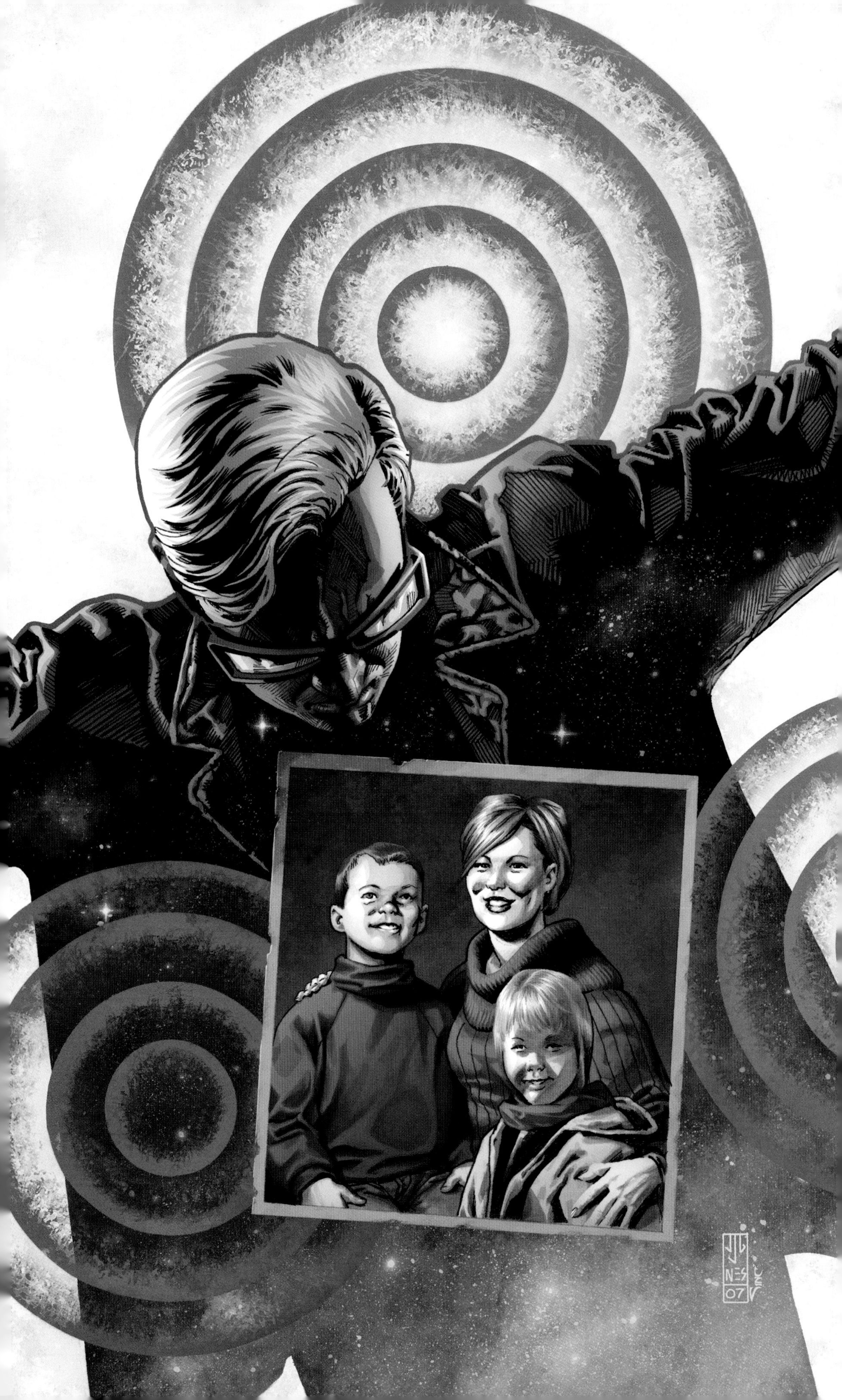

← Isis' tiara

← Blackened
Rose Petals

← Reflection
of B.A.
in blood
Pool

(Maybe his reflection
has him battling
Horseman?)

lightning
strike reflected
as well?

44

Isis' face
in Graphic
Blood pool

### WEEK FORTY-FOUR

I had several options for this one. I liked the sketch with Black Adam's reflection in a pool of blood next to Isis' tiara, but maybe this concept was a bit too similar to the cover of Week Fifteen.

Mark Chiarello really responded to the second sketch, which had Isis' face superimposed on a splash of blood spattered across a plain white background. It's a simple, effective image that I did with just pencils and red Doc Martin's inks.

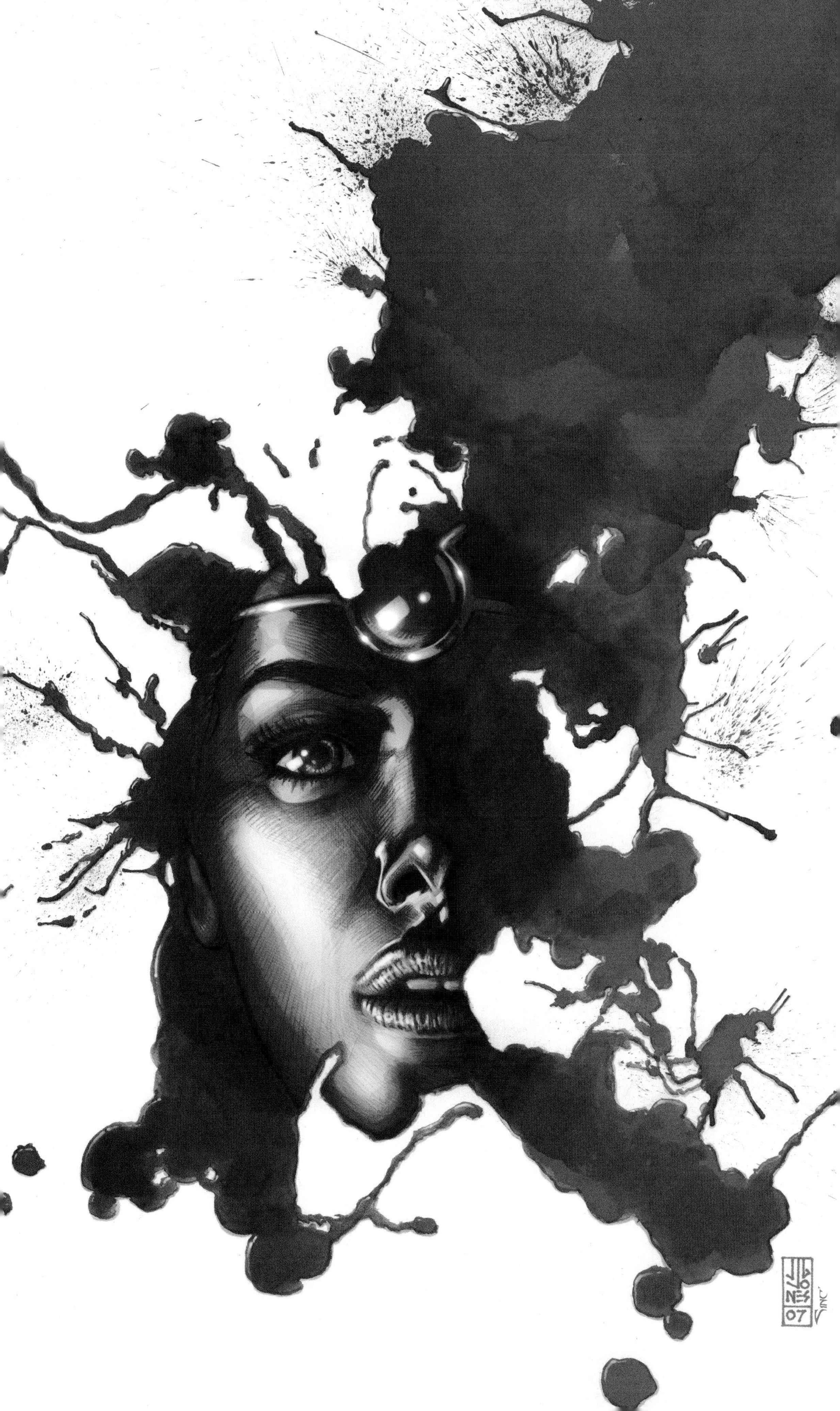

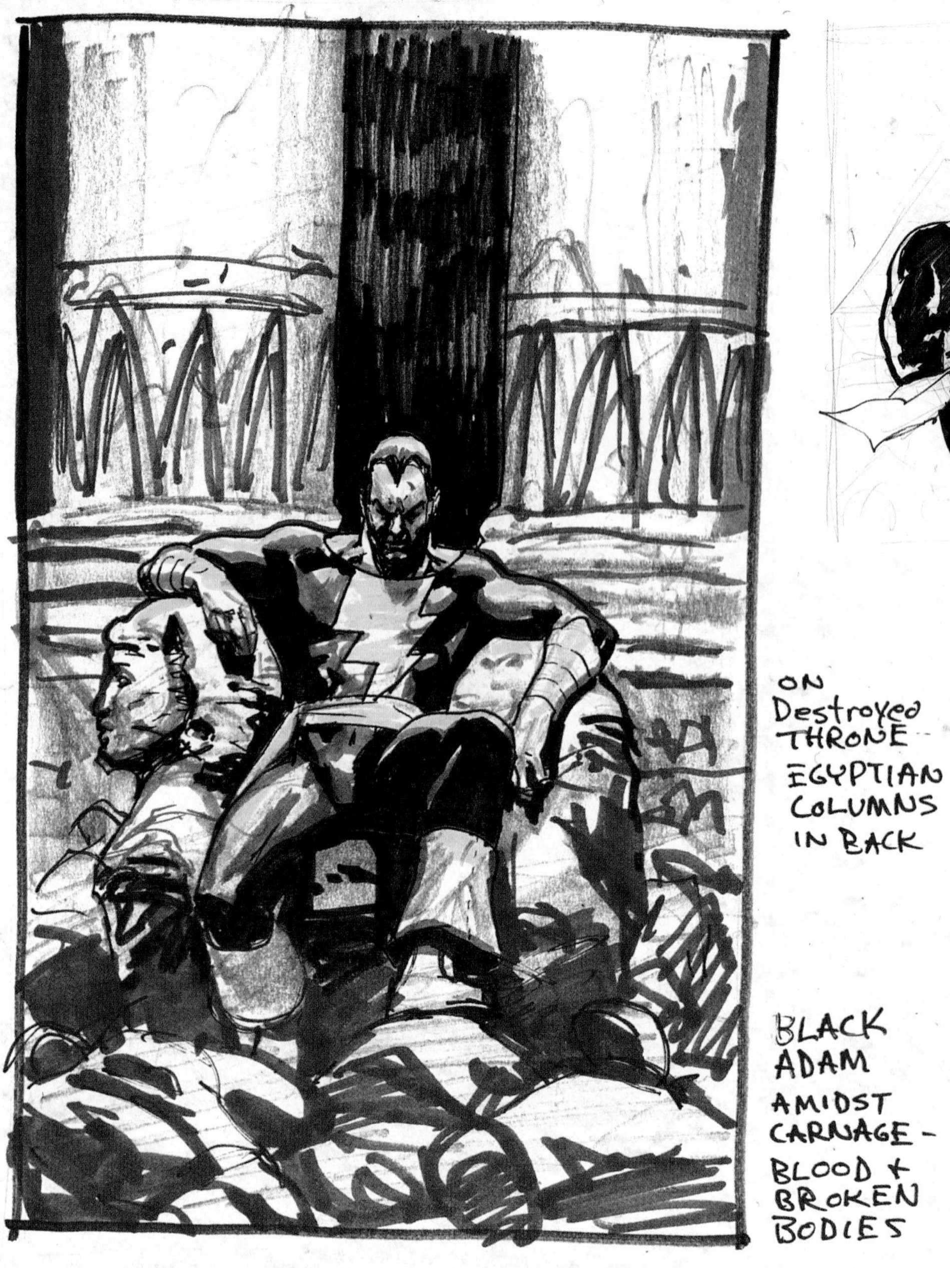
ON
Destroyed
THRONE -
EGYPTIAN
COLUMNS
IN BACK
BLACK
ADAM
AMIDST
CARNAGE -
BLOOD &
BROKEN
BODIES

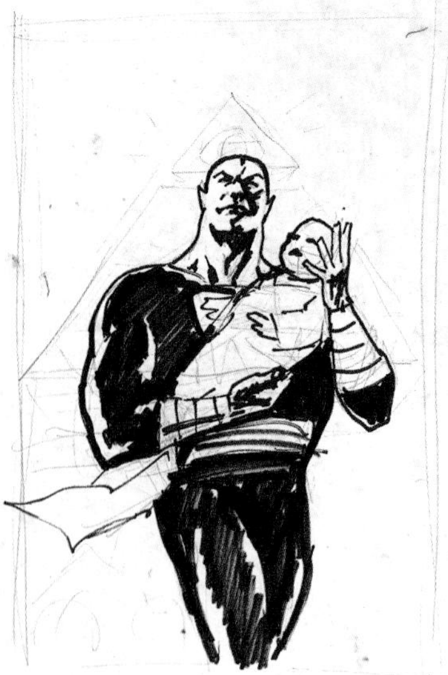

## WEEK FORTY-FIVE

In a blind rage following the death of his beloved Isis, Black Adam becomes Samson, pulling the temple walls down around him and destroying his enemies. How could I resist drawing a moment like this?

This was actually the very first 52 cover that I drew, and it remains one of my favorites from the series. I wanted a powerful, raw image composed in a simple, straightforward manner. The sunlight filters down onto the scene from the shattered ceiling high above, falling on Adam's shoulders and casting his features into shadow.

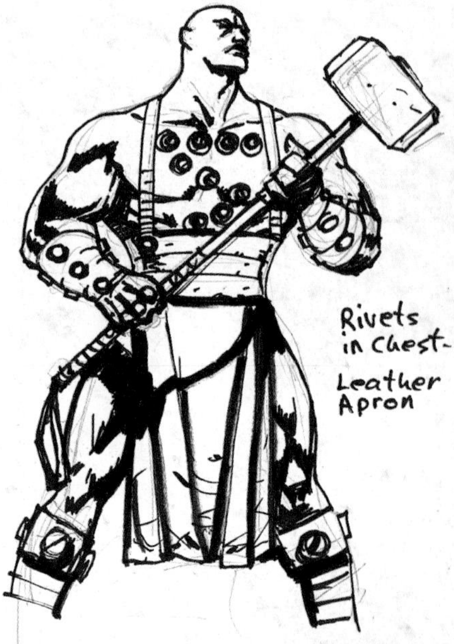
Rivets
in Chest-
Leather
Apron

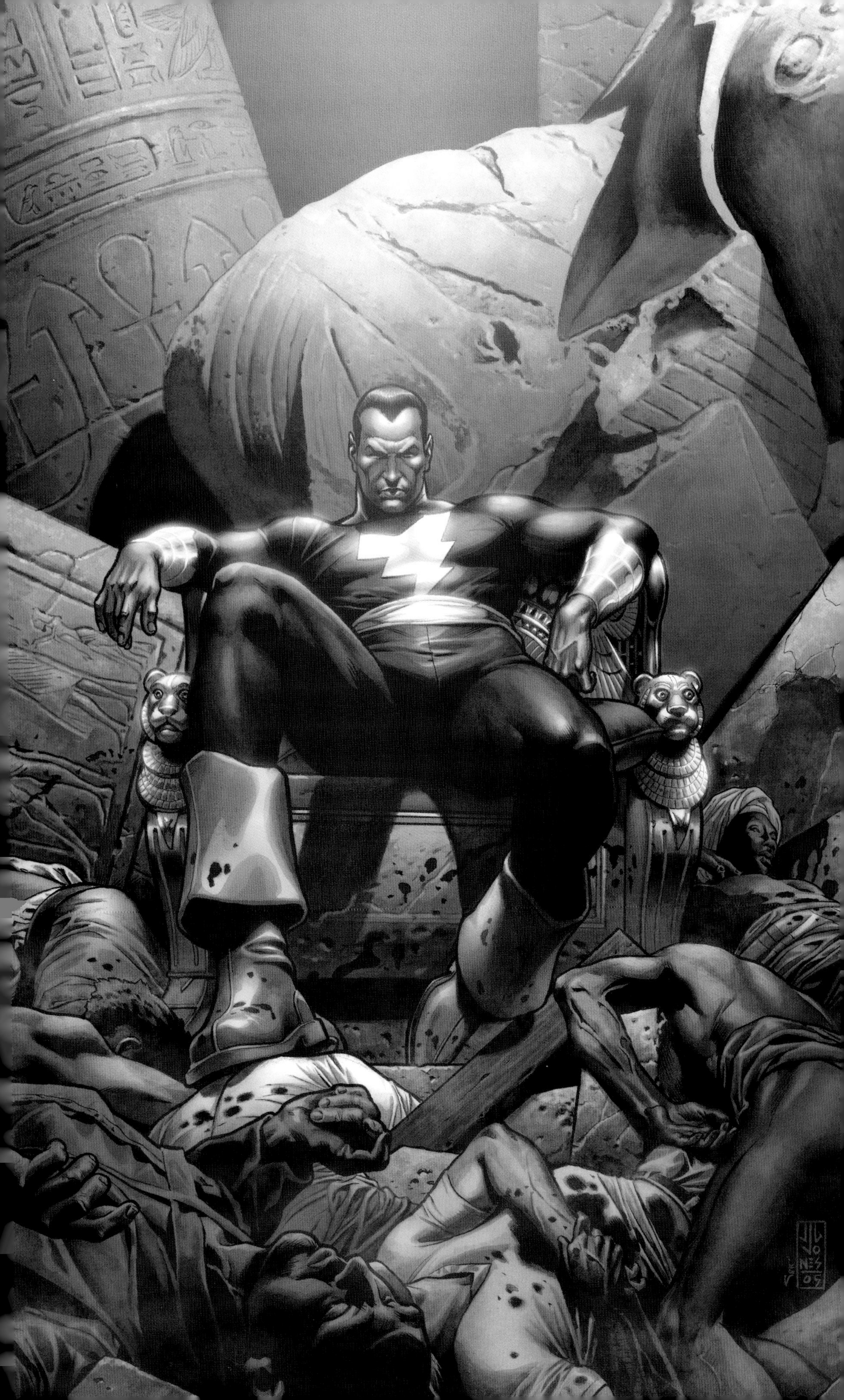

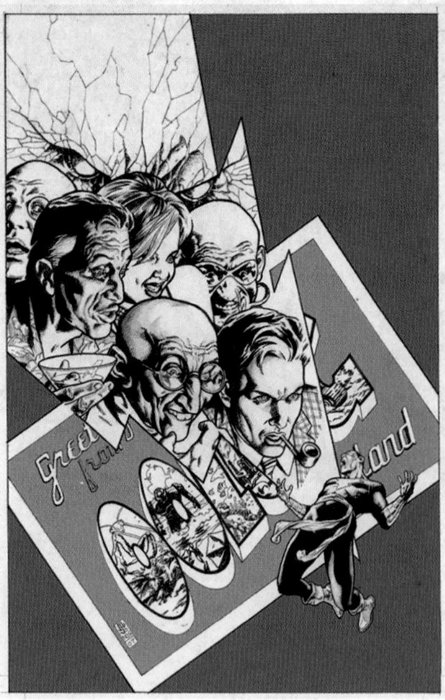
Greetings from Oolong Island

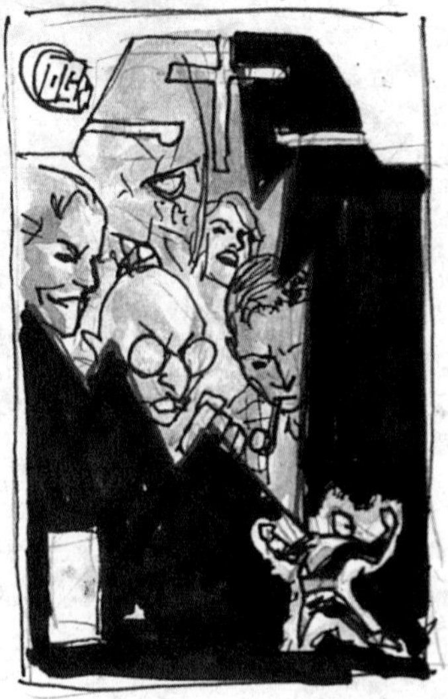
EVIL SCIENTISTS
INSIDE LIGHTNING
↓ BOLT
EGG FU
CALE
MORROW
SIVANA
MAGNUS
BLACK
ADAM
STRUCK
BY BOLT

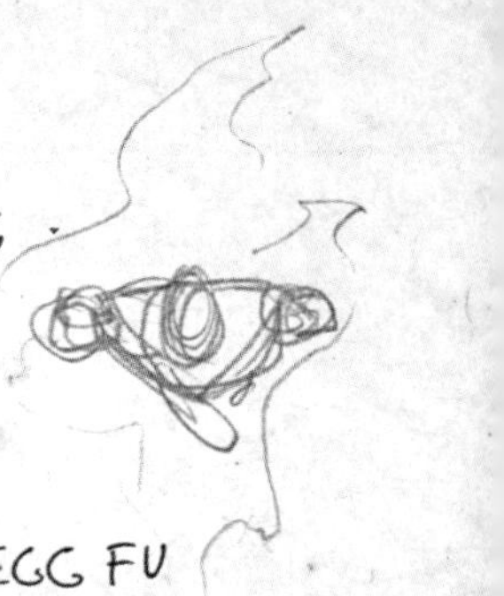

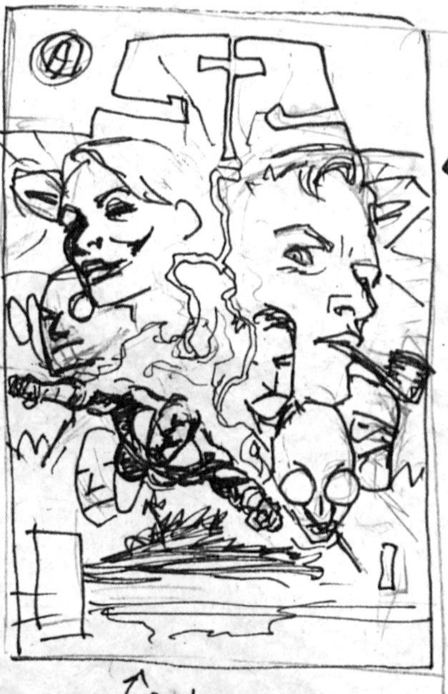
EGG FU face superimposed
on background
Lightning
strike in
center
V. CALE
MAGNUS
KRABB
MORROW
Black
Adam
in
flames
SIVANA
Oolong
Island
I WANT TO
WORK ON
THE PLACEMENT
OF THE HEADS
AND THE
SCALE OF
EACH, BUT
THIS IS THE
BASIC IDEA

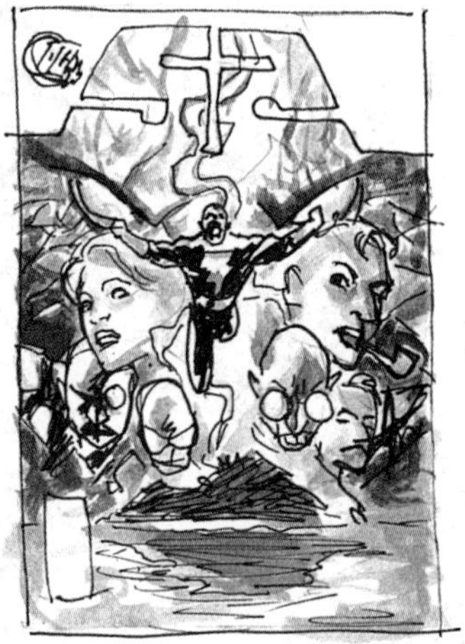
SAME CONCEPT-
SLIGHTLY DIFF.
COMPOSITION
46

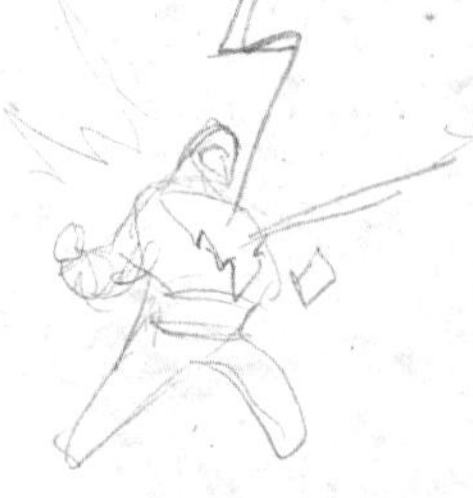
*maybe
revise
this one
for #50

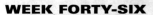

## WEEK FORTY-SIX

Sometimes we need to be saved from our own worst impulses. I did a number of prelims for this cover, but Mark Chiarello really responded to a little sketch that I sent in as an afterthought. He liked the dynamic simplicity of the stylized lightning bolt containing the images of the mad scientists as it strikes Black Adam full on the chest.

I had a ball drawing the scientists but still felt that the cover looked incomplete, so I added a postcard in the background that read, "Greetings from Oolong Island." Oolong Island, of course, is the home of the Mad Scientist Cabal.

Mark nixed the postcard from the final cover, returning the image to its original simplicity.

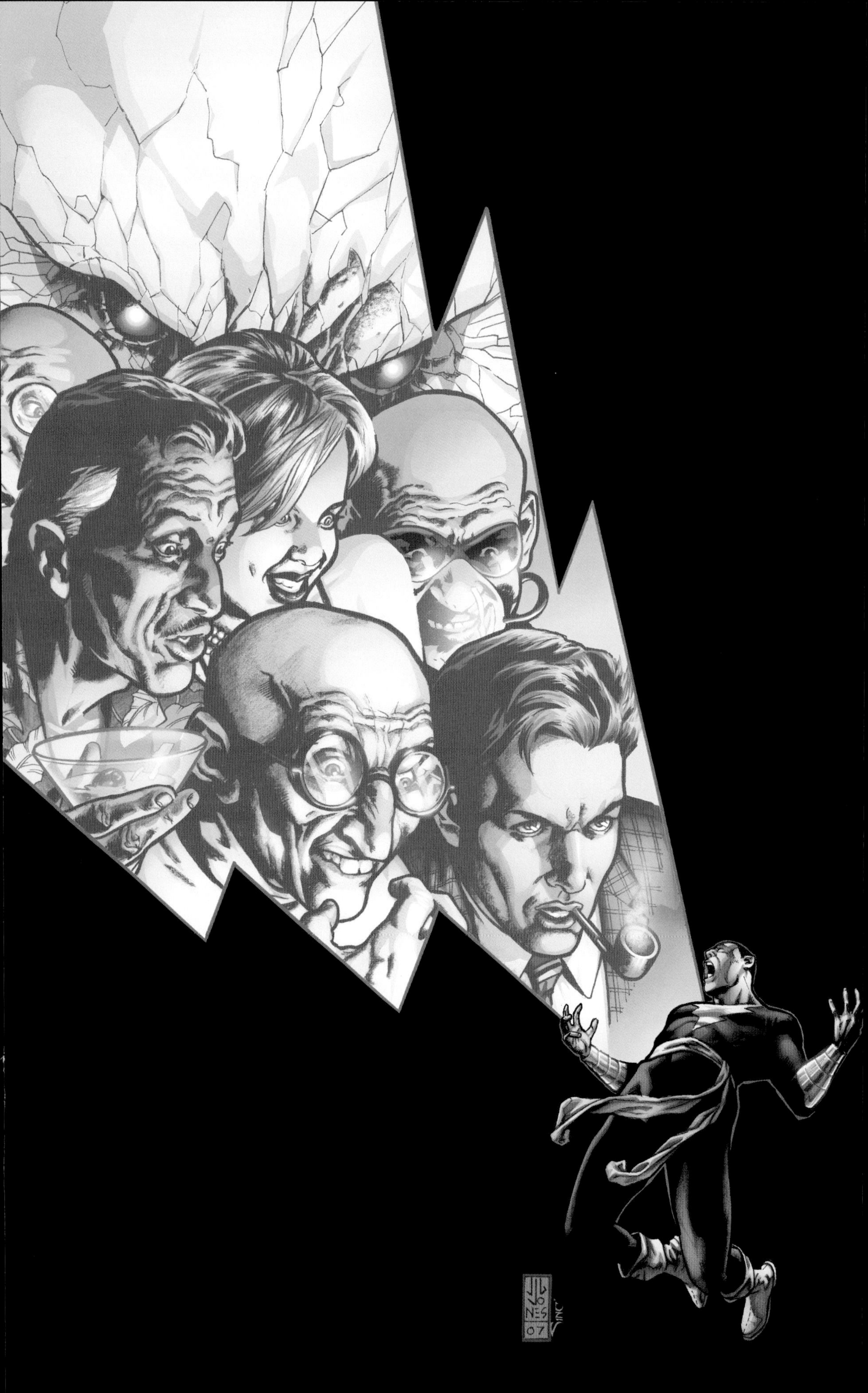

47

THE BASIC IDEA IS THAT THE SACRIFICIAL KNIFE IS THRUST INTO THE COVER OF THE CRIME BIBLE. THE BLADE IS CENTERED ON A GRAPHIC REPRESENTATION OF A HEART WITH LITTLE BAT WINGS. THERE ARE DROPS OF BLOOD ON THE BOOK, AND A SCREAMING BATWOMAN IS REFLECTED IN THE BLADE.

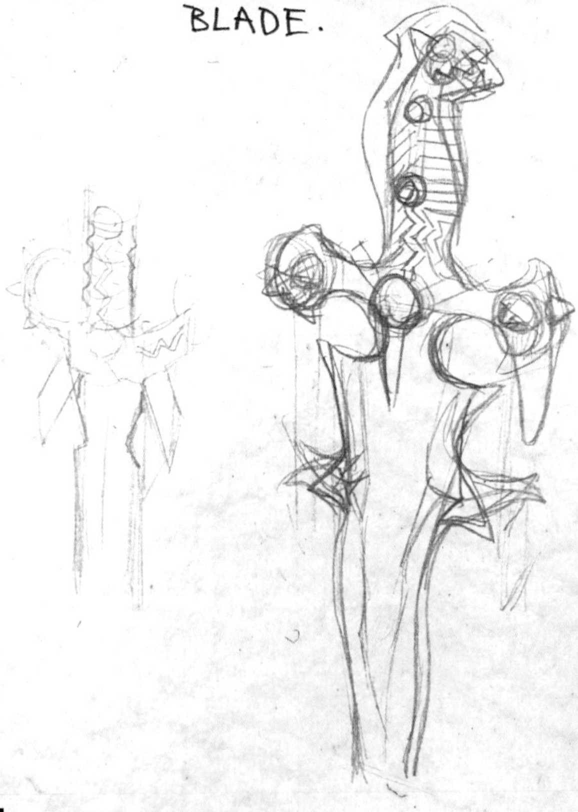

## WEEK FORTY-SEVEN

The little description scribbled next to the preliminary sketch sums this cover up perfectly. The only change I made was to swing the camera around to show the pages of the tome rather than the spine, making the object more easily identifiable as a book. The dagger was redesigned to reflect its origins on Apokolips.

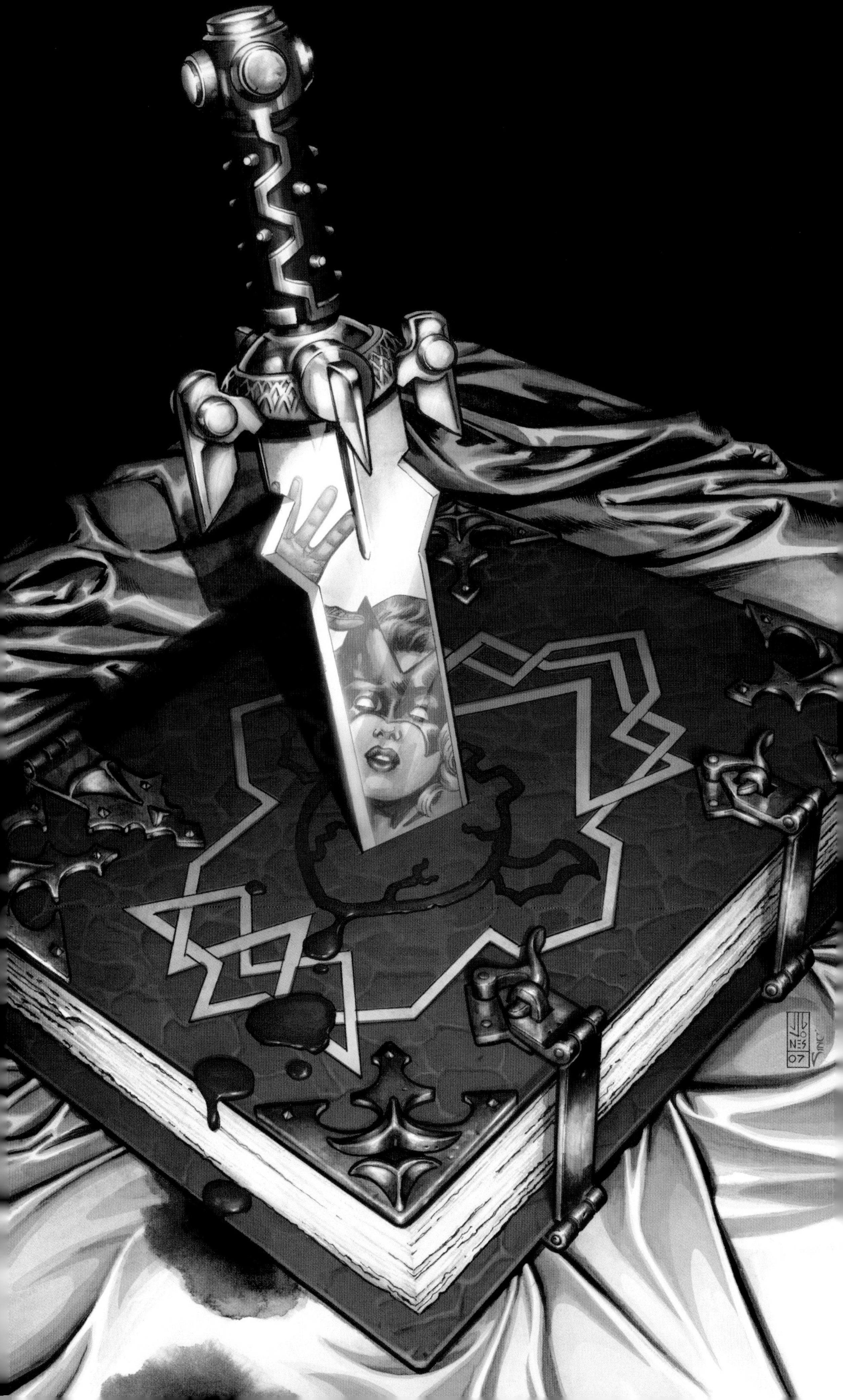

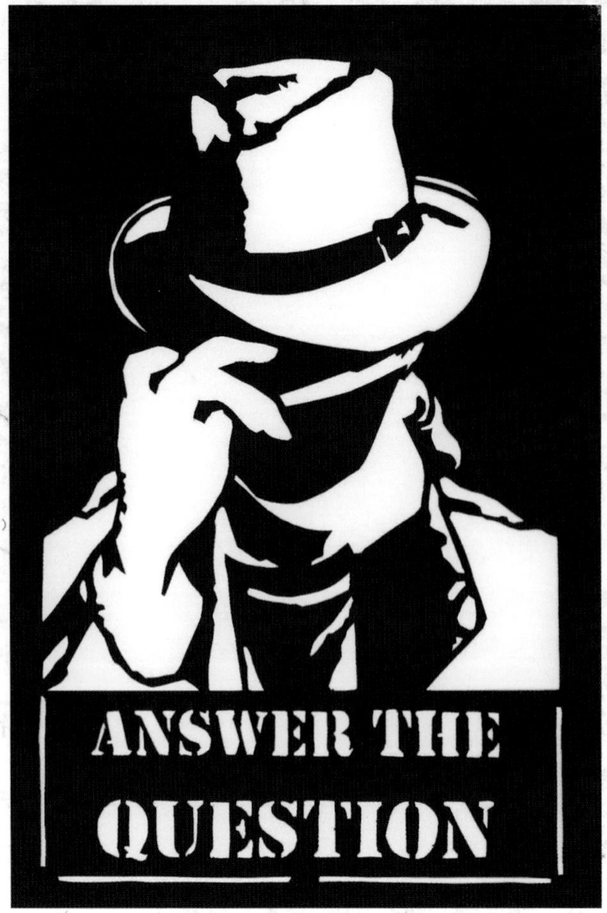
ANSWER THE
QUESTION

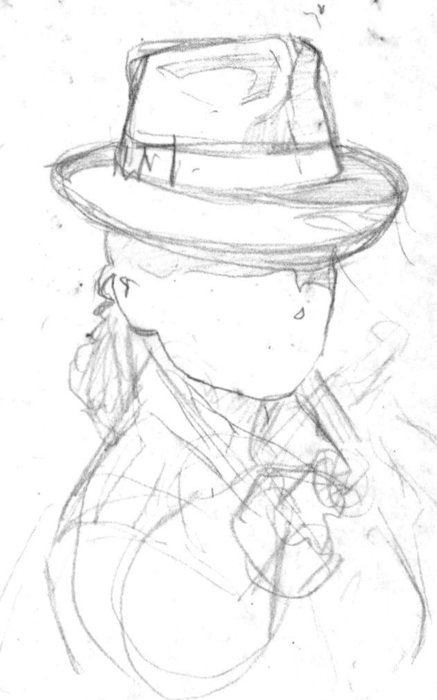

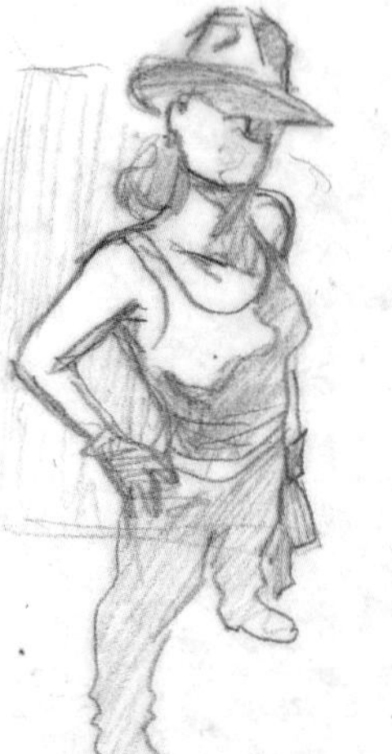

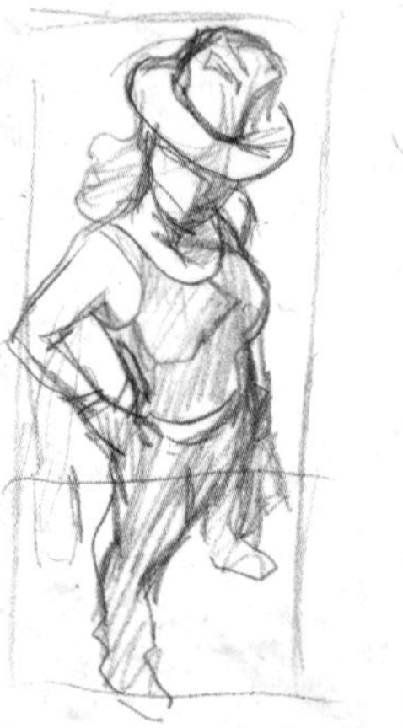

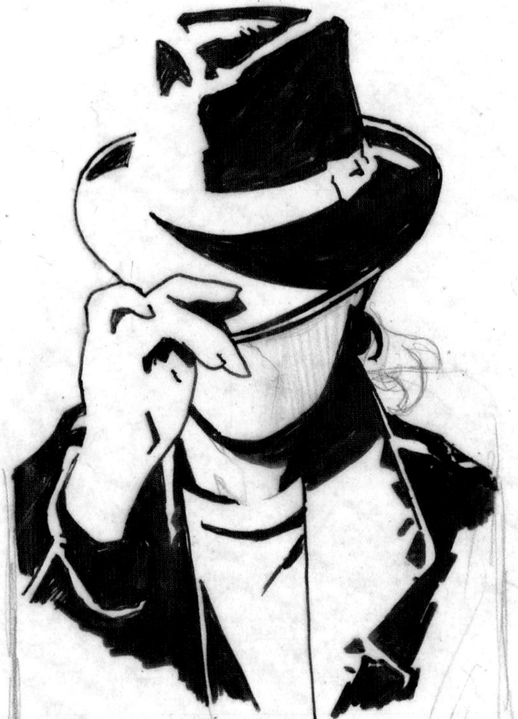

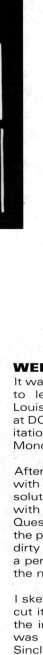

**WEEK FORTY-EIGHT**

It was a late Friday afternoon, and I was packing to leave for Christmas with my family in Louisiana. I got a panicked email from my editor at DC saying that we needed this cover for solicitation in three days. My flight was for early Monday morning, and I had nothing. Yikes!

After panicking, I settled down and came up with what I think was one of my more creative solutions for a 52 cover. Since this issue dealt with Montoya taking over the role of The Question, I thought that I would look at her from the perspective of the criminal subculture on the dirty streets of Gotham. Stencil graffiti seemed a perfect way to illustrate a street-level view of the new vigilante in town.

I sketched up a stencil on a piece of cardboard, cut it out with my mat knife, and spray-painted the image directly onto the art. The faux wall was painted on with watercolor, and I had Alex Sinclair add the inverted L-shaped shadow to ground the whole image.

For the final touch, Alex and I "tagged" signatures onto the finished artwork.

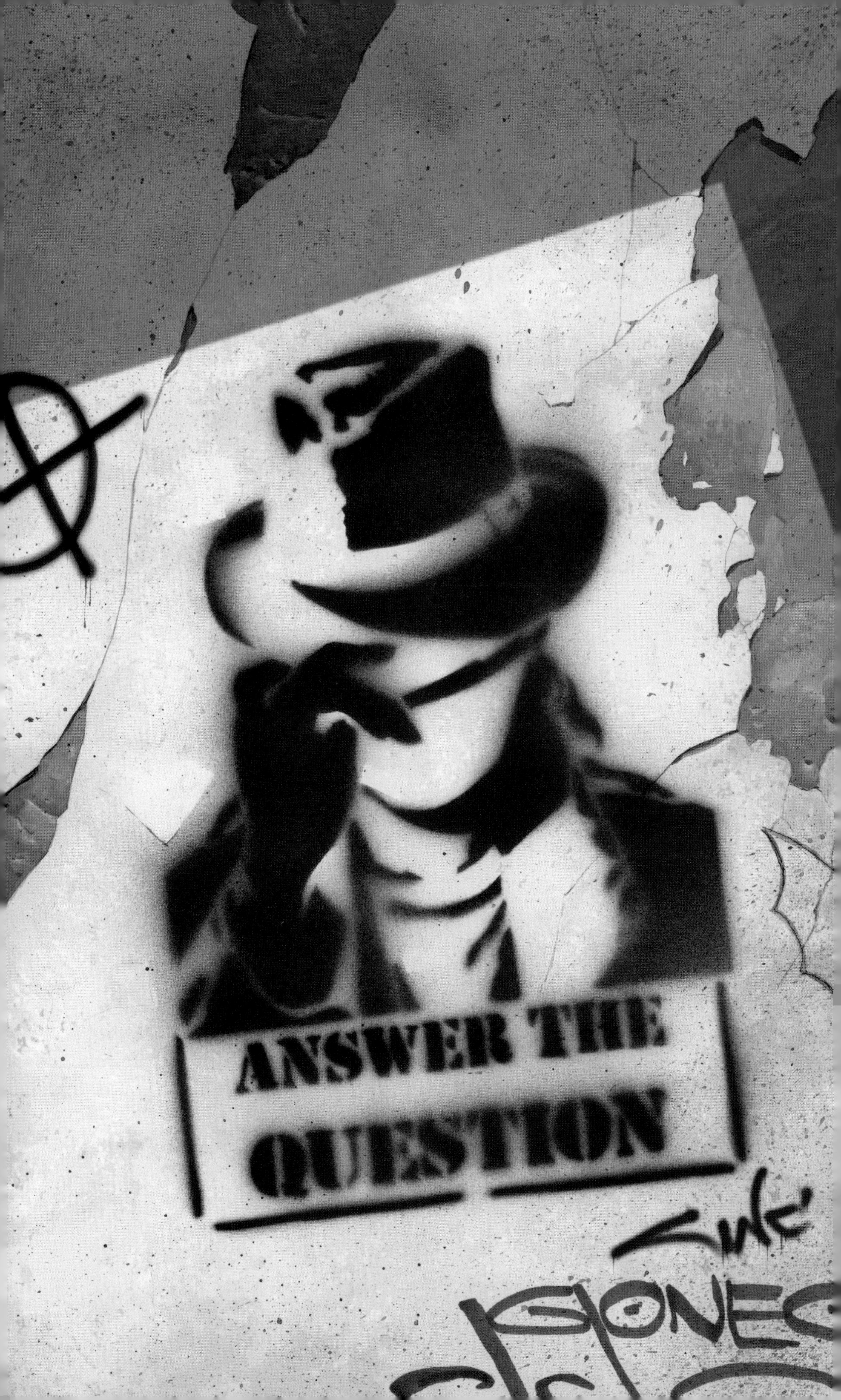
ANSWER THE
QUESTION

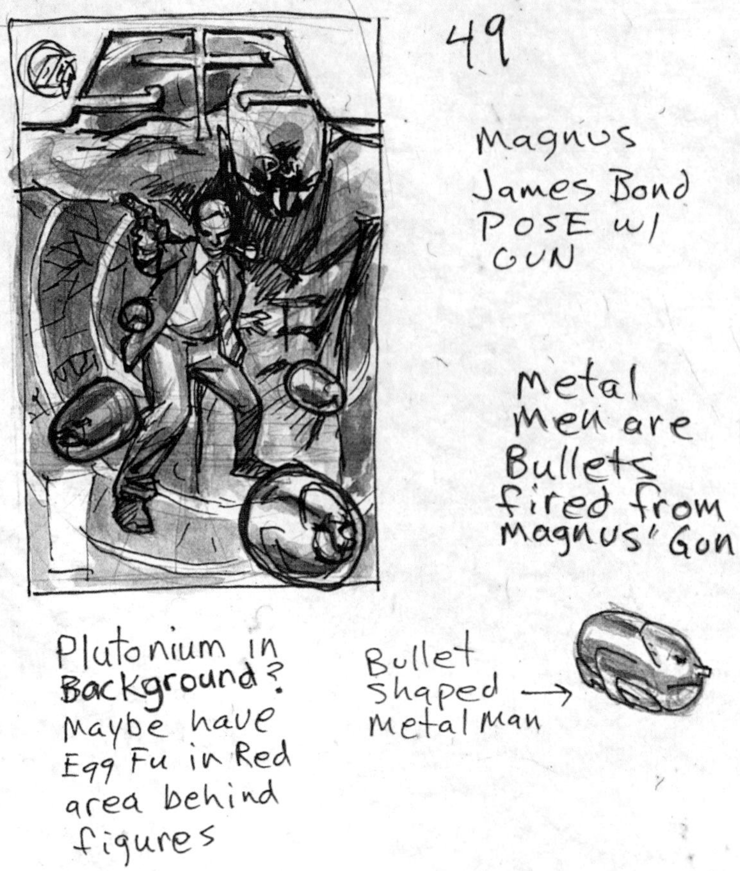

49

Magnus
James Bond
POSE w/
GUN

Metal
Men are
Bullets
fired from
magnus' Gun

Plutonium in
Background?
maybe have
Egg Fu in Red
area behind
figures

Bullet
shaped →
metal man

## WEEK FORTY-NINE

Barreling toward the finish line, I wanted to take advantage of this one last chance to draw the Metal Men. I love the idea of the Metal Men in the form of little bullets being fired from Doc Magnus's gun. I gave Magnus a James Bond-style pose and translated the rifling from the gun barrel into a disorienting spiral behind him. In the background, I drew the shattered form of Chang Tzu.

The final cover has a sort of trippy, zany, '60s flavor to it, and it was a lot of fun to draw. Alex initially colored this in a sort of dull tan with blue spiral, but I wanted something hotter and more energetic. He re-colored the piece using yellows, oranges, and reds, which did the trick. The final result was a much more exciting image.

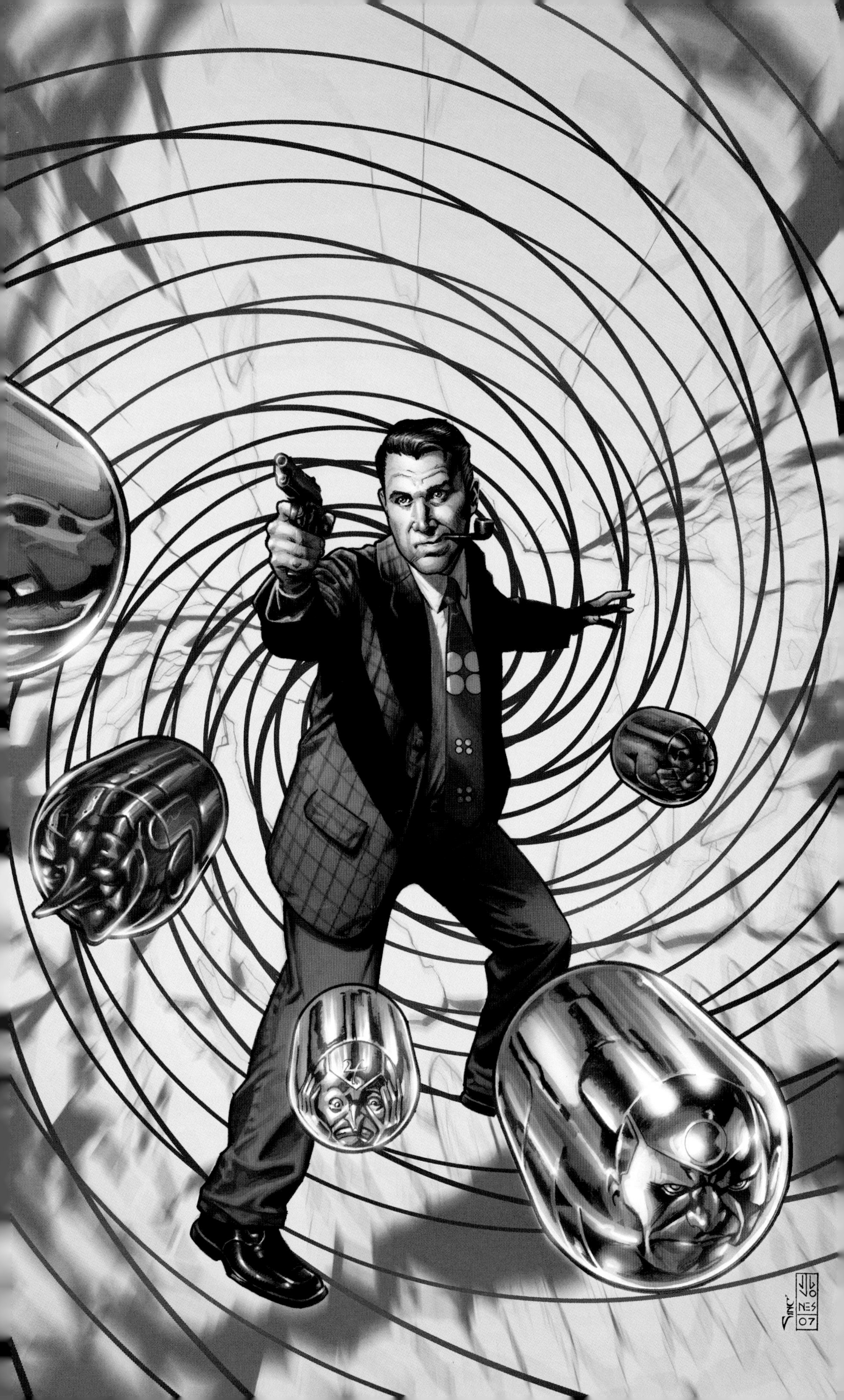

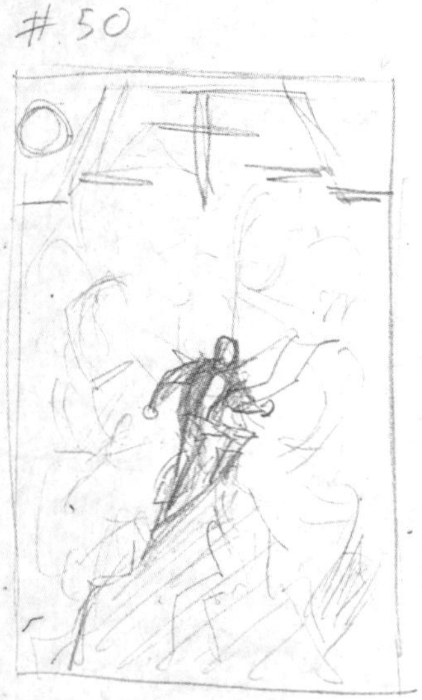
#50

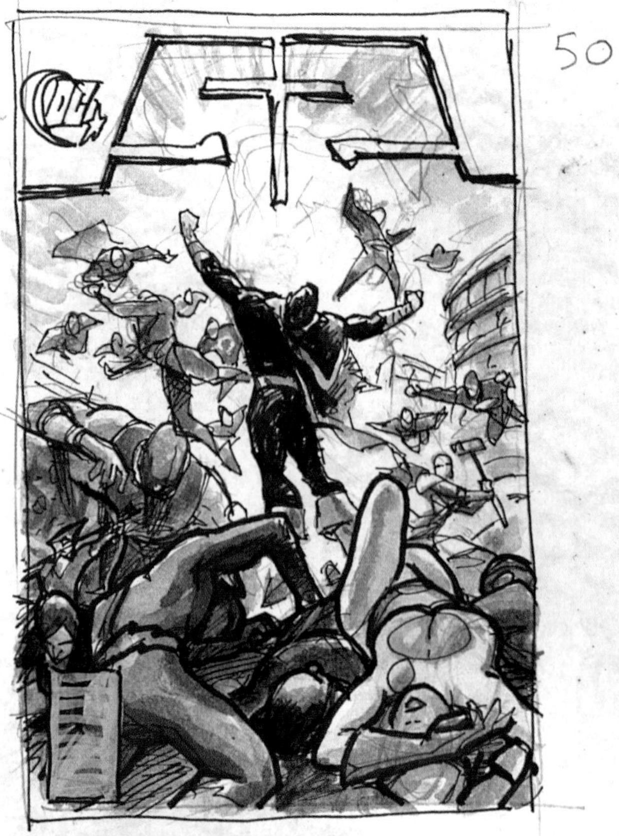
50

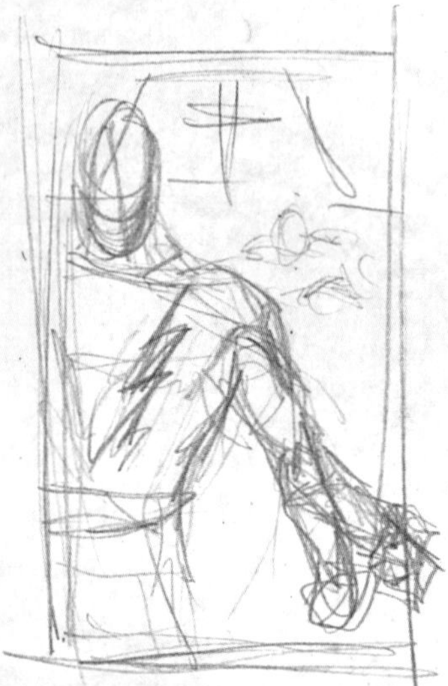

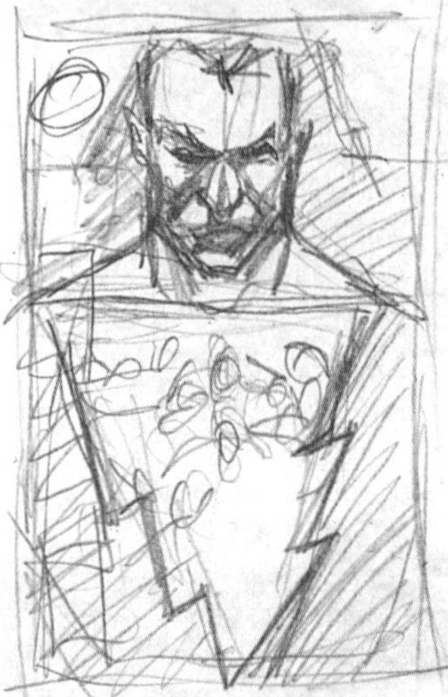

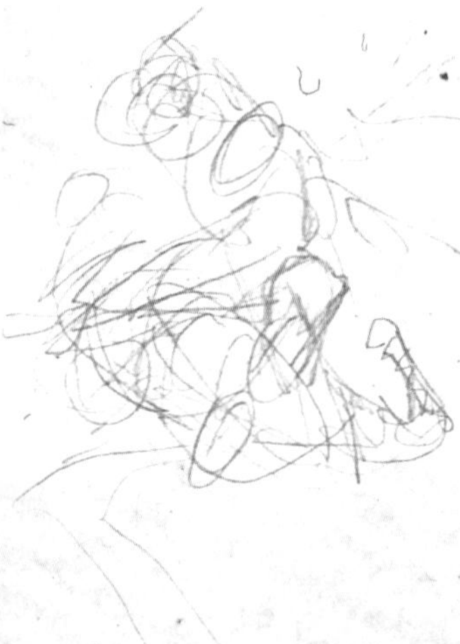

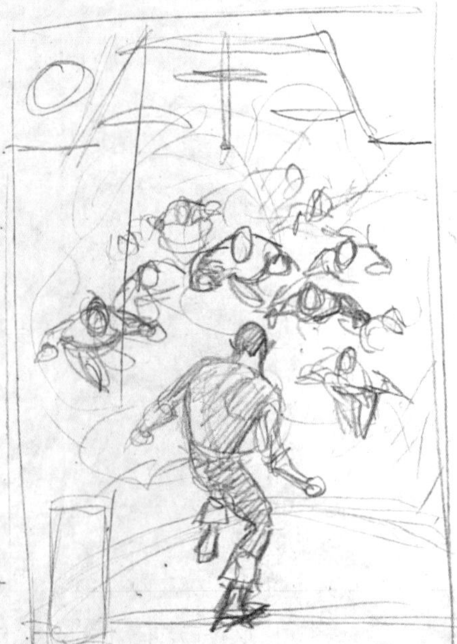

## WEEK FIFTY

This cover is a reworking of a sketch that I did for issue #46. I kept the unifying element of the lightning bolt, but changed Black Adam's pose and altered the background figures to fit the story in issue #50.

There's nothing fancy here: no references to old movie posters or Renaissance paintings. Just pure comic book fun.

The coloring is beautiful, if understated. A shadowy blue foreground set against a warm amber backdrop separates Adam from the collection of heroes lining up to take a shot at him. Another nice job by Alex.

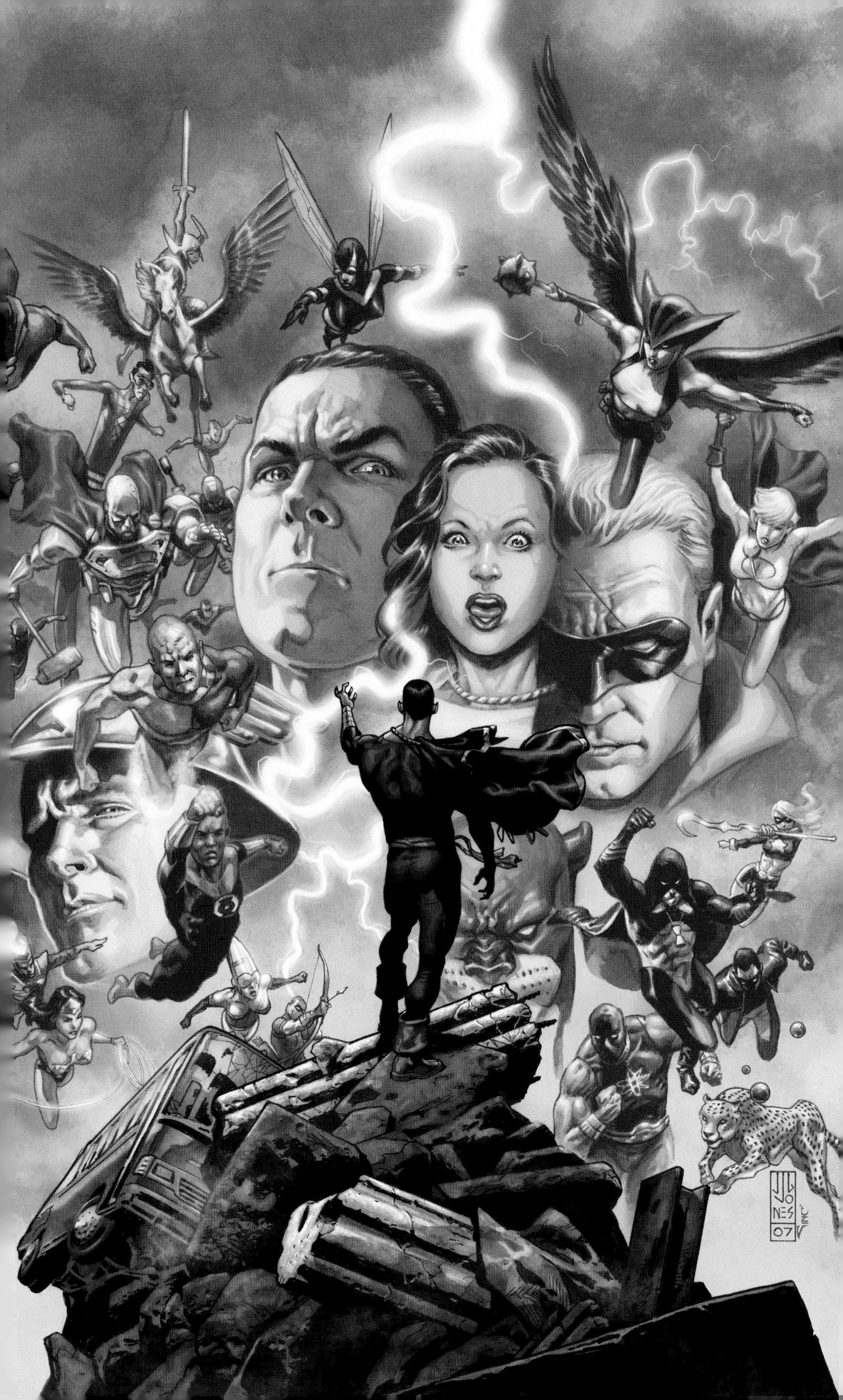

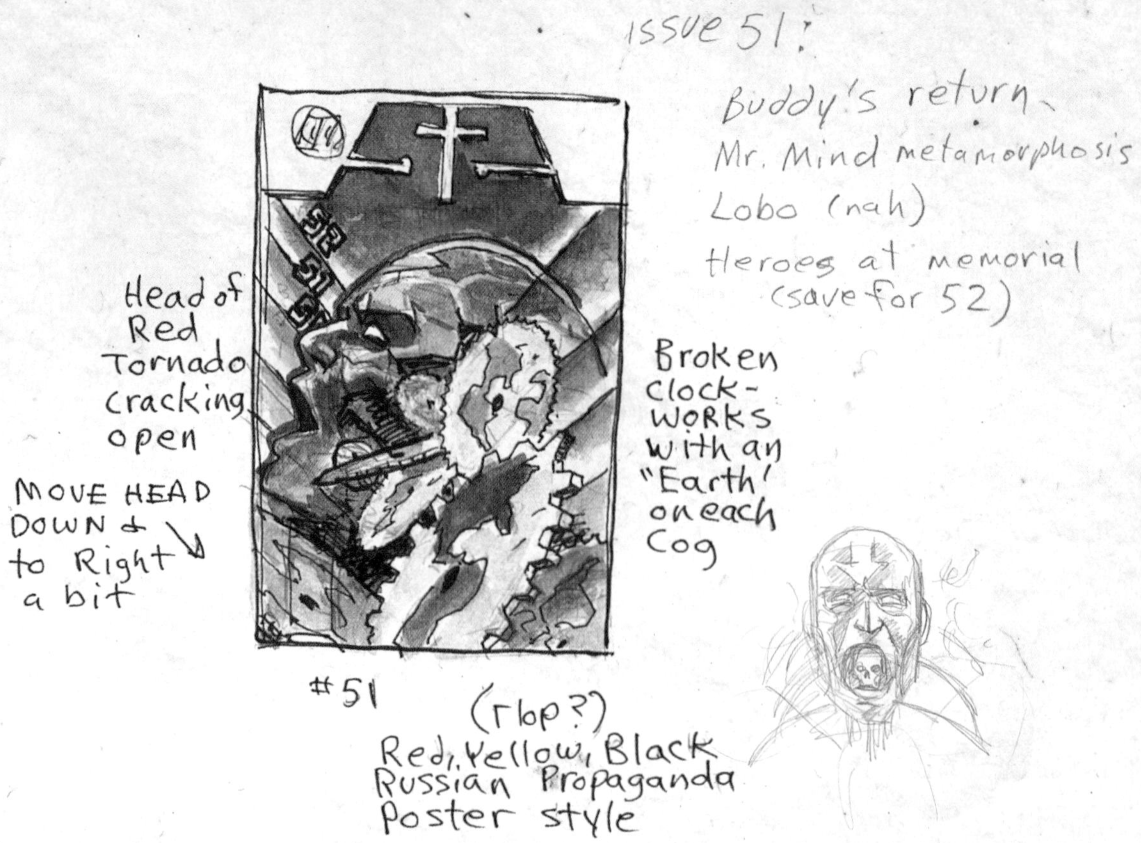
ISSUE 51:
Buddy's return
Mr. Mind metamorphosis
Lobo (nah)
Heroes at memorial
(save for 52)
Head of
Red
Tornado
cracking
open
MOVE HEAD
DOWN &
to Right
a bit
Broken
clock-
WORKS
with an
"Earth"
on each
Cog
#51
(rbp?)
Red, Yellow, Black
Russian Propaganda
Poster style

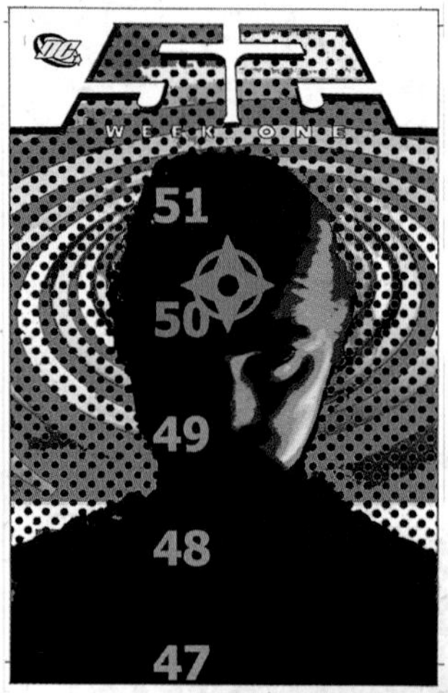
52
WEEK ONE
51
50
49
48
47
Take the old, unused cover sketch for #37

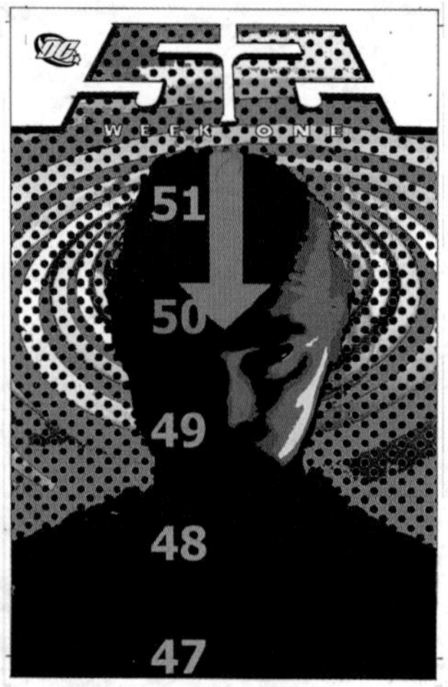
52
WEEK ONE
51
50
49
48
47
Remake the Supernova face into a Red Tornado

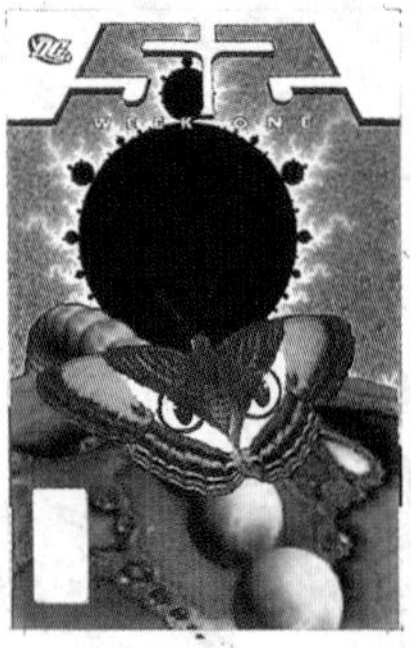

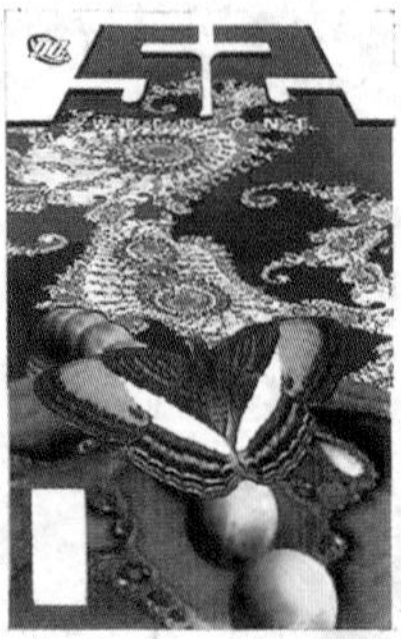

## WEEK FIFTY-ONE

I played with an infinite number of variations before finding a useful approach to this cover. I wanted to do something using chaos theory, fractals, or Mandelbrot sets, but in a way that did not tip the story for the reader.

After a bit of head scratching, it occurred to me that Red Tornado had the final piece of the 52 puzzle stored inside his synthetic robot brain. I translated the mechanical theme into a spray of broken clockwork cogs, each with a representation of an alternate Earth on its surface.

Once I had a direction, I combined the themes with the design sensibilities of Russian propaganda posters, as if Tornado is shouting his 52 Manifesto to the Multiverse.

Adding the countdown numbers was the final element, and the whole thing came together with the help of Alex's expert color.

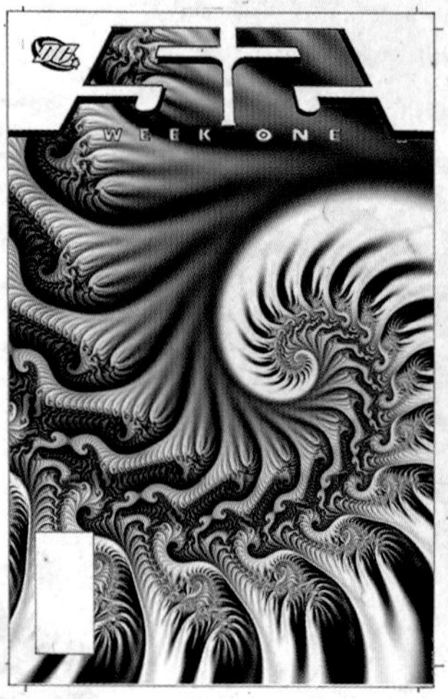
52
WEEK ONE
Maybe use this cool fractal image which symbolizes the 52 Multiverse.

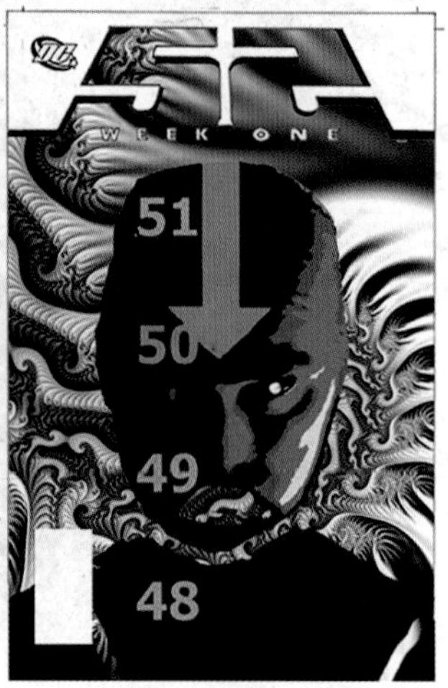
52
WEEK ONE
51
50
49
48
Add the head of Red Tornado

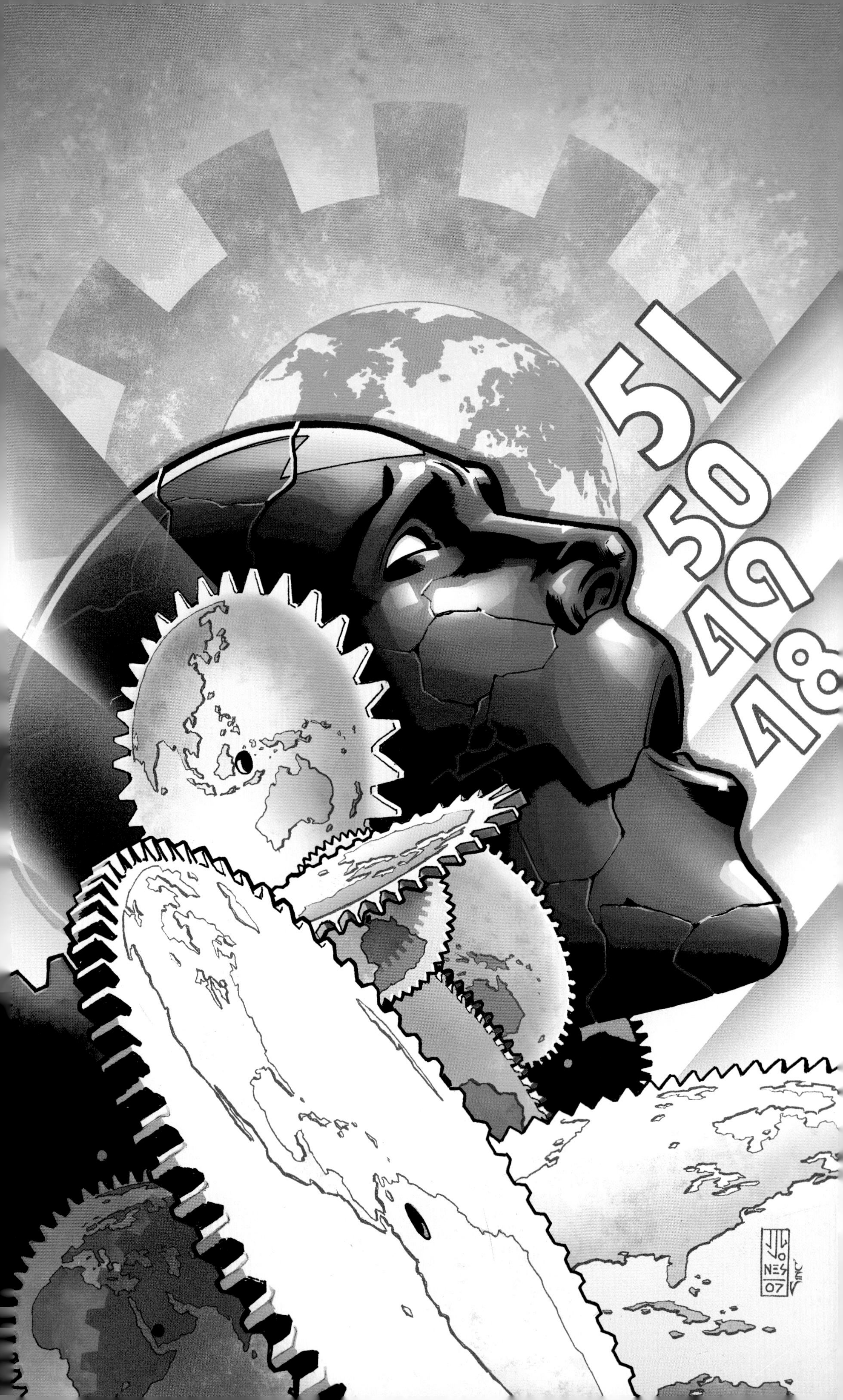
51
50
49
48

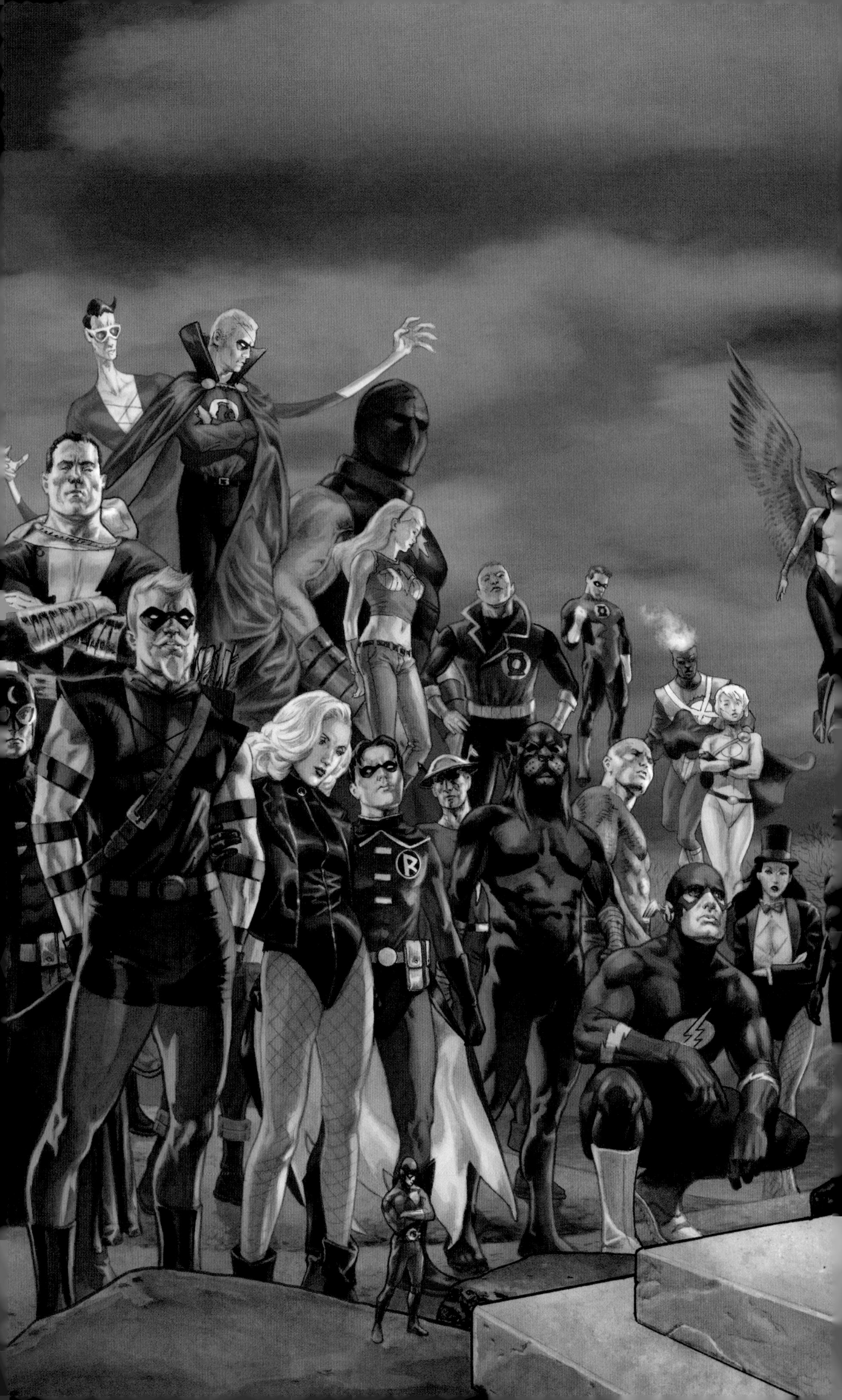

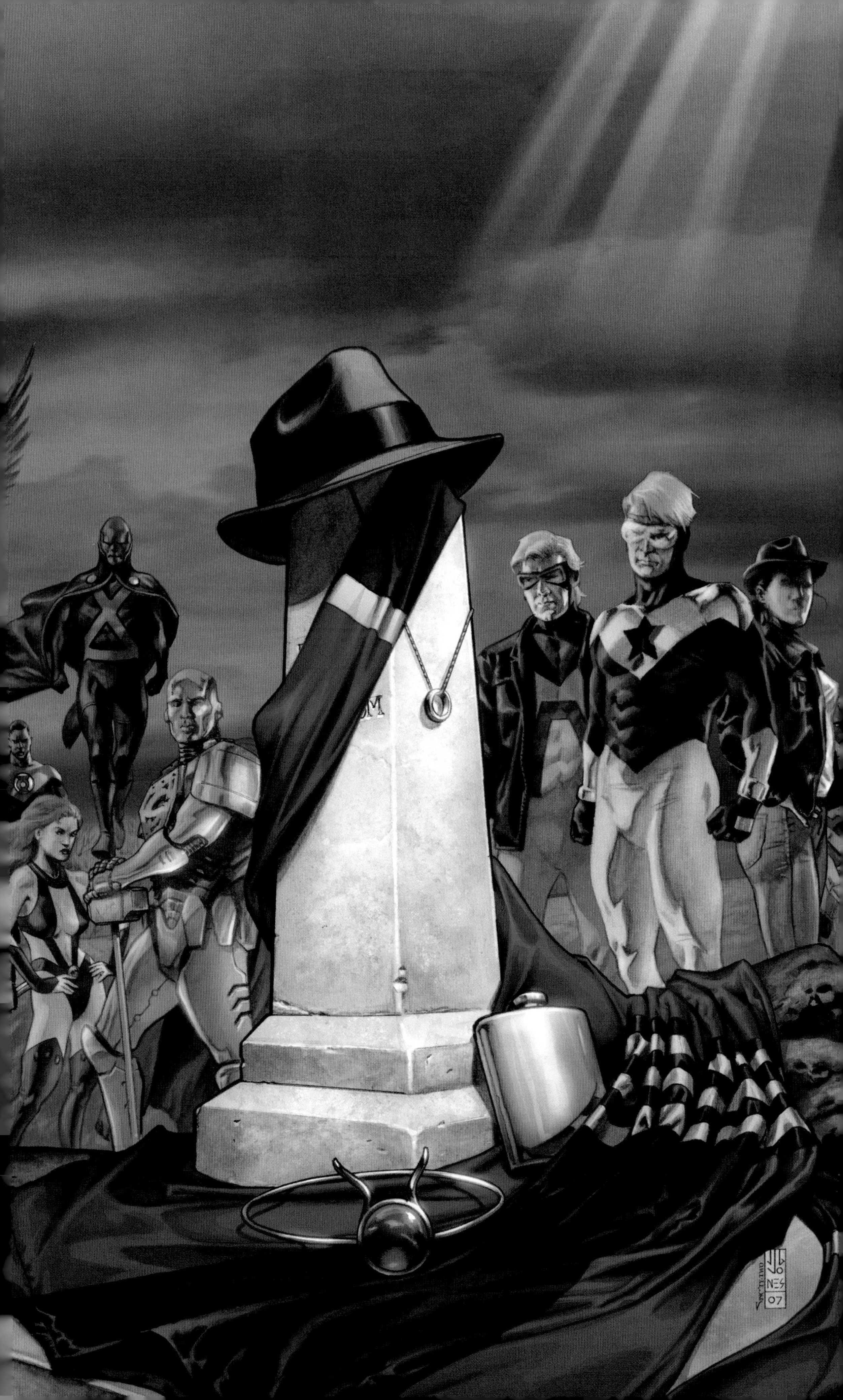

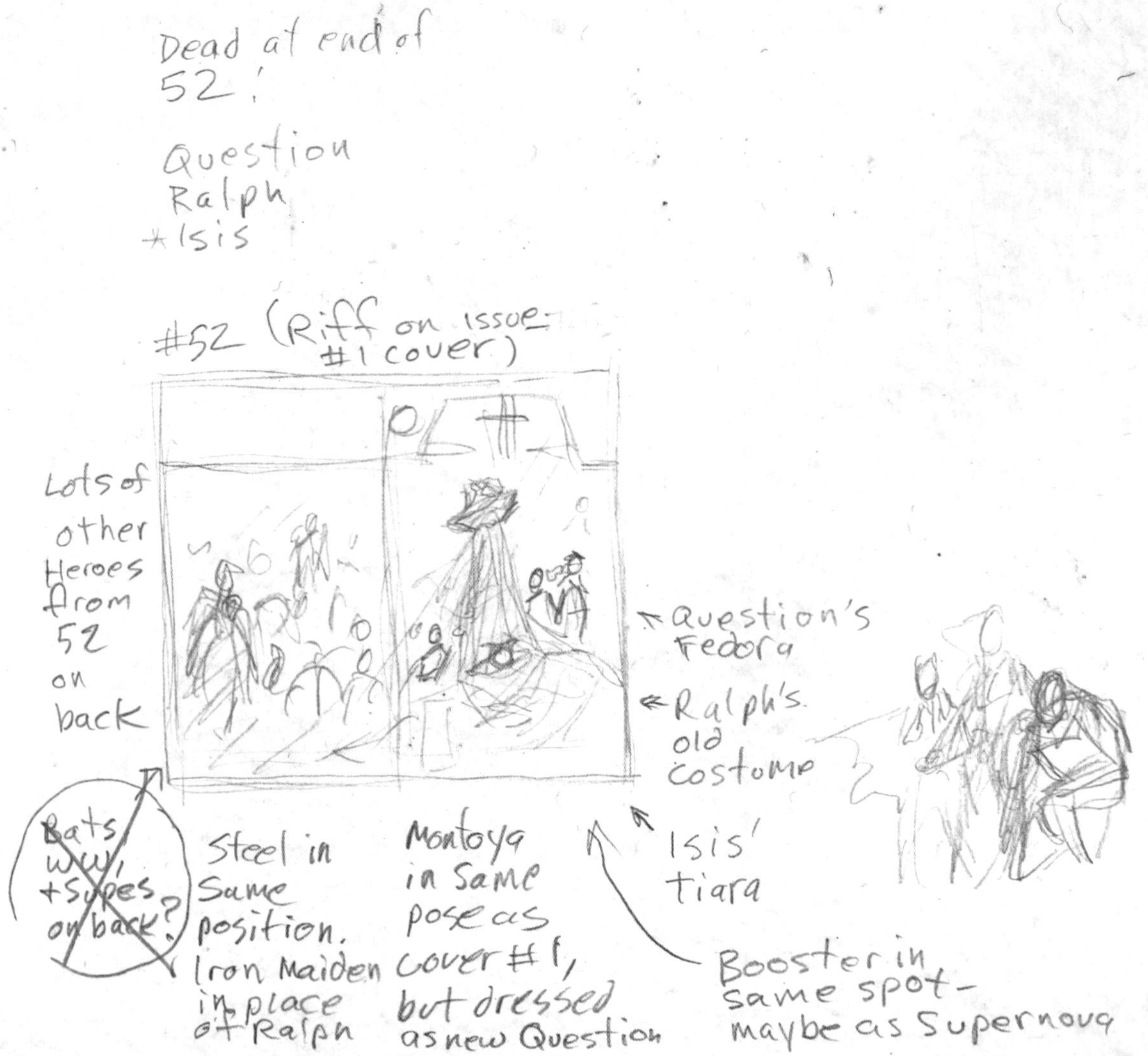
Dead at end of
52!
Question
Ralph
+Isis
#52 (Riff on issue #1 cover)
Lots of other Heroes from 52 on back
Question's Fedora
Ralph's old costome
Isis' tiara
Bats WW, +Supes on back?
Steel in Same position. Iron Maiden in place of Ralph
Montoya in Same pose as cover #1, but dressed as new Question
Booster in same spot - maybe as Supernova

**WEEK FIFTY-TWO** **(see previous spread)**

I wanted to do a parenthetical cover to close out the series, so I had the idea of reworking the elements of the first 52 cover for the final cover image. I replaced the elements of the missing heroes on the first cover (Superman, Batman, and Wonder Woman) with reminders of the heroes that we lost over the course of the year in 52.

Here we see the red Elongated Man costume, The Question's fedora, and the tiara of Isis. I threw in Ralph's gingold flask and his wife's wedding ring for good measure. I used similar poses for the heroes in the background, but here we have a lot more of the DC Universe. In fact, there are too many heroes for the front cover, so we decided to wrap the image around onto the back cover as well.

I wanted the same moody, somber feel as the first cover, and Alex did a fantastic job with the coloring chores, limiting the brightest areas to the foreground elements, and allowing the other figures to fade into the twilight.

I enjoyed each and every issue, and I'll miss the weekly challenge. Now that all is said and done, this has been the best job I have ever had.

# MORE UNUSED COVER CONCEPTS

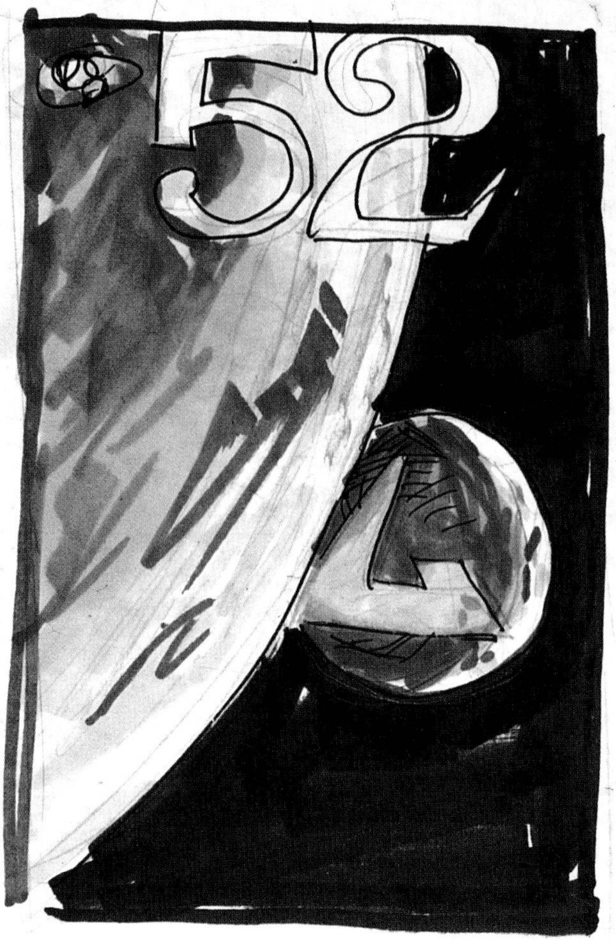
52
Earth
+
MOON
WITH
LEXCORP
LOGO
ON IT'S
SURFACE

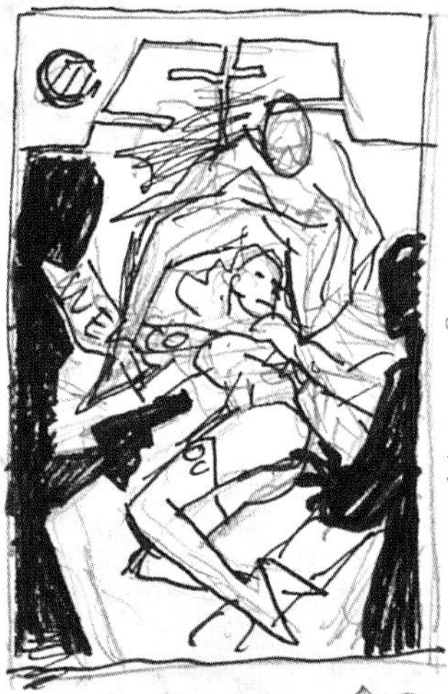
Buddy
Starfire
Wrapped
in
Welcome
Home
Banner
Bounty
Hunters in
silhouette

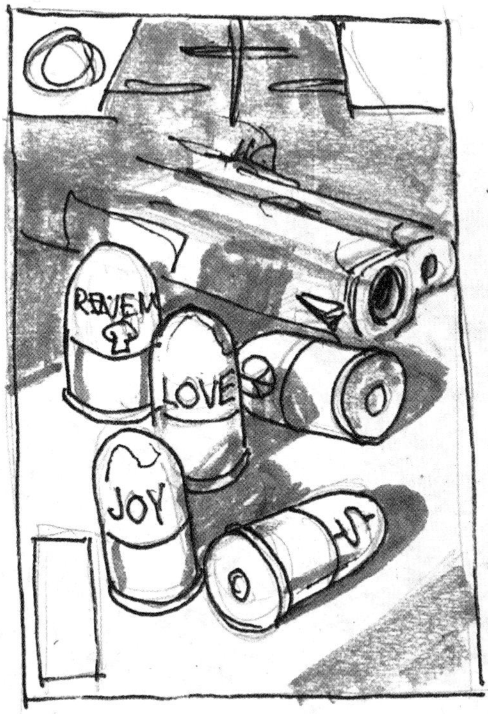
WISH
GUN
REVEN
LOVE
JOY

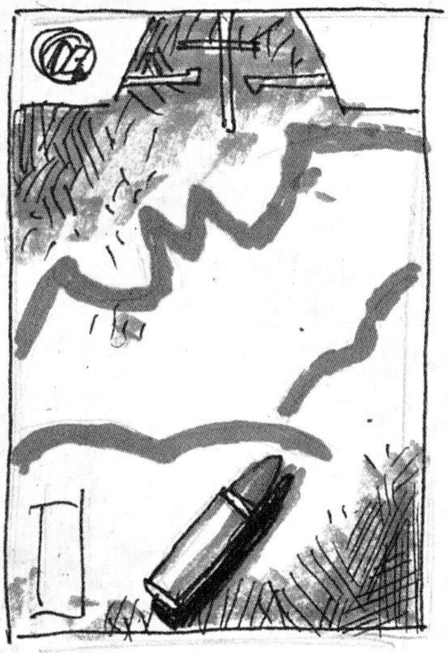
29
Batman/
Batwoman/
Nightwing
Lipstick
Drawing
of Bat
symbol

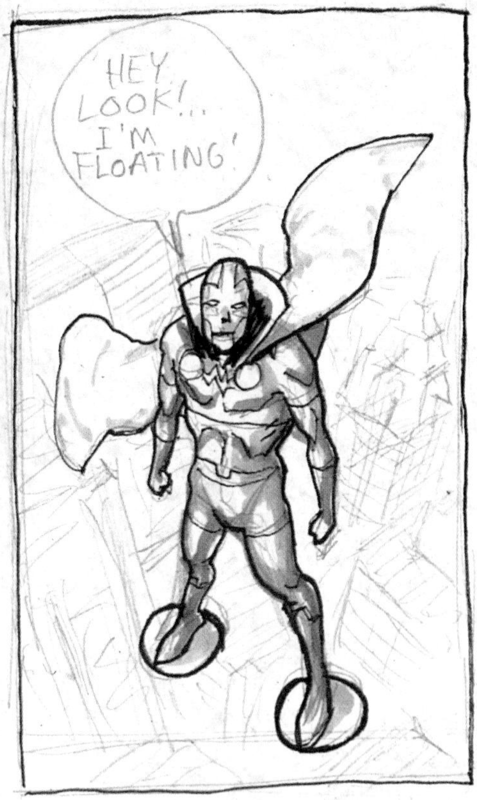
HEY LOOK!.. I'M FLOATING!

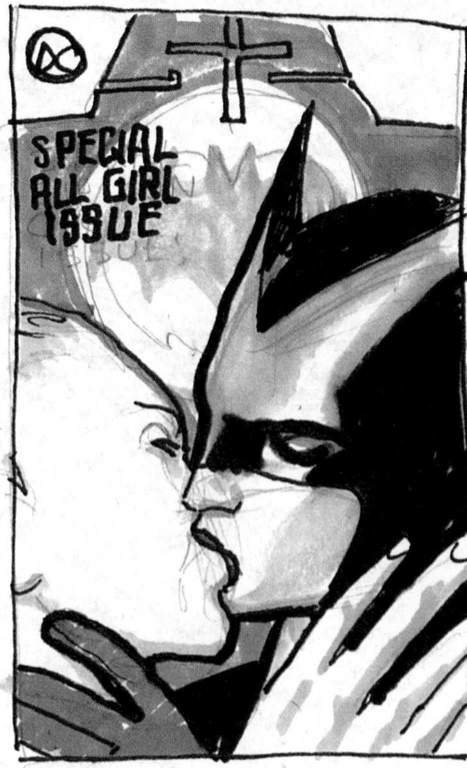
SPECIAL ALL GIRL ISSUE

THE COVER THAT COULD NOT BE SPOKEN!

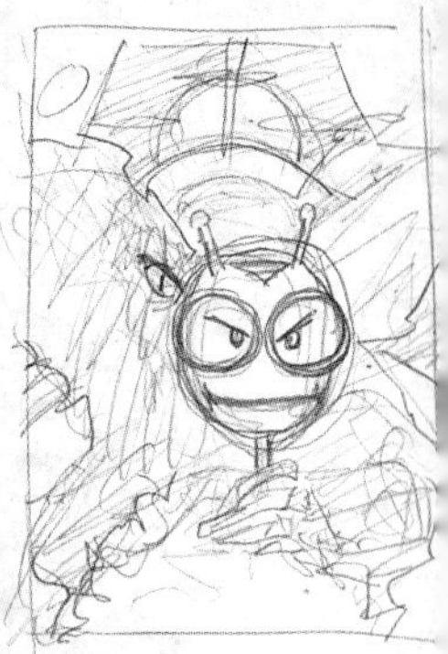

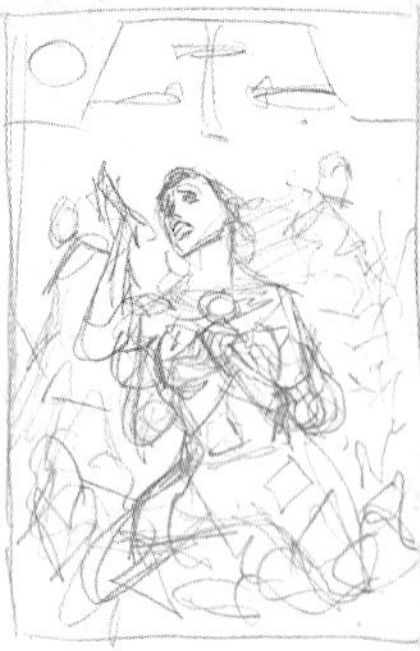

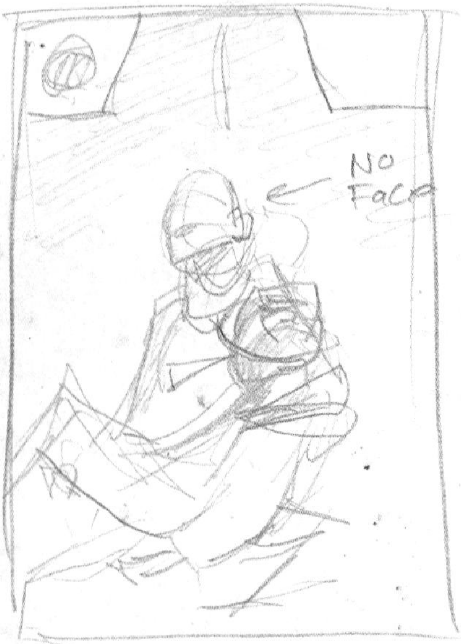
No Face

vic Dies- Renee becomes the Question

Holding Vic

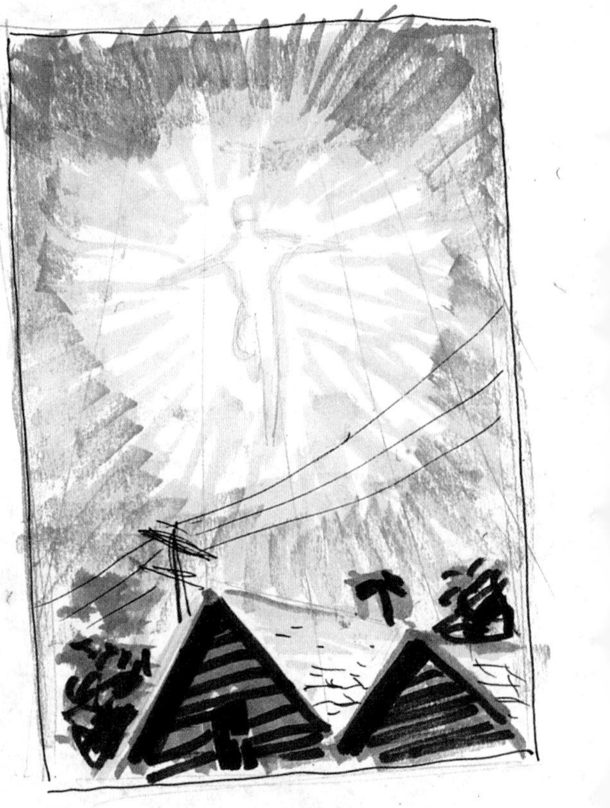

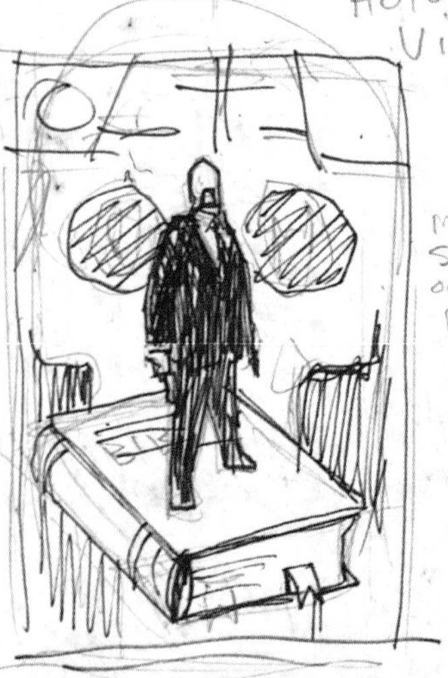

Manheim Standing on Crime Bible

Animal Man has absorbed the power of a sun-eater and descends from the night sky as a glowing sun

Roof of Animal Man's House

UP SHOT

# TRADE PAPERBACK COLLECTIONS

52 was such a big, sprawling story that it made designing the collected edition covers difficult. No single image would adequately capture the epic quality of each volume.

After a lot of discussion, we decided that the best approach would be four similarly designed montage covers. I used one of the major players as an anchor on each cover, with large headshots of some of the other principles behind. Then each was filled in with small, ancillary figures and maybe an indication of a location in the background to add atmosphere.

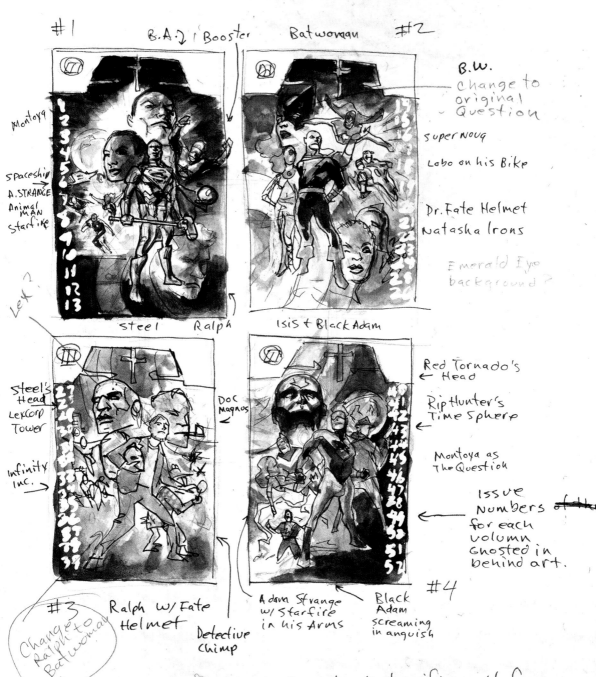

#1

B.A.? / Booster     Batwoman     #2

Montoya

Spaceship
A. STRANGE
Animal MAN
Starfire

Lex?

Steel     Ralph

B.W.
change to
original
Question

super NOVA

Lobo on his Bike

Dr. Fate Helmet
Natasha Irons

Emerald Eye
background?

Isis + Black Adam

Steel's
Head
LexCorp
Tower

Infinity
Inc.

DOC
Magnos

#3
Change to
Ralph to
Batwoman

Ralph w/ Fate
Helmet          Detective
                Chimp

Adam Strange
w/ Starfire
in his Arms

Black
Adam
screaming
in anguish

#4

Red Tornado's
Head

Rip Hunter's
Time Sphere

Montoya as
The Question

Issue
numbers
for each
volumn
Ghosted in
behind art.

*There should be a graphic element that unifies all four covers. Maybe it's an earth or 52 earths (not really). Maybe the evolved form of Mr. Mind in background or an earth with a clock face to symbolize time is broken. Help me out here.

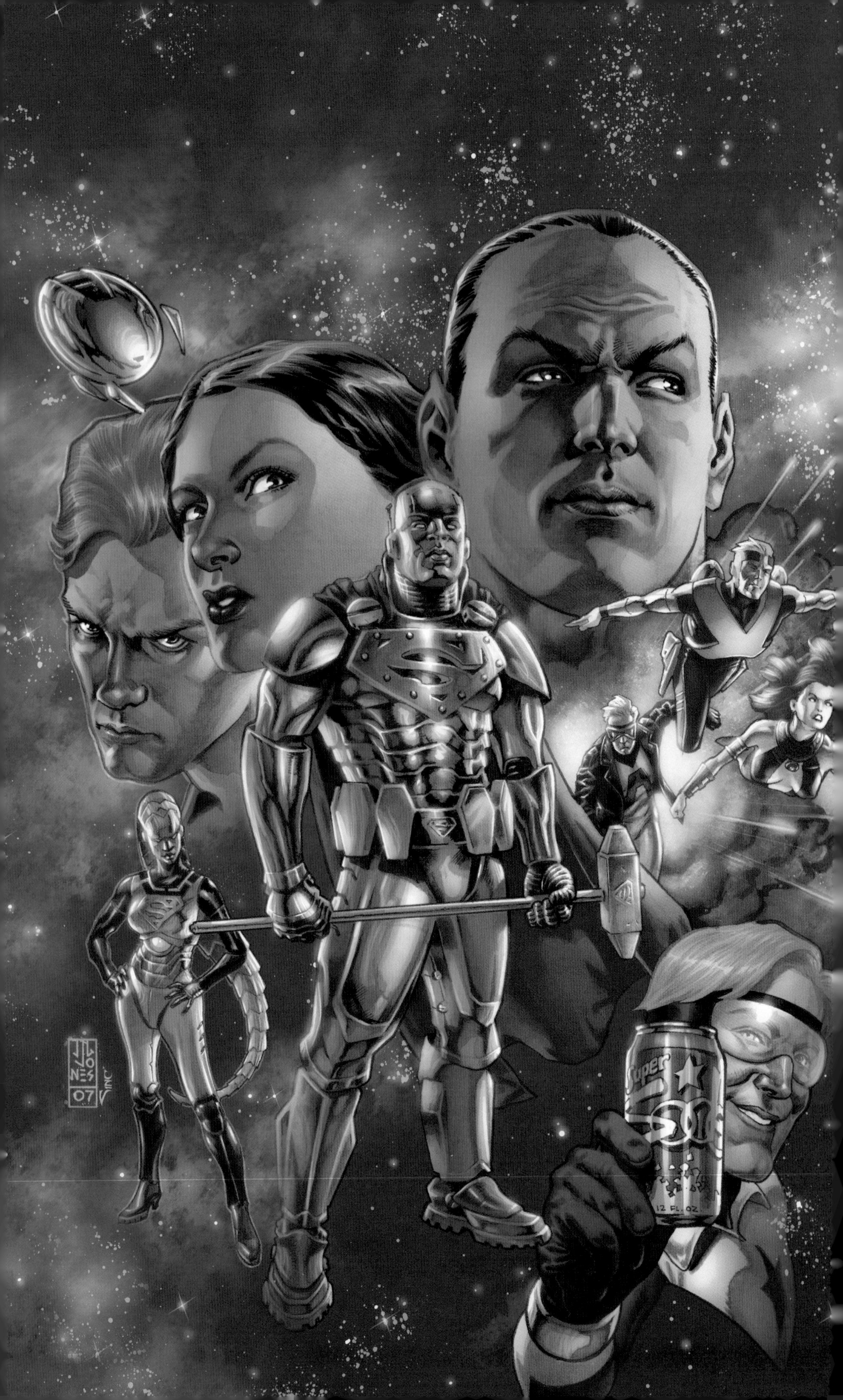
Super
12 FL. OZ

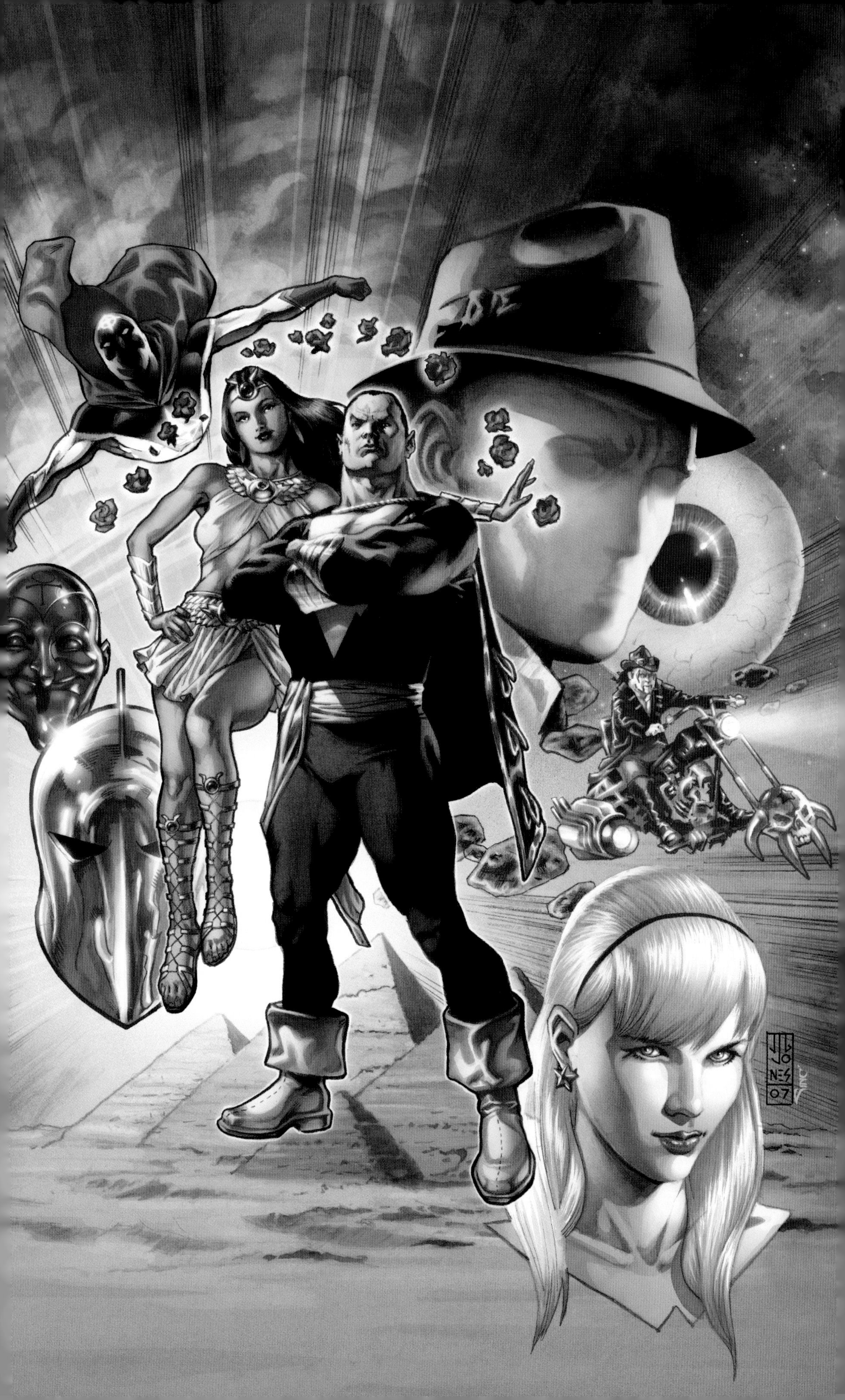

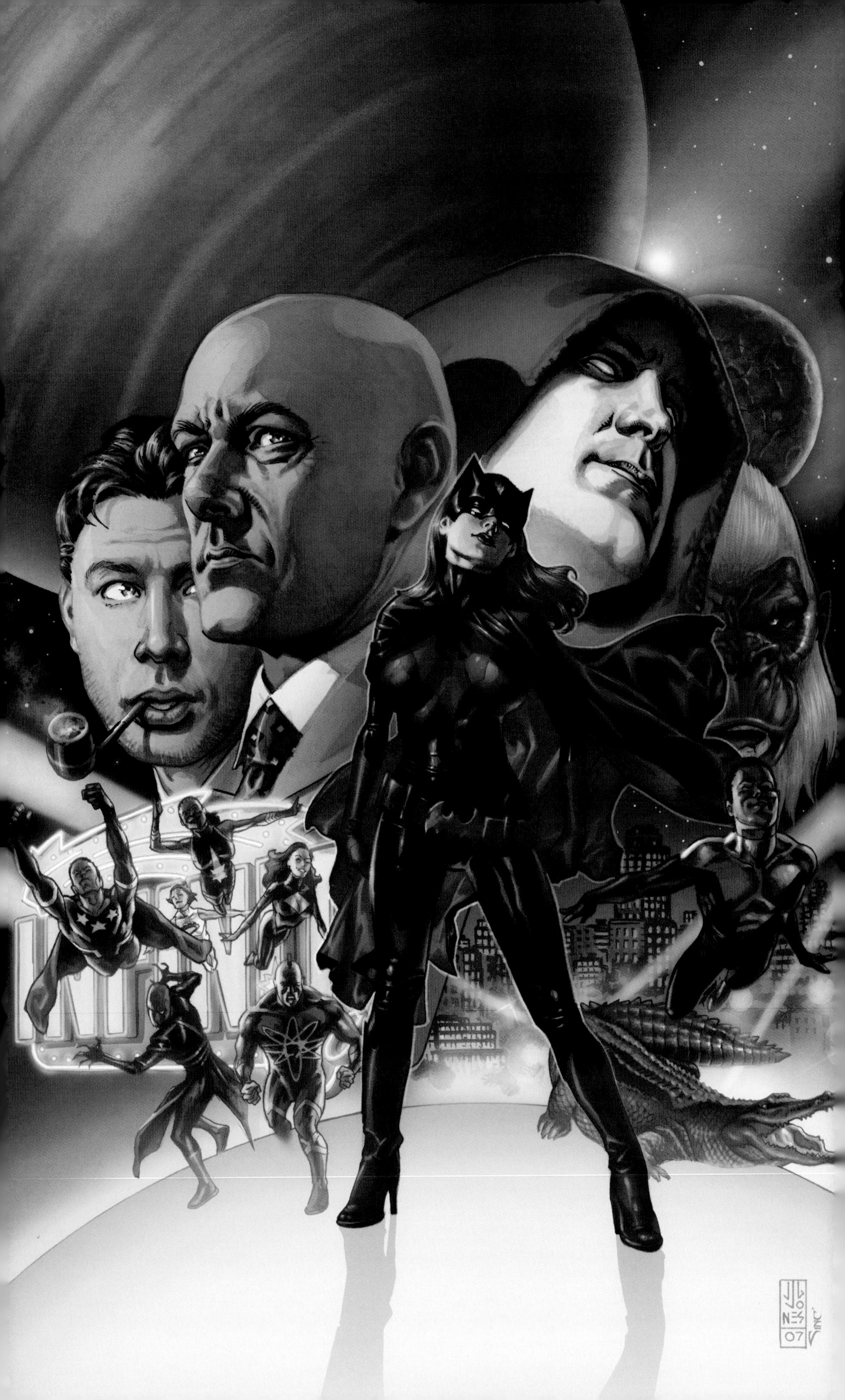

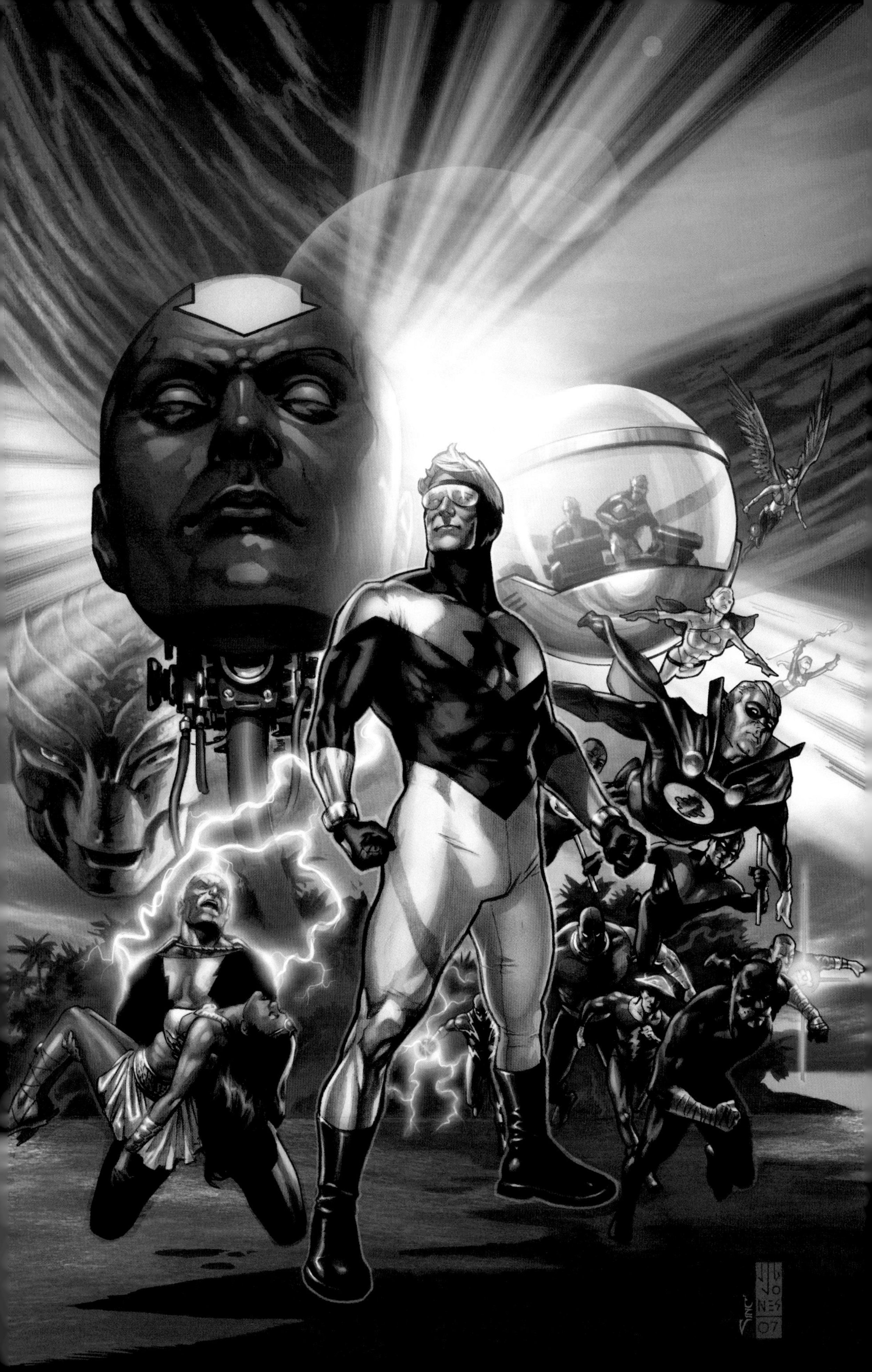

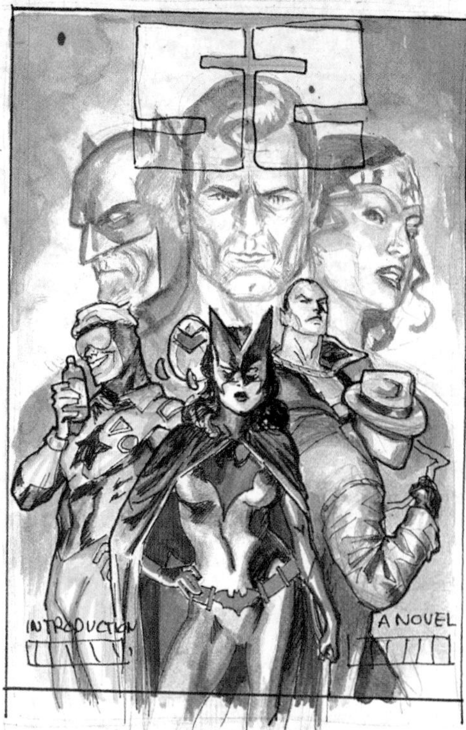
52
INTRODUCTION
A NOVEL
GHOSTED "MT. RUSHMORE" HEADS OF BATMAN, SUPERMAN, WONDER WOMAN IN BACKGROUND
BLACK ADAM
THE QUESTION
BOOSTER GOLD WITH SPORTS DRINK + Corp. LOGOS ON COSTUME - SKEETS BEHIND HIM
BATWOMAN

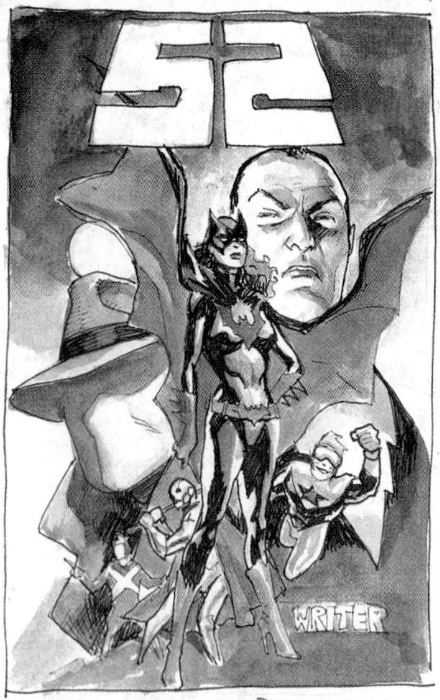
52
WRITER
BLACK ADAM
THE QUESTION
BOOSTER GOLD
ADAM STRANGE
STEEL
BATWOMAN

## 52: THE NOVEL

I did a number of sketches for the cover of the 52 novel. The editors had different concerns than those for a weekly comic. They were interested in a simple image using a few characters that would spark the reader's interest. They insisted on using Batwoman. Oh, and I had to include Batman, Superman, and Wonder Woman on the cover as well — even though they don't appear in the story.

In the end, they chose to use an image with the big three ghosted in the background above the figures of Booster, Batwoman, and The Question. I took much longer to design something they were happy with than it actually took to render the final image.

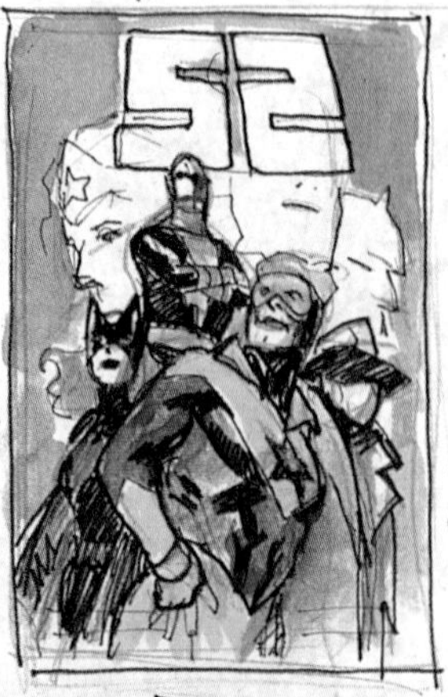
BLACK ADAM
52
WW, SUPES, BATS GHOSTED IN BACKGROUND
BAT WOMAN
THE QUESTION
BOOSTER GOLD

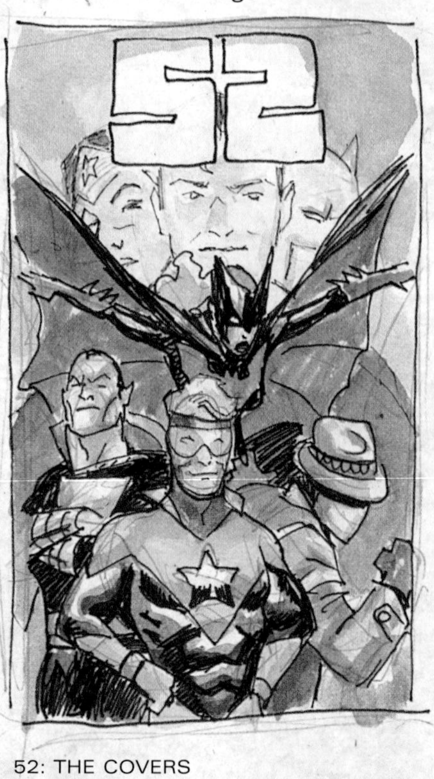
52

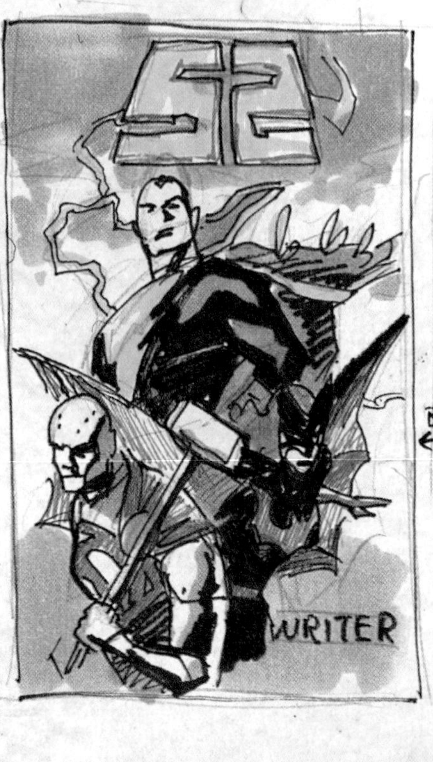
52
WRITER
Black Adam
STEEL
Batwoman

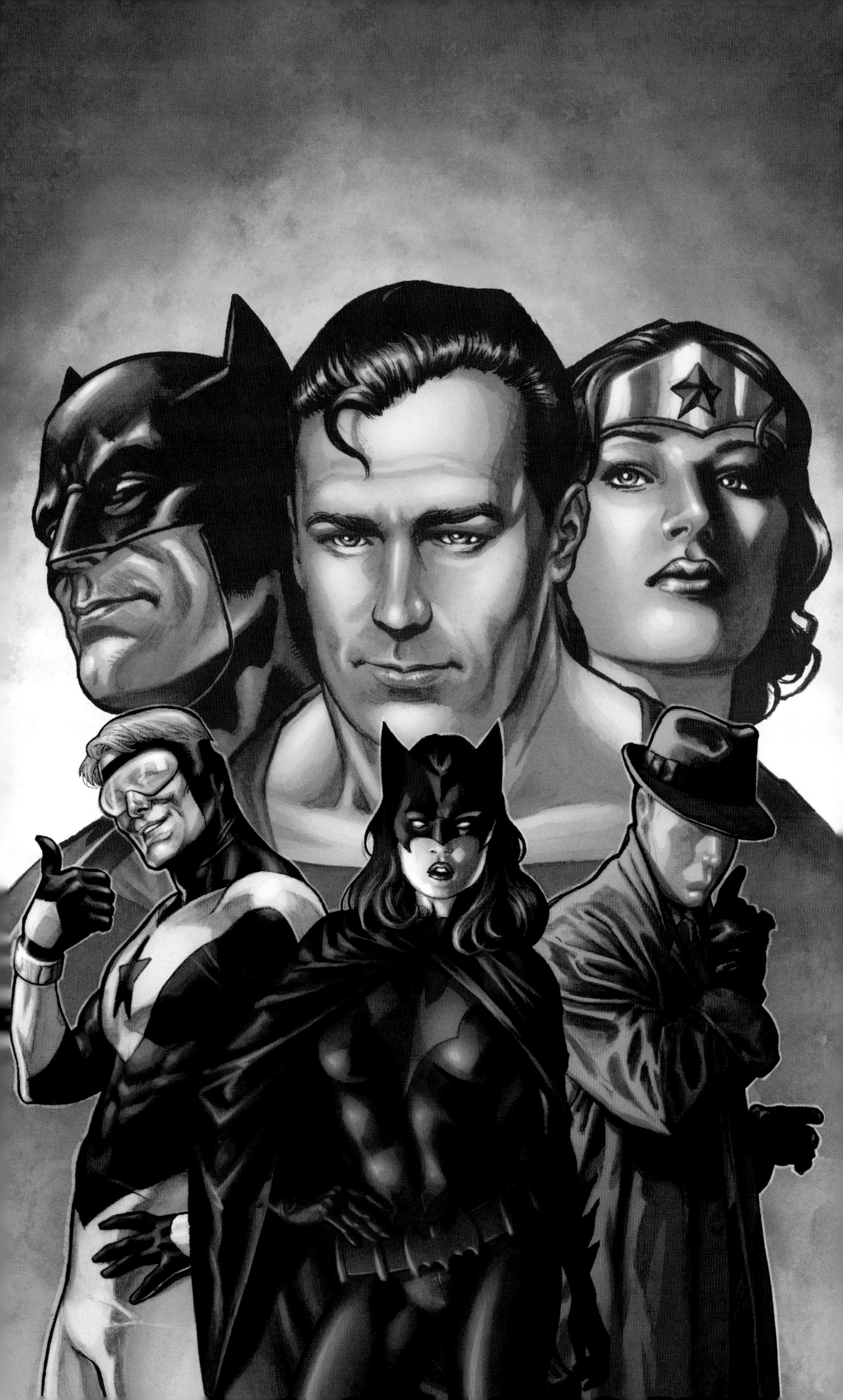

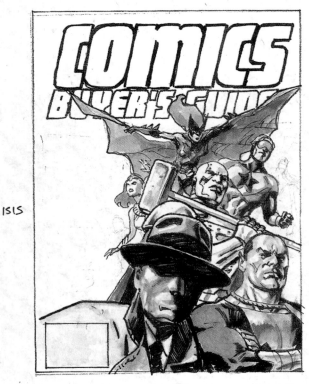

ISIS

BATWOMAN

BOOSTER
GOLD

STEEL

THE QUESTION

BLACK
ADAM

## COMICS BUYER'S GUIDE

It was a bit of a challenge to include so many characters from 52 onto one cover, leaving lots of room for the trade dress and type. I thought it would be fun to do a little full color painting for this, so I broke out the watercolors and stacked the figures up like heads on a totem pole. I left the background open because I felt that the image was cluttered enough with heroes, and it did not really need anything else.

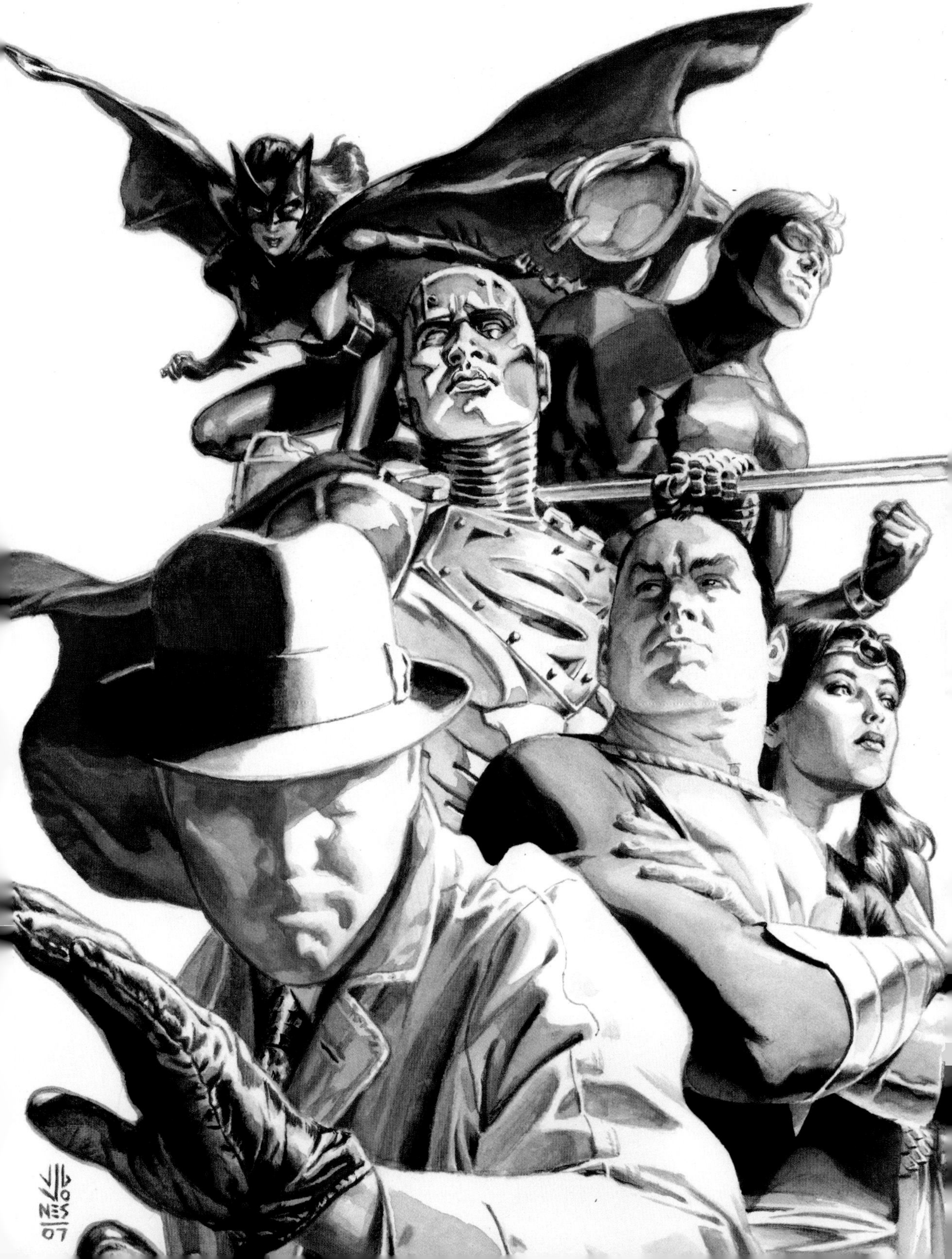
JG JONES 07

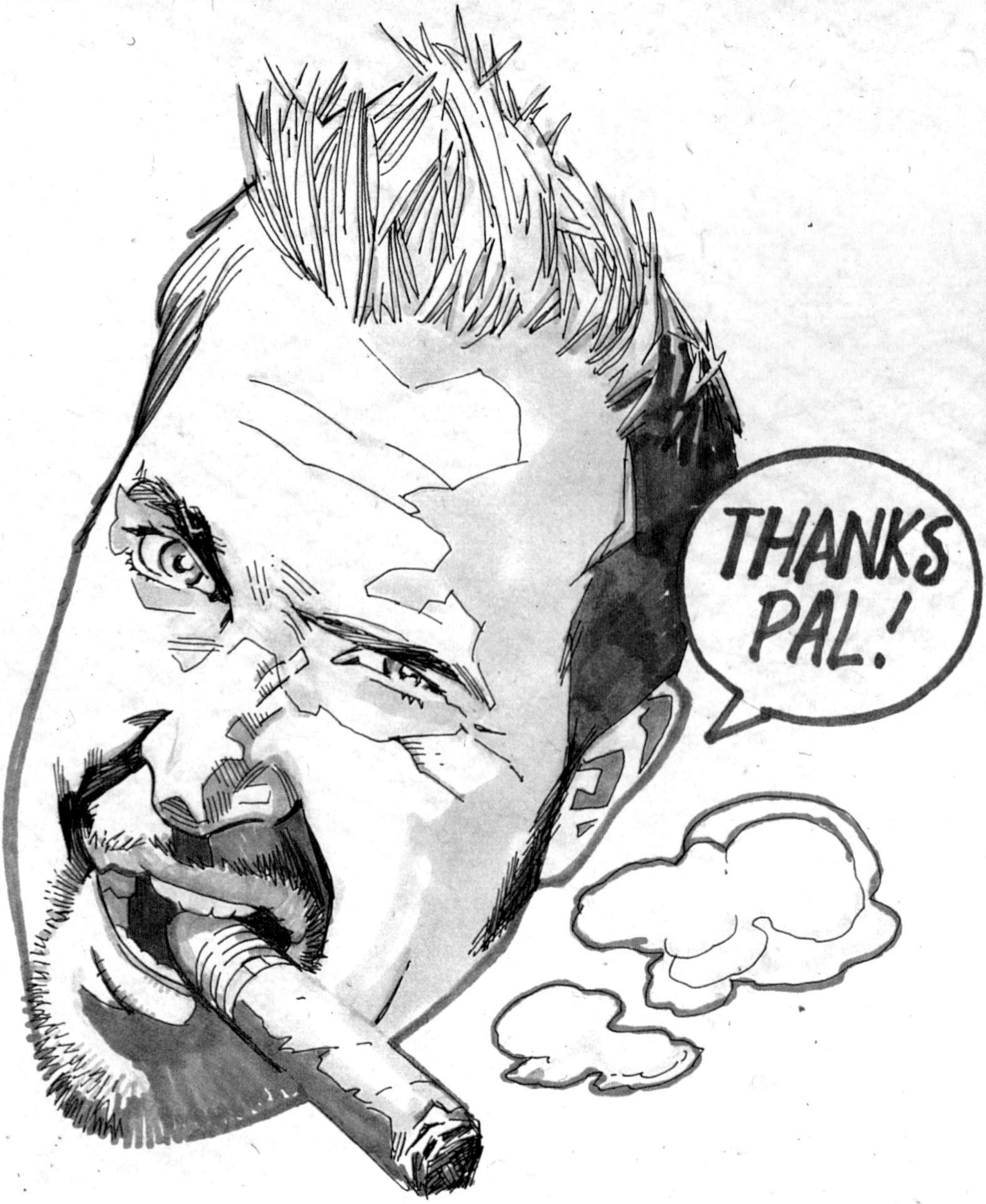
THANKS PAL!


## ACKNOWLEDGEMENTS

I'd like to thank a few people for making 52 the most fun I have had working in comics. Thanks to Dan DiDio for giving me the opportunity. Thanks to the Four Horsemen: Geoff Johns, Grant Morrison, Greg Rucka, and Mark Waid. Thanks to Alex Sinclair, whose magnificent color work made this less of a job and more of a treat. Thanks also to my editors, Steve Wacker and Mike Siglain. Finally, thanks to the fans for making 52 such a rollicking success. **— J.G. JONES**

Gotta send many many thanks to J.G. for trusting me with his art and allowing this to be a collaboration. Dan DiDio, Michael Siglain and Steve Wacker for actually believing I could pull it off (somebody had to!). And to my family for putting up with 52 weeks of me saying, "I'm busy this week." **— ALEX SINCLAIR**